WHY MEN DIE
FIRST

WHY MEN DIE FIRST

HOW TO LENGTHEN YOUR LIFESPAN

MARIANNE J. LEGATO,
M.D., F.A.C.P

palgrave
macmillan

First published in 2008 by
PALGRAVE MACMILLAN™
175 Fifth Avenue, New York, N.Y. 10010 and
Houndmills, Basingstoke, Hampshire, England RG21 6XS
Companies and representatives throughout the world.

PALGRAVE MACMILLAN is the global academic imprint of the Palgrave
Macmillan division of St. Martin's Press, LLC and of Palgrave Macmillan Ltd.
Macmillan® is a registered trademark in the United States, United Kingdom
and other countries. Palgrave is a registered trademark in the European
Union and other countries.

ISBN-13: 978–0–230–60517–6
ISBN-10: 0–230–60517–6

Library of Congress Cataloging-in-Publication Data is available from the
Library of Congress.

A catalogue record of the book is available from the British Library.

Design by Newgen Imaging Systems (P) Ltd., Chennai, India.

First edition: June 2008

10 9 8 7 6 5 4 3 2 1

Printed in the United States of America.

To Ivan Kronenfeld, who asked me two years ago
why I never talked about men.

Not only did he introduce me to a whole spectrum
of spectacular men—soldiers, boxers, policemen, educators,
and lawyers—but he reminded me when this book was
finished to thank them all for their spectacular bravery and
willingness to do all the difficult and brutally
hard things society asks of them.

CONTENTS

ACKNOWLEDGMENTS

Thanks to my son and daughter, whose comments helped to give my thoughts more clarity and to shape the sequence of this book. My editor, Luba Ostashevsky, did the difficult job of keeping me on track, simplifying my prose, and reminding me to talk about what brought richness and authenticity to the book: my patients. Nathalie Casthely's humor and intelligence were invaluable: She corrected biographical details and managed to find anyone I needed within a day. My agent, Frank Weimann, found the right home for this work and believed it was a new view of men that deserved to be considered. Carl Koerner's advice and counsel were essential ingredients for how—and with whom—my work in gender-specific medicine should take shape. And thanks to Sharon Baum, whose support and friendship have been so important to my work.

I mean this book to be a gift to all the men for whom I have been fortunate enough to care as patients, and for the others who shared their experiences and points of view with me. Many of them were decorated heroes; others were private heroes who did their duty every day to support, protect, and enrich the lives of the people they loved.

FOREWORD

It's time to talk about men—and in a whole new way, paying close attention to unique male qualities, particularly those that explain why *at all ages*, men die in greater numbers than women do. Since the time I was a medical student, I never once remember anyone asking why this is true; as one man said to me recently, "I never thought about why. I thought it was a given."

If it's true that men rule the world, it comes at a heavy cost. Women survive and live almost a decade longer. It's time to ask about the nature of men's vulnerabilities. Are they biological, that is, inbuilt and unalterable, or a function of the roles men play and how they play them? Men are trained not to complain, to shrug off pain and injury, and never, never refuse to do the most dangerous and difficult tasks required to keep societies stable. It turns out that these elements, too, contribute to premature death.

The biggest surprise of all, perhaps, is that men, from conception until death, are inherently more fragile and vulnerable than women. In virtually every society in the world, men die first. Women have a hardiness that men simply don't possess. As you will read about here, some of their vulnerability is the consequence of biology, schooling, and socialization. Men are expected to take risks. You go to war, you fight fires, bring order to our cities, sail our ships, and build our buildings. We encourage you to feats of daring and valor, and at the same time, we tell you never, never complain of or even mention the pain you might sustain in agreeing to do all these things. Certainly male biology, particularly in youth, seems fit for these risks. The adolescent and young adult male has a peculiar combination of recklessness, conviction of invulnerability, and a willingness to bear pain and deprivation. This combination can make men susceptible to committing violence. Statistics show that murder and homicide are among the top four killers of men from the time they are born until heart disease and cancers begin to claim those who survive into middle age.

The fundamental male biology makes you an underdog. You are less likely to survive the womb than your sisters; you are six weeks behind in developmental maturity at birth compared to girls. Men have four times the developmental disabilities of females. Men suffer more severely than women from seven of the ten most common infections that humans experience, as you simply don't have the vigorous immune systems that defend women. Men are likely to experience the first ravages of coronary artery disease in their mid-thirties, a full 15 or 20 years before women. And twice as many men die of the disease than do women.

One of the most important issues that face us all is the subject of depression: Women are said to suffer from this disease twice as often as men in virtually every country in the world. I think this is because men hide their pain. Women are permitted to talk about their sadness, to consult their friends and advisors about the experiences they have and how to deal with them. They seek and get counseling more often than their brothers. Men are forbidden this luxury: "Suck it up," men are told by their parents, teachers, and sports instructors—and by the commanders who send them into battle. I have asked many men if they think women underestimate the extent and depth of their sadness and the resounding answer is "yes."

It is time to spend some concentrated thought on you, on what in your biology makes you unique, and on how society conditions and trains you. It is time to think about how we can protect you from premature, violent death and debilitating illness.

WHY MEN DIE FIRST

CHAPTER ONE

THE STRONG, POWERFUL— AND MORE VULNERABLE—MALE

My physician father illustrated many of the biological and societal hazards of being male. My mother outlived him by a decade, mourning his absence every day. He was a formal, taciturn man who sometimes framed his conversations with me as though I were his student. Although he suffered through periods of deep depression, I never knew him to complain about the fact that he worked 16-hour days, or discuss any difficulties he may have experienced in his personal relationships. He made decisions without counsel; he never asked for advice but simply reacted immediately—I often thought impulsively—to any issue or crisis with a course of action he carried out as swiftly and efficiently as possible. He had enormous confidence in his surgical skills. I once watched him late one night in his study read a description of one of the most extensive and complicated surgeries in existence, a Whipple procedure for pancreatic cancer; he performed it successfully the next morning.

He was a short, muscular, and fit man, a first-generation American born of Sicilian immigrants on Mulberry Street in New York. When he was enrolled in school, his mother registered him under his Italian name, Giovanni Santo Francisco, and told his teachers his name was Santo. The moment she left, my then six-year-old father announced to all that his name was Sam, and he was known by that name thereafter. He apparently decided that an American name would make him more acceptable to the new world he was entering. The communal effort of his entire family was dedicated to educating him and having him become a physician, which he did with remarkable success. The town in which we lived called him "Uncle Doc"; every holiday the stairs to our door were filled with gifts of food and wine from his patients. He worked from 6 in the morning until 11 at night. Except for his annual hunting trips, he took no vacations.

My brother told me a remarkably illustrative story about him once: The two were hunting and came to the edge of a sunflower field. The plants were tall and tangled, difficult to walk through. My father, who was about 70 at the time, bent his head and simply started out, doggedly trudging through the field with no complaint, never pausing to rest and never commenting on how difficult the passage undoubtedly was. On another trip, my brother awakened to find him sitting on the side of his bed, smoking, at three in the morning. "What's the matter, Dad?" he asked. My father answered, pointing to his head, "Too much traffic." That was all he said. It would never have occurred to him to confide in one of his sons—or anyone else.

My father took risks, believed in doing his duty without complaint, and accepted the roles society asked of him without questioning them. When World War II engulfed the civilized world, he enlisted in the Army, although he was 42 and had three children at the time. It also did not occur to him to discuss it with my mother, who was horrified. He had a great sense of style and went off to Saks Fifth Avenue to have his uniforms made in preparation for what he always made us children feel had been a tremendous adventure. He served as a surgeon in Patton's Third Army and fought in the Battle of the Bulge. He took tremendous risks: His first act in any new area of combat, he told me, was to drive an ambulance, plainly marked with a red cross, between the lines. "Why?" I asked in amazement. "So I could find out if the enemy would fire on the wounded, in which case we would have to take special precautions to defend our vehicles and the men in them," he explained. Once, when several soldiers from his platoon were lying wounded at the foot of a hill, too badly hit to move, he ordered his medic to go down and bring them to safety. The medic refused. My father briefly considered shooting him for disobeying an order, then decided instead to go himself. He carried the wounded to safety while enemy fire shot into the side of the hill, missing him by inches.

He had enormous confidence and took on any medical challenge, from delivering a baby to performing complicated surgery without hesitation; most times, he was successful. He loved what he did and was full of fascinating sound bites about medicine. Once he told me that 80 percent of sick people will recover no matter what the doctor does, that 10 percent would die in spite of anything one could do, and that our care would make a difference in only 10 percent of the rest. I often think, as I refer one of my patients to a specialist for care, that my father would have handled the matter himself—he treated children as confidently as he treated the aged and he delivered babies as competently as he performed major surgery.

He loved to hunt. In his later years he went all over the world in search of challenging game. He had a large collection of very beautiful weapons of all descriptions, many of them from his favorite Italian gun maker, Beretta. The smell of gun oil filled the house on Sunday afternoons when he opened the cabinets that lined his study to take out one of his favorites to point out to me the beauty of the wood used to make the stock and the intricate tooling on the gray steel of the barrel. He always had a pair of hunting dogs for which we cared; sometimes he would use pointers, at other times English setters and even Brittany spaniels. He was always searching for the perfect duo. He taught us the value of a "soft mouth" in a dog trained to retrieve fallen birds and the importance of its holding a point steady without flushing the game before the hunters arrived.

My father's lifestyle was not conducive to a long and healthy life. He had what I came to consider the quintessentially male nature: He worked with an amazing tenacity at his vocation and he never asked anyone for help or complained about the burdens it placed on him. He took risks that were unnecessary, asked no one for advice or counsel, smoked three packs of Philip Morris cigarettes a day, ate huge amounts of pasta, oiled vegetables, and rich Italian pastries, and frequently finished his long day with a generous helping of Scotch on the rocks in one of the beautifully faceted crystal glasses he favored.

It all took a toll. He was often despondent and had outbursts of temper that were the result of what I now think was chronic depression. I think he would have considered the idea of confiding any of his issues to a psychiatrist, much less taking medication for his all-too-frequent sieges of depression, unthinkable.

He battled—and lost—his war with cancer, the effect of smoking. This was partly because he ignored the blood in his urine for two years before he decided to have a colleague look into his bladder. Even in the last hours of his illness, barely conscious, he tried to fashion what he was feeling into yet another medical lesson for me. My brother had just put an opiate into my father's mouth to ease his dreadful pain. "The physiology of pain is very complex," he murmured, his eyes closed. "Be careful how you use the medicine you're giving me, because the absorption can be very uneven." In a rare moment of revelation during those last exchanges he told me on the eve of surgery: "I will survive this operation. But after that,

I face the abyss." It was the closest he ever came to telling me anything at all about his inner life.

My father was doomed to die early by his behavior and attitude. All the qualities that made him such a wonderful man beloved by his patients and his community also contributed to his premature death. His self reliance was fueled by inner strength and firmness of character. He worked hard with little thought to his own health. We live in a culture where men aspire to this behavior and it causes their downfall.

———◆◆———

This is a book about the relative fragility of men. A male fetus is less likely to survive to term than a female. When he is born, a baby boy's lungs are especially vulnerable, so that boys are less likely to survive the challenges of the first weeks of postnatal life. The rate of violent death for baby boys is higher, too. At least 6 percent of males who die between the ages of one and four are murdered.[1] In their teen and adolescent years, 20 percent of boys who die do so because of suicide, murder, or reckless behavior. In fact, boys are physiologically inclined to die violent deaths. The area of the brain responsible for judgment and considered decision-making are less developed in adolescent boys than in girls.

Societal attitudes play an enormous role in this dreadful toll on men's lives. We encourage boys to "hang tough" and drive through pain, unhappiness, and discomfort of all kinds no matter what the personal price. We *discourage* them from asking for help or advice about how to alleviate the consequences of this societal pressure. The result is unrecognized, untreated depression in males of all ages.

Coronary artery disease reaps a grim harvest as well: The first symptoms of coronary artery disease appear in some men when they are only 35. It kills more than 24 percent of men and is the chief cause of male death after the age of 35. By contrast, it is only when they reach the age of sixty that women are as likely to have a heart attack as a man. Most women have no symptoms of heart disease until they are menopausal. Men have different and more vulnerable immune systems than women; they suffer more intensely from seven of the ten most common infections that afflict humans.

Despite the significant opportunities and advantages most societies afford men, they remain shockingly vulnerable on many levels. Researchers have largely ignored this phenomenon, with tragic consequences. Simply put, we have never turned a gender-specific lens on men. We have not thought enough—if at all—about why they are uniquely prone to disability and premature death.

THE PRICE MEN HAVE PAID FOR OUR EXCLUDING WOMEN IN CLINICAL STUDIES

Ironically, until the late 1980s, men were almost exclusively the subjects in medical research because it was assumed that the data collected from one sex could give accurate insight into both. We excluded women especially if they were still of child-bearing age, in an effort to protect their reproductive systems from the hazards of a clinical trial. We were also concerned about the dangers to a fetus conceived during the course of the research. Essentially, biological sex and gender were regarded as not relevant to human health: What was true of one sex, researchers thought, would be true of another. That assumption was one of the biggest mistakes in medical thinking. When we began to focus on women's health in the 1990s and compared the data to that harvested from men, we found completely unexpected and important differences between the sexes in every system of the body. Brains, skeletons, digestive tracts, endocrine systems—even the skin that holds us together—are different. Those differences affect both our normal functions and the ways in which men and women experience disease. As the expert panel convened by the National Academy of Medicine to study the issue remarked, "Sex does matter. It matters in ways that we did not expect. Undoubtedly, it also matters in ways that we have not begun to imagine."[2]

GENDER-SPECIFIC MEDICINE: THE NEW SCIENCE

As I watched the wave of interest in women's health sweep through the scientific community, I knew we were missing an essential point. As important as it was to "catch up" on what we knew about females, real progress would come from a broader and more inclusive effort to study the innate differences between the bodies of women and men. In 1997, we created a new area of study at Columbia University that I called gender-specific medicine: The science of how normal human bodily processes and the experiences of diseases vary as a function of biological sex. I remember asking my chairman at Columbia whether we could call our new program the Partnership for Gender-Specific Medicine. He answered: "No one knows what 'gender-specific medi-cine' is. 'Women's health' is the buzz word, and that's what we'll call your new program." He, too, resisted the idea that a comparison of the two sexes ought to be the focus of attention. Eventually, he became one of the strongest advocates for this new, cutting-edge science, and we worked together to show the tremendous importance of looking at our patients with a gender-specific lens, considering how their sex impacts the ways in which we can most successfully prevent and treat disease. My colleagues all over the world immediately saw the value of the new approach. Shortly after launching our center, I gave a lecture in Seoul, South Korea, and was excited to see my hosts unfurl a banner across the stage announcing the new Korean Society for Gender-Specific Medicine. Sweden, Japan, Germany, Israel, Malaysia, and Austria have joined the United States and are playing leadership roles in developing this new field of medicine.

The irony of our having studied only men in clinical trials for many years is that we have never appreciated, and therefore never focused on, their unique vulnerability. We simply used them as subjects to trace the course of disease and the impact of treatment on those diseases. We never questioned why they succumbed earlier than women at every age of life. It is time to ask why and what can be done to reverse the trend.

The reasons men die first are hardwired into their uniquely male physiology but are also the result of the demands society makes of them. Biological sex is determined by our genetic material—whether we carry the XX complement of sex chromosomes or the XY pair. Gender is a broader term that refers to the composite produced by the setting of a biological male or female in a specific social environment. Experiences impact us profoundly throughout our lives; we fashion our view of the world from what happens to us. The intricate dance between our genes, hormones, and environment creates and refines our unique persona throughout the course of our lives. Our agile, ever-adapting brains form memories, allow us to create the skills we need to interact with the world around us, and produce, for better or worse, all of our behavior.

WILL SOCIETAL CHANGES AFFECT OUR BIOLOGY?

Two profoundly important changes in our history have been the technological revolution of the past half century and the revolution in the roles of men and women. For millions of years, men's ability to provide food and shelter and to protect territory and property from marauders was essential to our survival. The environment demanded a willingness to take risks and to resist foreign occupations that threatened our lives. Men's roles as provider and defender were undisputed, and those who best filled these roles were evolutionarily selected for survival and replication.

The technologic revolution, however, has made physical strength and aggressiveness more and more irrelevant—at least in the most developed societies. The greater size, muscle mass, and bone weight of men and the ability of testosterone to mute physical pain are not as relevant in a society in which complex global businesses are successfully conducted without the need for speed, strength, or endurance. Women fill the most intellectually demanding traditional male roles with undeniable success.

There is no question that the balance of societal power in developed countries has shifted; women have insisted on freedom from constraints to their advancement of all kinds, including a warning that sexual advances in the workplace may spell disaster for the man who makes them. For a species whose survival depended on males' ability to fertilize as many females as possible, demands to mute sexual advances and aggression cannot be without consequences. The traditional role of father as family provider and his exemption from child care has changed so much that, in many families, women are the major earners. The feminist movement's success was contingent on the technological revolution, which changed the entire playing field for men and women and redefined what was essential for securing and keeping power. It could never have happened a century earlier.

As Charles Darwin showed, the environment winnows away all those ill-suited to the part of the world in which they live, leaving only those most successful at fitting into the existing geographical and societal milieu. If women prefer docile, less sexually aggressive men and males who have an affinity and tolerance for domestic duties, they will breed with such men. Changes in the nature of men will not necessary take millions of years to become evident. Using computer simulations of biological evolution, Nadav Kashtan and colleagues at the Weizmann Institute of Science in Israel suggest that if no new demands are made on a species for adaptation, "the population [becomes] stuck at fitness plateaus for long times." In contrast, these scientists found that if goals change, evolution speeds up dramatically. "Each time a goal changes, a positive local gradient for the new goal is generated . . . strikingly, we find that this gradient often points in the direction of a solution for the new goal. . . . when the goal switches, the networks rapidly find a solution for the new goal *just a few mutations away.*"[3] The study points out that the more complex the goal, the greater the species' speed of accommodation. The most efficient prods to evolution are a series of goals, each of which builds on its predecessor.

HOW LONG WILL MEN LAST?

In other species sexual identity is fluid; many animals go it alone, producing and fertilizing their own eggs. It's not surprising then, that biologists are wondering if the human race will always have two sexes. Scientists looking at humans' Y chromosome worry about its unique and distressing tendency to lose genetic information. The Y has gotten smaller and smaller over the last 300 million years of its existence. It's even been called a "profoundly degenerate" chromosome and "a genetic wasteland."[4] As one commentator put it: "The human Y chromosome is a genetic mess. It's accumulated so many mutations over the years that only a handful of active genes remain. When these decay, all men will be infertile and the human species will become extinct."

The original Y chromosome contained about 1,500 genes; almost all are now lost or inactivated.[5] This isn't surprising: The Y chromosome is under constant fire. In the first place, it's located outside the body in the scrotal sac (an evolutionary development that helped defend sperm from the too-high temperature within the abdominal cavity), where it is bombarded by radiation and other mutagens. A second problem the Y chromosome faces is the enormous number of cell divisions needed to create more than 150 million sperm every day. As one scientist put it, "The chances of errors . . . are astronomical."[6] Sperm also lacks the internal machinery to repair injuries. It is rich in molecules (unsaturated fatty acids) that keep it fluid enough to fuse with the egg it's fertilizing, but its membrane is delicately structured and therefore very vulnerable, and it is particularly susceptible to destruction from oxidation.

The assault on the Y chromosome has advantages to both sexes in spite of its cost: *The Y drives evolution* because mutations are so much more frequent in this chromosome. The ratio of male–female mutations in primates is 3–6:1.[7] So, the tiny Y enlarges the palette from which nature can select to ensure that we can adapt to our environment.

But how long can the Y survive? The prognosis seems so grim that Brian Sykes, professor of genetics at Oxford University, warns that if the assaults continue, there will be no more men in 125,000 years.[8] How can we preserve the two sexes? We may figure out a way to transfer the male-determining segment of the Y chromosome to a hardier member of our chromosomal family; our recently found ability to manipulate the human genome might provide a way to do this by direct intervention. If we're successful, we can go right on copulating in the usual way. But others wonder if we'll have to do without men altogether. Razor-tongued columnist Maureen Dowd writes:

The new research into sex chromosomes suggests that all that antler crashing over the centuries has tuckered out the Y. Men are now the weaker sex, geneticists say, and could soon disappear altogether—taking March Madness and cold pizza in the morning with them. Only another hundred thousand years—or ten million, if you believe the Y optimists—and the male chromosome could go the way of the dial-up connection.[9]

The biology is more complicated than it may appear, however: One of the facts about the sturdy Y chromosome that Dowd may not have taken into consideration is its unique ability to repair itself. Chromosomes travel in pairs, a fortuitous arrangement in which they can reach out to one another to exchange genetic material to repair the damage that inevitably occurs in the production of new cells. However, while women's sex chromosomes, the XX pair, can repair one another by exchanging parts, the male is in a very different situation. All but a tiny part of the Y chromosome has a protective coat that does not allow any exchange with the X. Some suggest that this is the Y's ingenious way to protect the unique and specific DNA that produces maleness and guarantees fertility. During the reproductive process called mitosis, when cells multiply and divide, mistakes in the copying of DNA often occur. Unable to turn to its partner, the X, for help, the Y has developed a unique mechanism to repair itself. The Y contains large segments of genetic material that read the same forward and backward; this is called a *palindromic structure*, like the sentence "Madam, I'm Adam." If some of the Y's components are damaged in the process of replication, the chromosome simply makes a hairpin turn on itself and apposes those palindromic sequences; it uses its own analogous parts to repair itself! What an astonishing reflection of the tendency of men to "go it alone," not asking for help and devising unique and ingenious systems of self-maintenance and repair!

Scientists Bruce Lahn and David Page of the Howard Hughes Medical Institute and MIT, respectively, have a more sanguine view of the Y's future than other experts. They point out that all the non-sex chromosomes contain "motley assortments of genes,"[10] but that the Y chromosome shows a unique and focused concentration on one theme: making the organism male. Far from being a "genetic wasteland," the Y chromosome is now known to contain 78 genes, almost double the previously known tally, and 12 of these are novel. Five have homologues on the X chromosome and are involved in cellular housekeeping in a wide range of tissues. The other seven are expressed only in the testis and have to do with the production of sperm and enhancement of sperm fitness.

THE IMPACT OF SOCIETAL CHANGE ON SEX

The problem of male fragility taps into the question of how society is changing. Our world has changed radically over the last 150 years. Mankind no longer needs to depend on strength and physical endurance to forage for food or even to build cities. Computers and the internet free us to sit anywhere and research, write, communicate, and conduct all our business. And the computer doesn't demand that the operator be male—or female, for that matter. It's gender neutral. Robotic science is producing machines so uncannily like humans that it is not inconceivable that each of us will have the opportunity to own an eminently compatible robot, shaped according to our own unique list of requirements, to replace our fallible, flawed, human significant other. In a recent provocative article in the *New York Times Magazine*, Robin Henig pointed out that several women preferred individually tailored robots as companions to the more difficult and demanding men with whom they had been living.[11] So what will be the consequences for men? Certainly your role in society is changing profoundly. Your unique characteristics as a man—your greater height and strength, for example—are unnecessary to perform many of the new roles that society is defining for you. Women are as effective as men in filling occupations and professions that were once

thought to be the exclusive province of men. I recently had orthopedic surgery and was astonished to find that the chief orthopedic
resident was a slightly built young woman. I told her that when I
was a medical student, orthopedic surgeons said that women were
simply not strong enough to perform the maneuvers required in
this subspecialty and violently opposed accepting any women into
orthopedic training programs. Yet, 30 years later, here she was,
only about five feet tall and weighing no more than 120 pounds—
not just a house officer, but the chief resident! Evolution may no
longer foster the same skills in humans that made the male of the
species able to wage successful physical combat, successfully tra-
verse large distances, and, in his prime, risk his life without hesitation to achieve a goal. If he is to survive at all, we have to take a
hard look at the very nature—and future—of the Y chromosome
and the other inbuilt vulnerabilities that make it less likely for him
to survive than his sisters.

In spite of the furor about our having studied only men for so
long, it is painfully evident that we have not used those studies to
address men's unique characteristics or vulnerabilities. It fascinates
me that activists' calls for more information about men's health sound
eerily similar to those formerly made for women: including concerns
about sexual function (fertility, erectile dysfunction, prostate cancer)
and physical fitness. Furthermore, we have not made a concerted
effort to assess men's value and what's uniquely important about what
they add to the human family. What makes men vulnerable (as they
surely are) and how to correct it—or at least take it into account—are
fundamentally important questions to consider.

As my medical practice has matured, I treat more and more
men. Typically they are the last to admit any weaknesses. Mitchell,
a dazzlingly handsome 42-year-old, loves life, women, and
making deals. He fills the waiting room with his larger-than-life
presence and booming laugh. He is utterly charming, entertains us
all with jokes, and always brings samples of his latest products to
show us. He has high blood pressure that I've persuaded him to

control with two different kinds of medicine. About every three months he'll stop taking one of his drugs and report that on his home machine his blood pressure is fine. I always point out to him that he takes his blood pressure when he is quietly at home, resting, rather than during his hectic, highly competitive workday. He worries that his medicine is the reason he's begun to experience erectile dysfunction, and we've agreed to change his drugs several times to address that issue. He has had lifelong issues with anxiety but has never talked about them with anyone. He thinks it would be unmanly to admit to anything that compromises the perception that he is a completely competent male.

Harry, a 60-year-old with advanced heart disease and severe arthritis in both hips, is finishing a complete physical examination with me that revealed a stone-hard, irregularly shaped prostate. I ask him to see my colleague for a biopsy. An angry outburst is the response: "I hate doctors! I've seen enough of them! I'm not going to any more of them!" I wait for him to finish, understanding his fear that yet another threat to his life has arisen and that he simply wants it gone. As he quiets a little, I ask him to think about it. He says he will, but I doubt that I will see him again until some constellation of symptoms once again overwhelms him. As he leaves the office, I have to remind myself that I can't control my patients— I can only advise and protect them from the increasingly serious issues they face as they age.

Andrew, a 33-year old, tall, muscular entrepreneur, is unable to sleep because he is pursuing three huge deals at once. He asks me for a pill "to tide him over" during this trying time. I worry about how to help him manage his challenges so that they don't produce the palpitations and squeezing chest pain of which he is already complaining. I send him for cardiac testing and, sure enough, the beginnings of coronary artery disease have established a significant beachhead—well before his thirty-fifth birthday.

Arthur, a 66-year-old retired CEO, is still in the swing of business. He has a tight web of connections with powerful businessmen throughout the world. He also has diabetes, for which he will take no medication; he is convinced that he can conquer his elevated blood sugar by exercise and diet. His coronary arteries were filled with atherosclerosis when we sent him for imaging, and I hoped that perhaps the pictures from those tests would persuade him that controlling his diabetes is an essential next step. He is still deciding what to do. It is not lost on me that he considers his own opinion much more compelling than anything I advise.

Recently, I visited the hospital room of a 52-year-old man who had been in pain and whose abdomen had been expanding for months before he agreed to see a doctor, and then only because his wife threatened to call the police if he didn't get medical help. He proved to have a particularly aggressive cancer. The night before surgery to remove it, he lay in bed, a drain in his swollen abdomen, watching a football game. "I'm going to kill this thing," he told me. "I'm going to smash it and lick it." I asked him if he was in pain: "No," he answered. "Just uncomfortable." He died the next day on the operating table without regaining consciousness; the cancer, bigger than a watermelon, had metastasized to every organ in his abdominal cavity. I don't know if anyone could have saved him if he had come for help at the first sign of trouble. But I do know that only the agony of his wife's distress finally brought him to admit, months after the initial symptoms, that he was seriously ill. And by then it was much too late.

Confronting age, vulnerability, and illness is never pleasant, but for men there seem to be special issues: The need to seem powerful, in control, and able to handle what life dishes up is pervasive. Boys are told to "Suck it up" beginning with their first hurts and disappointments. Most men ask for no quarter—and give none—as they struggle to grow their careers, provide for their families, and earn enough money to survive. Asking for counsel is unmanly, while ignoring pain and even the most patent symptoms of illness is routine in the patients I treat. Whining, as they see it, is for women. Not for real men.

We need to understand the biological and social forces that shape the deadly vulnerability of men. It is time to focus on men's specific issues, which come not only from their unique biology but from the social roles and expectations imposed on them. The consequences are profoundly important and their causes often go unrecognized. Arthur Miller painted an unforgettable portrait of the suicide attempts of Willie Loman, a failing salesman broken by depression. Willie's wife, Linda, reports that Willie's frequent "accidents" may not, in fact, be accidents at all:

> "The insurance inspector came. He said that they have evidence. That all these accidents in the last year weren't accidents. One of the 'accidents' had been observed by a passerby: She says that he wasn't driving fast at all, and that he didn't skid. She says he came to that little bridge, and then deliberately smashed into the railing, and it was only the shallowness of the water that saved him."

Her son Biff answers: "Oh no, he probably just fell asleep again." Linda's poignant answer: "I don't think he fell asleep."[12]

CHAPTER TWO

BEGINNINGS

SURVIVING THE WOMB AND THE FIRST WEEKS OF LIFE

The odds of any individual sperm successfully wooing and capturing the egg would daunt even the most daring gambler. Even the most hardy, fit specimen stands little chance of winning. In the normal process of sexual intercourse, a sperm that makes the home run and successfully penetrates an ovum competes with about 250 million others. The winner has to possess speed and the ability to read the signals provided by the chemicals secreted by the egg: Without these chemoattractants, as they're called, the sperm, running and tumbling on its journey, would lose its way.[1]

Once it reaches its target, the sperm releases chemicals that digest the thick protective membrane that surrounds the egg and crosses over into receptive territory. Upon being broached by its eager suitor, the egg immediately closes the door to the competition. Its membrane undergoes a series of changes that make it impossible for any other sperm to penetrate. If the victorious sperm is carrying a Y chromosome, the fertilized ovum develops into a male; if it receives another X to match its own, the result is a female.

If the resulting zygote is male, it has a higher chance of self-aborting. As noted earlier, more girls than boys survive in the womb. At the time of ovulation, not all the eggs, known as oocytes, are fully developed. Interestingly, the Y-bearing sperm is more likely to fertilize a flawed egg than an X-bearing sperm.[2] The impetuous Ys simply don't have the capacity to determine which are the healthiest, most competent ova, as the X-bearing sperm do. Some of the vulnerability of the XY embryo, then, may be due to the poor judgment of the Y-bearing sperm that indiscriminately fertilizes an imperfect egg.

The Y-fertilized egg also has less chance of surviving into a blastula and then an embryo because lethal mutations are more likely to exist on the Y than on the X chromosome. The sperm are produced rapidly, in large quantities—each ejaculation carries with it between 40 and 600 million of them!   and reside outside the body, where they are much more vulnerable to radiation and toxins that corrupt their DNA. This is, of course, vastly different than the situation for the ovum, which lies well within the abdomen, sheltered from such assaults. It is well known, for example, that the greatest incidence of male birth defects occur in areas with the greatest use of pesticides.[3]

The quality and amount of semen in ejaculate has been decreasing throughout the world over the past 50 years; the reference value for a normal sperm count has decreased threefold since the 1940s. Associated with this decrease in the amount of sperm produced is a rise in testicular cancer, which has increased two- to four-fold over the past 50 years.[4] Some suggest that the decrease is the result of environmental toxins that impact the unborn child.[5] Other investigators suggest that an increase in maternal estrogens is responsible.[6] Even a small increase in environmental toxins can have a disproportionately harmful effect on sperm because of the very high content of fat in seminal fluid, in which sperm are packed. Fat is a preferential storage place for toxic materials.

THE BIOLOGICAL CLOCK ALSO TICKS FOR MEN

Men never ask me about storing their sperm while they are still young to ensure that they will be able to create healthy children when they find a mate or decide to have a child on their own. My women patients often ask me about preserving their eggs to use later in life if they want to preserve their options. Contrary to our firmly held belief that men, no matter what their age, don't suffer from the limitations of a biological clock that defines their period of optimal fertility, age does affect the quality of semen. Compared with 30-year-old men, for example, 50-year-old men have less semen volume and sperm motility, and the percentage of normal sperm drops sharply.[7] There is a 20 percent increase in the time it takes to conceive when the father is older than 50.

SURVIVING GESTATION: THE VULNERABILITY OF BOYS

One might expect a 50–50 chance of becoming one sex or the other, but that's not the way it works out. Interestingly, in good times, when no natural disasters or environmental toxins intervene, the ratio of boys to girls conceived can be as high as 1.7 to 1. The ratio of miscarriages of boys to girls after 16–19 weeks of pregnancy is 248:100. By the time pregnancies mature to term, the ratio of males to females is about equal. In fact, the sex ratio at birth is remarkably constant across various human populations, with 105 to 107 male births for every 100 female births.[8] The high preterm mortality of boys is due to several factors[9]:

- Boys experience higher rates of infection than girls in the womb. Boys may have a less-competent immune system with which to fight infection, which is certainly the case in adult men compared with women. Men are less able to mount an inflammatory, protective defense against invading agents than are women.

- Mothers are sometimes allergic to the male fetus they carry. Their immune response takes the form of an inflamed placenta, thus compromising fetal nutrition and making miscarriage more likely.

- Two-thirds of fetuses with immature lung development are male. Lack of proper lung development in the second trimester is an important factor in producing premature rupture of the membranes and early labor.[10] Androgens delay lung maturation and the production of surfactant, the material that lines the inner surface of the lungs and makes gas exchange efficient in the newborn.[11]

- Girls have higher levels of sympathetic hormones than boys. These help them at the time of delivery, enabling them to generate higher heart rates to cope with the demands of the last hours of labor. This protects them from anoxic damage to the brain and other tissues, in contrast to boys, who often develop slower-than-normal heart rates in the same phase of labor.

- Abnormal fetal size, either overly large or overly small, is associated with more cerebral palsy in boys.[12]

- Mothers who carry boys have a higher rate of gestational diabetes and produce larger-than-normal babies. These mothers also suffer failure to progress during labor and have sons whose umbilical cords prolapse or have true knots, compromising blood supply to the fetus.[13]

- Human chorionic gonadotrophin, a hormone that influences the amount of blood supplied to the uterus and placenta, varies in concentration as a function of the sex of the baby. It is less abundant in the third trimester of pregnancy with males, meaning that blood flow supplying the placenta and uterus is lower in those cases.[14]

- Maternal stress during pregnancy exacts a high toll on boys. Scientists Dawn Owen and Stephen Matthews of the University of

Toronto believe that a male fetus whose mother is stressed has an impaired ability to defend himself against stress. He cannot respond to intrauterine challenges by regulating the production of stress hormones in his own adrenal glands as well as a girl can.[15] Even if the baby does survive to birth, the data suggest, boys are less able than girls to mount an adequate response to stresses after they are born. Steroids are given to mothers whose fetuses seem to be in danger of miscarrying; these scientists point out that the ability of males to handle multiple doses may be much less than that of females. Thus, the effort to improve fetal survival with steroids may not be as useful for boys as for their sisters.

OTHER FACTORS IN THE BOY-GIRL RATIO

Some of the vulnerability of boys at birth is neutralized by a preference for sons in some countries; some cultural groups prefer males. In India and China alone it's estimated that there are 80 million fewer females than were expected to be born, and there is concern that the excess of males who are now reaching adulthood (most of whom are in lower socioeconomic classes) will not be able to find partners, which may actually threaten social stability. As Therese Hesketh of the Institute of Child Health at University College London points out, "in many communities today there are growing numbers of young men in the lower echelons of society who are marginalized because of lack of family prospects and who have little outlet for sexual energy."[16]

Whatever the consequences, over the next 20 years in parts of China and India, there will be a 12 to 15 percent excess of young men. Since women will have the upper hand in choosing among them, those left will tend to be the least desirable. In

China, for example, 94 percent of all unmarried people aged 28–49 are males, and 74 percent of those have not completed high school.[17]

Nature itself varies the ratio between males and females in any population, depending on environmental conditions. For example, an interesting fact is that during wartime more boys are born than females. Increases in male births during and after war has been documented for both world wars[18] and for the Korean and Vietnam wars.[19] Scientists attribute this to more frequent coitus during wartime; the earlier in the cycle an ovum is fertilized the more likely it is to result in a male fetus. The quality of cervical mucus is an important determinant of whether the Y- or X-bearing sperm gets through to the ovum: The Y-bearing sperm is better able to penetrate the thick cervical mucus that predominates at the beginning of the menstrual cycle than the X-bearing sperm.[20] If fertilization occurs early in the period of contact between the ovum and sperm (under six hours) in the laboratory, we know that the likelihood of a boy increases significantly.[21] Prolonged interaction is more likely to produce females.

The proposal that the relatively more abundant harvest of boys during war is an effort to replace the males lost during the conflict is untenable, because the births are never enough to replace all the lost men: The preponderance of male births doesn't last long enough. The usefulness of a sex ratio skewed in favor of boys during wartime is explained by Harvard biologist Robert Trivers and his colleague Dan Willard of the mathematics department at Harvard.[22] They point out that the health and nutritional status of the mother is the determining factor of the sex ratio in a population. In most societies, the largest, healthiest males have the highest success in mating successfully with the available females; their frailer, smaller brothers are more often excluded from procreation.

$$\boxed{\text{SURVIVAL AT BIRTH AND INFANCY}}$$

Once they exit the womb, boys have less hope for survival than girls. They are 1.5–2.0 times more likely to die at birth.[23] In 2001, overall infant mortality for boys was 23 percent higher than that for girls.[24] The bad news for boys doesn't stop there: They continue to die in greater numbers than girls not only throughout childhood but, as we will see in other chapters of this book, into adult life.[25] Many scientists believe that at least part of the female advantage is the "double dose" of genes girls have as a result of having two X chromosomes; if one gene is damaged there is a potential backup on the second X chromosome. As we have seen, the Y chromosome of boys has to go it alone. If an X-localized gene is spindled, bent, or mutilated, it can't turn to the Y for a corrective piece: The Y genetic complement is devoted principally to maintaining fertility. In XX pairs, even though most of the genes on one of the X chromosomes are "silenced" in an evolutionary effort to maintain an equality between the sexes, some genes on the silenced X escape and continue to function, serving as a backup pool for errors on the dominant X.

> Low birth weight and prematurity are the two most important predictors of newborn mortality. The impact of both is more severe for males: Very low birth weight boys suffer a much higher rate of death than do their low birth weight sisters. A study done in 2000 by the National Institute of Child Health showed that mortality for such males was 22 percent and for girls 15 percent.[26]

Immature lung development due to inadequate amounts of surfactant, the lubricant that lines the air sacs and allows the lung to inflate normally, was the most important cause of higher mortality in boys. Maternal diabetes is another important cause of lung immaturity in boys: These babies have higher levels of testosterone, which blocks the production of the surfactant.[27] Smoking during pregnancy has a bigger impact on the male fetus; it retards growth and even produces males with significantly reduced head circumference.[28] Boys grow faster and achieve larger size than girls under normal conditions, but drug use (heroin and cocaine) during pregnancy that significantly decreases birth size affects males more than females. Male children of drug-addicted mothers show higher rates of developmental difficulty than their sisters.[29] Brain hemorrhage, significant congenital malformations, aspiration pneumonia, infection, and urinary tract infections are also more common in this population of newborn boys. This disparity in survival has persisted despite improved methods of ventilating these tiny babies, giving steroids to the mother before she gives birth, and, more recently, using surfactant therapy to help the lungs of male children develop.

It is possible that appropriate response to threats in the environment is developed later in boys than girls and that this contributes to boys' greater vulnerability. For example, fear expressions develop significantly later in boys than girls and clearly are important to survival.[30]

THE SEX-SPECIFIC BRAIN

From the moment they enter the world, boys are different than girls. Ask any parent. When my daughter was handed to me, her eyes were closed, and it seemed to me that she spent the first three days of her life lying quietly asleep, almost as if she were reluctant to engage with the new world she had entered. My first encounter with my day-old son was entirely different: He lay in my lap, looked into my face wide-eyed with an enormous smile, and animatedly pumped his arms and legs in response to what I said to him. I thought him enormously energetic and adventurous. He was definitely up for the game from the first moment he took a breath. I can still see him in my laboratory, which he often visited as a toddler, enthusiastically performing mysterious "experiments" in which he would mix various liquids in a beaker to see what would happen. "I don't know whether this will work or not," he told me one afternoon about a particularly complex brew, "but it's worth a try!"

The differences in the male and female aren't just the result of hormones. It's clear that genes also shape the sex-specific brain as they do all our sex-specific tissues. Researchers got an important clue that this is the case because of an amazing bird, called a gynandromorph, discovered in a colony of finches at New York's Rockefeller University. Half of it is male and the other female. The pictures of the bird are truly astonishing: The right side is decorated with brightly colored male plumage and the left with the less spectacularly colored female feathers.[31] Scientists found that the cells in the right half of its brain and body were genetically male (that is, they had the bird equivalent of an XY chromosomal pair—called ZZ in the bird). The other half were genetically female—in spite of the fact that both halves of the brain and all the other organs of this remarkable bird were exposed to the same hormonal environment. The right side of this amazing creature's brain contained the male-specific song center characteristic of the finch, which generates the sounds the male uses to woo the female.

ACQUIRING A MALE BRAIN

The specialization of the brain according to gender begins from the moment of conception. The male brain is the result of the impact of the male-specific Sry gene on the Y chromosome, which acts directly to shape the embryonic brain.[32] The same gene stimulates the formation of the testes by the sixth to seventh week of development in the womb. These produce testosterone, which is certainly abundant in this just-started little boy: After 16 weeks of gestation, he has as much of the hormone as an adult male![33] These high levels gradually recede, so that by the twenty-fourth week of life in the womb, the levels are equal to those of early puberty. The early cascade of testosterone interacting with male-specific genes has a huge impact on the male fetus's brain, hard-wiring it to be distinctively different from that of the female. Hormones continue to impact brain structure and function throughout life, particularly at crucial periods of development like puberty, when there is a surge in hormone production that impacts all the organs of the body.

The finished brain is not formed solely by the multiplication of cells. The final structure of the brain also depends on an orderly system of neuronal migration, pruning (which reduces the amount of grey matter), and the creation of the insulating sheath of myelin that coats neuronal axons, called white matter. By two years of age, the brain has achieved almost 80 percent of its adult weight; this rapid period of growth, which begins well before birth, is due to a vigorous production of synaptic connections between nerve cells. After age five, there is no significant increase in brain size.

The changes in brain development are different in girls and boys: Between 6 and 18 years of age, boys lose 19.1 percent of their grey matter while gaining a 45.1 percent in white matter. Girls reduce grey matter by only 4.7 percent and increase white matter by 27.4 percent during the same developmental period. One of the last areas to mature is the prefrontal cortex, which has to do with working memory, inhibitory control, and the regulation of behavior. This is particularly delayed in adolescent boys, as we will discuss in another chapter, and explains their unique vulnerability to risk-taking and impulsive behavior that can often prove fatal.

> The brains of adult men are 10 to 20 percent larger than those of women and, as in childhood, have more white matter (involved in sending and accepting messages to relatively distant sites) than women. This relatively more abundant store of white matter is thought to be the reason men are more adept at spatial tasks.

The boy's brain is different in its anatomy, chemical composition, and functional organization. But is there something about the unique composition and function of the male brain that creates more vulnerability to illnesses and premature death than is the case for the female?

Boys, as we all know, often express emotion physically. For example, boys may react with violent behavior in response to a threat. Ruben and Raquel Gur, a husband and wife team at the University of Pennsylvania Medical Center's Department of Psychiatry, suggest that this can be explained by the higher metabolic activity in the evolutionarily older parts of men's brains. Even at rest, men have higher baseline activity in this older part of the brain, called the limbic system, which makes them particularly alert to objects or people entering their field of vision from the periphery. Interestingly, this state of alertness is never higher than when they are involved in the first stages of seduction. They are focused not only on sexual conquest but on protecting the object of their interest from competitors. I once watched a couple, clearly involved in the first stages of infatuation, in a crowded restaurant. A man at the adjacent table passed close enough to them to nearly topple their bottle of wine. Inexplicably, the male member of the couple flew into a rage that baffled everyone; the unintentional near disaster had been averted, but the instinct to protect and mark the female he was courting as his own was clearly in full force.

The complexity and size of the human brain are directly related to our intellectual competence, which is a different order of magnitude than that of any other animal. Apparently, brain growth of exceptionally intelligent children has a unique pattern. Philip Shaw, a psychiatrist at the National Institute of Mental Health, scanned the brains of 300 healthy children.[34] He found that in the average child's brain, the cortex grows thicker during early childhood, but at about age seven or eight it begins to thin out. Very intelligent children have a delayed but more pronounced peak in cortical thickness that begins to be apparent at about age 13. They also have a more vigorous pruning process. The thought is that the brains of gifted individuals are more plastic than average, and do more fine-tuning in the parts of the brain that support higher levels of intellectual function. Changes in brain anatomy are most striking in the prefrontal cortex, the seat of the most complex mental processes, including abstract thought.[35] It's conceivable that the microcephalin (MCPH) family of genes, which is thought to control neuronal multiplication and differentiation, is particularly competent in these gifted individuals.

Testing of large numbers of males and females reveals that more males exist at both poles of the normal distribution of intelligence: There are more very bright boys—and more very limited boys—than girls; variability in intelligence is greater in boys than in girls.

Harvard psychologist Steven Pinker makes a compelling case for hard-wired differences in the brains of males and females.[36] He lists six fundamental differences in priorities between the sexes that ultimately influence what they choose to do in life:

- Boys like playing with objects rather than with other children, in contrast to girls. This makes a difference in the eventual choice of careers. As Pinker puts it, "the occupations that fit best with the 'things' end are physicist, chemist, mathematician, computer programmer, and biologist." This proclivity for concentrating on things rather than social networks or interrelationships with others may help to explain the underestimated scope of depression in men and, moreover, compared to women, the much greater likelihood that they will commit suicide.

- Boys take more risks. This is an undisputed male characteristic that makes them willing to engage in more dangerous pursuits, and contributes, particularly during their adolescence, to the high incidence of "unintentional injuries that cause nearly 50 percent of their deaths before the age of 25."

While it is impossible to say how much each of these differences owes to biological differences and how much to experience, expectation, and training, Pinker points out that there is excellent evidence to suggest that biology is responsible for some part of them:

- There are large differences in the concentrations of sex hormones in males and females, as well as in the receptors throughout the brain for these hormones. There are also significant differences in cerebral anatomy, metabolism, and blood flow to the brain. Behavior emanates from the brain, and it is counterintuitive to believe that the sex-specific brain does not possess sex-specific abilities and conduct.
- Almost all of these sex differences are universal, no matter what the culture in which men and women exist: Women are more likely to be involved in the care of children and men are more likely to travel over a greater spatial range than women. Men of all societies that have been tested also show a greater ability to understand the characteristics of three-dimensional objects in space.
- Another fascinating observation is the failure of community efforts to stamp out gender differences. Pinker cites the Israeli kibbutz

and "various American Utopian communes a century ago" as examples of these. It seems to me, however, that our contemporary society is homogenizing gender differences more successfully, in that women now fill places in society that were once the exclusive province of men.

- Sex differences are not the exclusive province of humans but can be seen in other mammals. Even male vervet monkeys prefer to play with trucks.
- Sex differences emerge early in childhood and some are apparent even in the first week of life; newborn boys are more interested in objects and newborn girls in faces.
- Later in life, the rough-and-tumble play characteristic of boys is true of girls who have been masculinized by congenital defects that subject them to unusually high levels of testosterone during development. Finally, the fact that environment alone cannot create a male or a female is clearly borne out by children who are genetic males but who are raised as females; such children have a clear sense of themselves as male, exhibit characteristic preferences for aggressive and rough play in childhood and in adult life, and choose a lifestyle (including marriage to a female) commensurate with their genetic sex.

EXPERIENCE AND BRAIN DEVELOPMENT

The experiences of very early life may alter brain development in permanent and profoundly important ways. As a medical student at New York University College of Medicine, I was sent to the wards of Bellevue Hospital for training. Learning at Bellevue was one of the greatest gifts I could ever have received. Our district was supposed to cover 42nd Street to Houston Street, river to river, but no sick patient was ever turned away. When every other hospital bed in the city was filled (as they often were in the dead of winter), Bellevue was the last port of call, and beds were brought up from the bowels of the hospital storerooms to fill the hallways with the sick for whom no one else had room. Often neglected or abandoned children who had no other place to go came to us until the state could find a facility for them. Many were listless, tiny for their age, and completely unresponsive to any of us. I remember the chief resident writing on the charts of many of these children the diagnosis of "Dwindles." I asked him what that meant: "They are simply dwindling away because no one has touched them, spoken to them, fed them, or cared about them since they were born." Another euphemism for such a child was "FTT—failure to thrive." One of the duties of the medical student (called the "clinical clerk" in the archaic language of our discipline) was to prick the heels of these babies for blood samples. The most deteriorated would not even cry out, and I found their silent indifference to the pain I was causing them more heartbreaking than any protest healthier children made at my approach.

The way mothers treat their newborns sets the brain's thermostat for reacting to a disturbing experience. An unpleasant experience prompts the release of a stress hormone, cortisol. When it first appears in the bloodstream in response to stress, cortisol increases our attention, focus, and ability to learn. If the levels remain elevated for a longer time span, though, depression results and our ability to remember and think clearly, with concentrated attention, is compromised.

Experiments with animals reflect the importance of parenting on a child's stress response, a response that persists even into adult life. For example, mother rats lick and groom their pups, and do so even more intensively when the pups are taken away and returned after a brief absence. When they are handled, the pups increase their vocalizations, stimulating the mother to more intensive contact with their (presumably agitated) babies. It is clear that this early affection from the mother helps form a brain that is less reactive to stress later in life.[37] If the babies are removed from their mothers for longer periods (hours at a time), the mothers are indifferent to them, at least when they are first returned to the nest. These neglected pups develop into adults who show excessive stress to noxious experiences.

This maternal attention actually promotes gender-specific changes in the areas of the brain that have to do with social behavior and anxiety.[38] Mother rats seem equipped to address the importance of increased attention to baby male pups. They spend more time licking the anogenital areas of their sons, presumably because of the higher salt content of male pup urine. Rats treated this way have more reproductive success as adults. Mother rats also retrieve male pups before their female offspring if the babies are taken away from them; the best-developed male offspring are favored by the mother.[39]

The parental response to distress in the newborn is obviously crucial to developing a pattern of response to stress later in life. Telling boys to "deal with it" when they are distressed or in pain rather than reassuring and comforting them may create anxious, depressed adults. Thoughtful attention to the suffering of young children can teach them to articulate their problems and help them create solutions and develop resources to cope with similar issues in the future. Silencing their expressions of grief or pain simply contributes to a sense of isolation and powerlessness. Even in dealing with adults in my own practice, I find it useful to ask the patient to tell me exactly what is causing them pain and then to help them decide exactly what they are going to do about it. Simply allowing them to complain is not useful, but coupling the complaints with that powerful question, "What are you going to do about it?" is extremely effective.

In an interesting observation, Wiedenmayer and Barr described the response of baby rats to the presence of a hostile male unrelated to them. Such "intruder males" often kill pups because doing so stops lactation in the mother, rendering her ready to conceive again.[40] In the presence of the new male, the rat babies immediately develop elevated levels of stress hormone, stop vocalization, avoid the adult intruder, and "freeze" in an effort to escape his attention.

I think of this research whenever I read about a child subjected to repeated violence or murdered by a stepfather or visiting male. We human beings are not, after all, so different from or superior to the rest of the animal kingdom. Even in situations where the new male is not hostile, there is a period of quiet "sizing up" until a sense of safety has been established. I remember inviting to dinner two of my relatives whom my children, then four and nine years old, had never met. These relatives had caused me considerable pain when I was younger—as my children knew. My son and daughter were absolutely silent during the entire dinner, to my amazement. Amusingly, the guests told me that "my children knew their place"; they didn't understand how wary they were.

The impact of psychological trauma on brain function is profound and has an effect no matter what the age of the victim. Children who are abused have a reduction in volume of the hippocampus, a part of the brain involved in learning and memory. Male Vietnam combat veterans showed similar effects: They suffered memory problems along with an average 8 percent reduction in hippocampal volume.[41] The medial prefrontal cortex, another part of the brain that regulates emotional responses to fear and stress, is also affected by abuse. Abused children have less-robust academic achievement in school and develop the hallmarks of post-traumatic stress disorder, including delayed recall of memories so painful that they are initially suppressed.[42] A 1997 survey by the Department of Health and Human Services documented that boys experience 48.5 percent of childhood abuse; they are more likely than girls to experience *physical* abuse as well as general and medical neglect.[43] The data on boys may be skewed by the fact that they tend not to talk about abuse; more probably suffer it than is reported. Worse, boys are three times more likely to die from maltreatment than girls.[44]

The magnitude of sexual abuse of boys is underreported and underrecognized.[45] A 1998 comprehensive survey of existing studies showed that 16 percent of men 18 years or older reported sexual abuse by an older male; these men were more likely to be nonwhite and from families that were poor, physically abusive, and headed by only one parent.[46] The median age of first sexual abuse was about 10 years of age; 58 percent of the boys were younger than 11. Ninety-four percent of perpetrators were men; of the women who were perpetrators, about half were teenage babysitters. The consequences for the abused boys were horrendous: Rates of depression were four times that of the general population, threefold for bulimia (perhaps an unexpected sequella for boys), and twofold for other disasters, including runaway behavior and legal problems. Suicide attempts were 1.5 to 14 times higher in abused compared with non-abused males. The use of addictive substances was also more frequent: Sexually abused boys in treatment centers were more likely to use alcohol before the age of 10 and marijuana before 12. Cocaine use was 10 times that of non-abused boys. One of the most important observations of this survey was the fact that sexually victimized males were not likely to report the experience; prior to the studies, only 15 percent had ever told anyone about their experience.

In spite of the greater numbers of abused boys, whatever the unpleasant experience, males seem more resilient than females: Testosterone has an important impact on the response to a stressful event. Normal adult male rats show a marked improvement in performance when they experience an unpleasant stimulus. In contrast, if they were castrated at birth, their ability to learn a defensive response to an unpleasant stimulus was impaired. In females, a stressful exposure dramatically impaired their performance in adult life unless they were exposed at birth to testosterone, in which case their performance actually improves, similar to that of a male.[47]

There are some effective strategies for reducing the incidence of child abuse. In a 2000 statement, the Canadian Task Force on Preventative Health Care observed that the best preventative measures for minimizing child abuse were home visitation for disadvantaged families during the perinatal period through the child's second birthday.[48] First-time mothers younger than 19 were particularly targeted for such visits, as were single parents with low socioeconomic status.

The percentage of families headed by single mothers has more than doubled between 1970 and 1994. Almost 31 percent of families have no father or husband in residence.[49] This absence of an adult male has a significant impact on boys: Boys in inner-city, single-parent households are more likely to have emotional, behavioral, and academic problems. At least some of these issues arise through the absence of an important secondary caregiver rather than the presence of family dysfunction; an effective secondary caregiver such as a grandmother can neutralize the difficulty, and children in such situations function equally well as children in two-parent households. Single mothers seem to be more severe in their discipline of adolescent sons and are less effective at monitoring their activities. The tone of the warning or discipline matters less than the effectiveness with which the discipline is enforced; not surprisingly, boys get into trouble more frequently when their mothers are more tolerant of their bad behavior. The right mix of control and autonomy-granting behavior is more difficult for single mothers than two-parent units.

A newer variation in family structure is on the rise: The number of stay-at-home fathers has tripled in the United States over the past ten years to almost 160,000.[50] According to a recent study of 213 such dads, they are not male housewives but retain an interest in and pursue male pastimes like fishing and fixing automobiles; they are apparently as content as other, more traditional men with their roles. I have many couples in my practice where husbands fill traditionally female roles in the household; without exception, both parents maintain that the children thrive in such an environment. Not only is more attention for the children possible than would be the case with only one parent, but two points of view are healthy and enrich the quality of how issues are handled in the family unit. Even more interesting to me is the fact that these men seem to enjoy the extended contact with their children enormously and do not resent the time they are required to spend with them at all. They have, for the most part, a strong sense of their own masculinity and feel that the functions they are serving are valuable and rewarding to them and to the children.

BOYS AT RISK: WHEN THINGS GO WRONG

One of the most challenging periods of my training involved working with developmentally disabled children under the tutelage of Dr. Louis Cooper, Professor Emeritus of Pediatrics at Columbia University. He sent me to a center run by New York State on Morton Street in Greenwich Village. There I was able to see scores of these young people. My first visits shocked me. The children required constant care and vigilant supervision, for clearly their behavior was not only often violent but completely unpredictable. Some of their mothers had rubella during the first trimester of their pregnancies, which had a devastating effect on the brain development of their fetuses. None of these young people were able to speak; many had a whole constellation of physical disabilities in addition to their intellectual limitations, and not one of them had any vestige of the personal beauty or attractiveness of normally gifted children. I can still hear their grunts and

loud cries and remember the outbursts of uncontrollably aggressive behavior and their grotesque grimaces. Their fate was completely dependent on the competence and dedication of the
people who cared for them. Some of these children would
become ill and require hospitalization on Dr. Cooper's service.
Somehow, he brought order out of chaos for these children. The
kind and degree of mental limitation each had was carefully
assessed by his talented staff, who developed ingenious methods
of soothing these frightened children, afflicted not only by acute
physical illnesses, but also by fear of a new, strange environment.
I remember thinking that the saddest feature of these youngsters
was their inability to understand or construct language; watching
Dr. Cooper interact with these children I understood in a way I
had never considered before how important a physician's calm-
ness, touch, facial expression, and tone of voice were in reassuring a sick patient.

> Developmental disabilities are astonishingly common in this
> country; one in every six children younger than 17 years of age
> (an overall prevalence rate of 16.7 percent) is affected if one
> includes delay in growth or development.[51] The evidence that
> males are far more vulnerable to developmental disabilities is
> overwhelming and universally accepted.

In a recent essay, Sebastian Kraemer reminds us that developmental disorders, including reading delays, deafness, blindness,
seizure disorders, hyperactivity, autism, clumsiness, stammering,
and Tourette's syndrome are three to four times more common in
boys than girls.[52]

Premature babies are at special risk. Neil Marlow and his colleagues at the School of Human Development at the University of
Nottingham studied 308 surviving children in the United Kingdom

and Ireland. They found that in the children they studied about 22 percent of babies born at 25 weeks or less gestation did not survive. Of the 78 percent that did survive, fully 86 percent had moderate to severe disabilities that were still evident by the time the children were six years old. In boys, the disabilities were not only more frequent, but much more severe.[53] These investigators make the very interesting suggestion that the immune mechanisms of these disabled children were also disturbed, and that the brain tailoring that is such an important part of normal function was disturbed as a result. All of their patients had a family history of autoimmune disorders, and the children had a higher than normal incidence of autoimmune diseases. The researchers also concluded that intrauterine testosterone might have played a role in creating an abnormal brain; exactly what happens to explain this is not known.

Animal models of both severe autoimmune disease and disorders in the migration and placement of neurons in the developing brain show that if the defect is simply the result of brain cell formation, migration, and ultimate positioning, putting the animals in a stimulating environment as soon as they are born has a significant effect on improving their ability to learn.[54] If, however, the disordered brain anatomy is pervasive and severe, as is the case with an autoimmune process that attacks and destroys the brain itself, intervention is not effective. Clearly, brain structure and function are not cast in stone, but respond to the environment throughout life.

Children with developmental disabilities—and the societies in which they function—pay a high price for their handicap. Einfeld and colleagues reported that in at least 40 percent of these children there is an added burden of major behavioral and emotional disturbance.[55] Effective mental health therapy for those affected as well as support and training for their parents or caregivers ease the burden of what these authors properly term a sizable and neglected public health problem.

Developmental disorders of brain function are common and treatment is expensive, not only for the individual, but for society as a whole.

Attention-Deficit Hyperactivity Disorder (ADHD)

The disruption of the normal map of brain development has profound effects on function and behavior. The most common childhood psychiatric disorder is attention-deficit hyperactivity disorder (ADHD). In a recent study of 152 affected children, investigators at the National Institute of Mental Health showed that such children have a generalized decrease in brain volume of about 3 percent, predominantly in white matter.[56] Those children with the most severe symptoms have the greatest loss of brain substance. Interestingly, in those children who received medication, the white matter content of the brain was apparently restored to normal, unlike that of untreated patients.

The diagnosis of this disorder is so frequent that I have questioned its validity. However, magnetic resonance imaging (MRI) of the brain in these children definitely shows a lower than normal brain volume. Surprisingly, this deficit is most dramatic, not in the part of the brain that supports cognition, but in the cerebellum, which controls the coordination of movement and balance. Even more interesting, the deficit in white matter is not as marked in medicated children, implying that medication corrected the initial defect and the *normal subsequent growth of the brain was not disturbed.* The authors of the study point out that the fundamental developmental processes of later childhood and adolescence are probably not disturbed, and that the symptoms we see in patients are caused by defects that are *fixed and occur far earlier in development.*

Autism

The public's concern and fascination with autism is understandable: Although there is confusion about the precise criteria for the diagnosis, it can be defined as a developmental disorder that begins before the third year of life and includes abnormalities in cognition, learning, attention, and the processing of information that comes through the senses. In a moving autobiography, Temple Grandin, whose insights into the autism she herself suffered are compelling, describes the autistic child's nearly unbearable sensitivity to touch.[57] The spectrum of temper tantrums, sensitivity to sound, and fascination with repetition are all portrayed in this memorable book. The autistic person has profound problems with communication and socialization. There is a whole range of related disorders that fall into this general category, including Asperger's syndrome, a less-disabling malady in which there is generally high cognitive functioning but some of the same difficulties in social integration and relationships as in classic autism.

People with Asperger's syndrome can be high achievers, particularly if their skills relate to work that does not involve interpersonal relationships. One of my patients, a brilliant financial analyst, works long hours and earns a tremendous salary at his firm. He never meets my gaze, and his interchanges with me are always as brief as he can make them. He cannot explain his symptoms when he is ill; he appears, tells me that he knows something is wrong with his health, and lets me know what medication he thinks will be most useful for what ails him. There is a painful lack of the warmth and exchange that characterize encounters with my other patients, and I am acutely aware that he will never be moved by any of the personal qualities that bond me with others.

Males are overwhelmingly more affected by Asperger's than females, by a ratio of ten to one. A careful survey of children with classic autism by investigators at the National Center on Birth Defects and Developmental Disabilities at the Centers for Disease Control and Prevention showed that males were four times more affected than females, and the more profoundly handicapped children were likely to be male (4.4 males to 1.3 females).[58]

In a very interesting interpretation of the nature of autism, Simon Baron-Cohen, professor of psychology and psychiatry at Cambridge University and director of its Autism Research Centre, believes that females have "empathizing" brains that make them sensitive to the feelings and motives of others and that the quintessential male's brain is interested in "systems" rather than people. He views autism as an extreme of "male brainedness."[59] Males, he argues, are often most effective when they *do not* feel impelled to take into account the feelings or opinions of others. He uses the example of the general who may order the murder of captives to ensure the survival of his army on relatively limited resources during wartime. Furthermore, he believes men are best at "systemizing" mechanical systems and objects; for example, if they understand how to produce and optimize projectile weapons they are at an advantage in winning territory and other prizes from their competitors. He cites the facility men have with negotiating, remembering the features of their journeys through space, and the importance of the ability to sense, remember, and utilize the characteristics of hunted prey. Excellence in trading requires an analysis of the market and the value of objects within it. Most of all, the male interest in securing the most *power* within a social system ensures his ability to copulate with the most females. The latter, in turn, seek the protection of these most competent males and their superior genes.

These traits of male and female brains are evident in employment to this day: Men emphasize their rank within the corporation and the degree of power they wield within the system in which they work. Salary is representative of power, and they rate it as of primary importance. In contrast, women place greater value on the ambiance of the workplace and their relationships with other workers.[60] Baron-Cohen comments that, even today, men's positions in the social hierarchy affect their ability to procreate; he points out that men with higher social status are more likely to be married, and tend to have more children.

——•◆•——

All the data show that negotiating intrauterine life, emerging safely, and surviving the first weeks of postnatal existence are more challenging for boys than girls; fewer males survive, and those who do are more likely to be handicapped by developmental disabilities than girls. I am constantly reminded of a pediatrician who told me that her first thought when she is told that a newborn is in trouble is to hope that it isn't a boy, because a boy's survival is so much less likely. It might be argued that societies who assign more care and resources to male children are not acting in an entirely inappropriate way, but boys' biological vulnerability may well justify extra resources and informed, targeted attention to their needs.

CHAPTER THREE

EDUCATING BOYS

HOW WELL ARE WE DOING?

Boys suffer from a narrow definition of masculinity in our culture. Their emotional responses are squelched by society's expectations that they grow into tough, stoic, and invulnerable young men. They also have cognitive needs that some educators believe are not being met. Most psychologists believe that boys and girls have significant innate differences in skills and a different developmental sequence of the brain, but MIT's Elizabeth Spelke believes that societal pressures are the sole force in forming the sex-specific characteristics attributed to males. While it is true, as noted, that, from the first, boys prefer objects to people, and that they are less verbal, yet more competitive and rough and tumble than their sisters, Spelke thinks these are not innate preferences or behavioral patterns. She believes that we (beginning with parents) shape these characteristics, by projecting onto boys and girls our own prejudices and thus impacting the way their brains actually develop. Rebutting Spelke, Harvard cognitive psychologist Steven Pinker put it this way: "Those who don't believe that boys and girls are different from birth on constitute a unique group: 'childless.'"

I find it amazing that we doctors often omit critical information about neurobiological development when discussing how best to help children learn. A strategy for the optimal education of both sexes should take into account the differences in cognitive skills and the different timing of brain development in boys and girls. Certainly, the two sexes can be taught in the same environment, but different teaching strategies will maximize learning by both.

First of all, the success of any teacher depends on her ability to assess the strengths of her students, to engage them in exploring knowledge, and to foster a mutual sense of excitement and wonder at the amazing complexity and beauty of the world. The first teacher I had was my mother, who taught me to read when I was only three. I remember she taught me the alphabet in a single afternoon and then, as I stood by the side of her chair, we went through pages of print of increasing complexity. Her serenity, patience, and close attention to my progress were key ingredients; I had the keen awareness that we had embarked on a great adventure and that my progress was as exciting to her as it was to me.

During my long career in medicine, I have taught people at all levels; to me the greatest successes are achieved in very small groups, where both student and teacher engage in a common exploration of the subject at hand. Invariably, I learn as much as my students; their untutored eyes often uncover something I had never observed before, and they ask questions about things I had never thought of asking myself. Nothing is as fascinating as the eye of a naïve observer; it challenges and expands even the most accomplished professor's view of a subject, which often becomes fixed and limited. If, as we have shown in the previous chapter, boys' and girls' brains develop at different rates and men and women have sex-specific brains, what should it mean for how men are raised and educated?

TIMING IS EVERYTHING: THE GENDER-SPECIFIC DEVELOPMENT OF THE BRAIN

Even the order of our birth has an impact on cognition: Regardless of sex, the firstborn child in a family has a modest but significant superiority in IQ scores.[1] Spelke would no doubt say that this is the result of the relatively greater attention parents give to their first child; certainly my children point out that there are hundreds of pictures of my daughter in our photo album but significantly fewer of her younger brother. But other differences are innate and immune to environmental influences: There is a definite difference in timing of brain maturation and in the development of sex-specific specialized skills in boys and girls. The well-known "chattiness" of little girls compared to their much more taciturn brothers is a case in point. A patient of mine described how her two-year-old granddaughter seized her hand, pointed to an empty chair next to her own, and demanded that her grandmother sit with her and "Talk!" Her brother, on the other hand, captured his grandmother and pulled her across the room to watch him manipulate a new truck that fascinated him. Harriet Hanlon and her colleagues at the Virginia Polytechnic and State University studied the electrical activity of the brain between 2 months and 16 years of age in over 500 children.[2] Girls developed the areas of the brain involved with language processing, fine motor skills, and social skills well before boys, between birth to age six, while boys showed increasing ability to assess spatial relationships and coordinate gross motor movement during the same period. Boys caught up to their sisters in terms of brain development dedicated to language skills by ages 14 to 16, while girls developed their skills with spatial relationships between 8 and 16 years of age.

C. Richard Clark and his colleagues at Flinders University in Australia traced the development and change in cognitive functioning over the lifespan in 1,007 subjects ranging in age from 6 to 82.[3] They confirmed what virtually all studies show: Girls, who had a better memory for spoken instruction than boys but were less adept at visuospatial learning and memory, reached an optimal performance earlier than boys. The superior ability of women to use language is viewed by some evolutionists as a compensation for their smaller size and less developed muscular strength compared with men; they gain an environmental advantage through persuasion and argument as opposed to men, who compete in a more direct, physical way with other men for dominance or resources. I often watch a group of my colleagues discuss a case. The women are much more likely to seek out and accommodate the opinions of others about a difficult diagnosis or therapeutic plan; the men issue an opinion about what should be done without relying so much on consultation and, in general, assemble the available data and reach a decision quickly.

———◆———

Societal expectations and the differential treatment of boys and girls have a profound effect on development. One of the elements of successfully educating preschool and early school boys is to avoid brutalizing them when they suffer injury or hurt, whether it is physical or emotional. It is a mistake to urge boys to stifle their tears, complaints, or protests in an effort to "make men of them." I saw a boy who could not have been more than two years old lean out of his stroller and tumble to the pavement; predictably, he burst into astonished tears, more surprised than hurt. His mother dragged him to his feet by one shoulder, put him roughly back into his carriage, and admonished him: "Stop the crying.

Boys don't cry." This kind of treatment costs boys dearly. They learn to suppress their emotional responses to pain, and the consequences are long term. As one psychoanalyst once said to me: "Those early experiences are written in cement."

The impact of the environment on brain development is complex and only partially understood. Among some of the more interesting findings is that musical training in young children can enhance their ability to solve mathematical problems.[4]

The hundreds of surveys of male and female cognitive abilities all reveal pretty much the same thing: the larger the group tested, the more apparent became the small but significant differences between the sexes. But there is a tremendous amount of overlap, and early fostering of natural gifts is critical. Janet Hyde of the Department of Psychology at the University of Wisconsin points out that the most important difference between prepubertal boys and girls is the higher activity level and physical aggressiveness of boys.[5] Even then, she reminds us, the overlap between the sexes urges separation of classes not by sex but by baseline levels of activity. In general, boys expand the space in which they learn; their work spreads out over the tabletop to a greater extent than is the case with girls. Boys are noisier and more physically active, and, in fact, boys are said to make up 90 percent of the behaviorally disabled.[6]

Depression in men is grossly underestimated; men assume it is cowardly to admit anxiety, to complain, or to ask for help when they feel troubled.

> A much better strategy when a boy is in pain is to acknowledge the emotion he is feeling as appropriate but also to couple that acknowledgment with a crucially important question: "What are you/we going to do about this?"

Rather than the admonishment she delivered, after comforting her weeping son, the mother of the child in the stroller might well have shown him the importance of his safety strap and of keeping his hands and feet well inside his carriage. Simply ventilating is not helpful; developing solutions is a way that any injured person, even a very young one, can regain a sense of power over their environment.

Another useful strategy for use with very young boys is to engage them in conversation. Their ability to use language is not as great as their sisters', and conversation helps to encourage them to chat. An ideal time for this is during the walk to school; don't invite their sisters, because there is a chance they would take charge of the conversation completely. A car ride is another ideal situation in which to encourage talking. The ever-present earpieces attached to their iPods should be banned during these rides so that they learn the importance of verbal exchanges.

Boys schooled with girls are often awed by their sisters' superior accomplishments, which is usually the rule until children are in midadolescence; girls are bigger and more verbal, and achieve higher marks within the conventionally didactic atmosphere of the classroom, where a facility with language and an ability to remember spoken words is rewarded. The unique gifts of boys should be noted and acknowledged. Howard Gardner's contribution to thinking about intellectual ability was important because he pointed out that there are as many as seven different kinds of cognitive ability, and that all should be acknowledged and developed.[7] Most school environments concentrate on, test, and reward only two: linguistic intelligence (which involves expertise in using spoken and written language) and what he called logical-mathematical intelligence (which involves the logical analysis of problems, mathematical reasoning, and expertise in scientific investigation). But he reminds us that the others are equally important, including kinesthetic intelligence (the facility to use and coordinate movement in the environment) and interpersonal intelligence (a profoundly important sense of how to engage and utilize the skills and collaboration of others). It is a way of pointing out that our ability to manipulate the environment (which is the only definition of intelligence I have ever thought useful) depends on an assortment of skills that most people possess in one combination or another, and that the best education is one that helps people develop using a broad and inclusive understanding not only of their strengths but of their areas of less-developed competence.

Some inclinations, talents, and abilities don't fall into stereotypical categories in spite of society's notions of what is gender appropriate. Boys' and girls' training doesn't always overcome their attractions to a field not considered to be sex-appropriate. One of the men I watched grow up met his father's iron opposition to his deep interest in fashion and design, evident from the age of five. Obligingly, he went to medical school, but he never practiced medicine. He's now a rising executive in the fashion industry, happy to be there, fulfilling his unquenchable interest in form, color, and design, and content with having satisfied—and survived—his family's pressure to do a "manly thing."

SINGLE SEX EDUCATION: IS IT THE BEST ANSWER?

The special needs of both sexes from preschool to the end of high school have been discussed for decades, and the debate about whether or not single-sex education is more effective has never stopped.

Michael Gurian, an expert in education and a family therapist, has written a comprehensive set of recommendations based on sex-specific brain biology and brain maturation that is worth commenting upon.[8] Some of his observations have tenuous links to the recommendations he makes. He comments that the brain is "just over 60 percent fat and requires omega-3 acids to promote optimal brain performance," for example; I do not know of any data to support this contention. Nevertheless, his recommendations for structuring an optimal learning environment at all levels of precollege education are sound.

In his comments about the preschool and kindergarten classroom he notes the tendency of boys to be more physically aggressive than girls and advances the view that "bumping, prodding, and pushing each other" is a way boys nurture each other. He advises teachers to monitor boys for cruel behavior but urges them not to "shut down" aggressive behavior in boys. He is a proponent of the outdoor classroom at this stage of education, stating, "young children are as much creatures of nature as culture and nature is our great ally in teaching them." He comments that boys need more physical space for their lessons than girls. To address the difference in linguistic competence at this age, he notes that boys improve their language skills if the words are set to music and are accompanied by body movements. Above all, the forging of close links between parents and teachers and a consistent set of rules for behavior at home improve learning for both sexes, but particularly for boys. Finally, the use of psychotropic medications has no place in this early education classroom because, Gurian believes, it interrupts the "natural flow of brain development within human society" and allows parents to continue disruptive management techniques instead of working on effective, one-to-one bonding. Gurian makes gender-specific suggestions for the optimal education of both boys and girls, and he suggests teaching each sex the skills of the other[9]—a recurrent theme among educators at all levels of instruction, as we will point out later in this chapter.

When discussing the composition of the middle school student population, Gurian points out that boys and girls prefer to do things with members of their own sex. In single-sex environments, girls achieve more in math and science, boys thrive in reading and writing, and discipline improves. He discusses the cruelty of students to each other, which is very prominent in the early to midteens and which must be monitored, but he believes that the attacked child may learn to strengthen a personal flaw. Directed physical activity has special importance at this stage of development. He writes: "For boys generally, this is crucial to learn to self-manage testosterone: thus it is even more vital for high testosterone males."

Most educators are in favor of school uniforms and believe that they minimize "identity attention," as they call it. Gurian writes: "The issue of students' rights is relatively low on the priority list because we come to realize that students' rights are better safeguarded by the protection of solid learning and maturity enhancement than by superficial attention to individualizing, dominance and mating behaviors."

Not all educators would agree that single-sex education is the only way to train boys and girls. Sometimes it isn't possible or practical to segregate youngsters according to gender. While it may be helpful to use different techniques in teaching, especially in the early years of education, combining the two sexes can be very helpful.

Brother Brian Cartey, founder and headmaster of the innovative De La Salle Academy on Amsterdam Avenue in New York City, was inspired to begin the school because schoolchildren who excelled in their Catholic grammar schools were not making it through high school in the same system. The model of grammar school training was the auditory lesson plan; children were not trained to read and digest the important points of a text, skills so important to success in high school. Boys in particular were bored to death; they became unruly and pests in high school. So Brother Brian founded a new middle school, focused on the needs of sixth- to eighth-graders.

In the process of combining girls and boys in the same classes, he became an expert on sex differences; he told me that middle school girls were bigger, more confident, and had qualities of leadership that boys of the same age simply didn't have. The boys, he felt, actually profited from working alongside girls and learning from them, even when their developmental stages were quite different. He believes that the girls are developmentally two years ahead of the boys and are the moral leaders of the class. Boys, on the other hand, teach the girls not to be mean, petty, or vindictive. Girls, he says, "are possessive. And they never forget." I found it fascinating that there was no physical education period in his curriculum, because there was literally no space for it in the small building that housed his classes. When I asked him about the consequences, he said simply that it was easy to channel and direct the physical activity of the students.

In an ideal world, Brother Brian favors single-sex education until college. Because girls consistently set the standard and out-achieve the boys in their classes from the time they are in elementary school, boys can feel left behind. He believes that pubescence, particularly for boys, is a challenging time unless the child has been able to develop a strong sense of himself and understand the nature of his own gifts and talents. These years are a crucial time, he thinks, in human development: Brother Brian believes that by the time a student is in the eighth grade, the adult persona is essentially formed.

His gender-specific philosophy seems to be working well. Independent high schools have discovered the stellar results of Brother Brian's academy and many of the most prestigious seek out his eighth-graders for admission.

General Joe Franklin, the former commandant at West Point who supervised the court-ordered integration of women into the student body, feels that there are still discrete differences between young men and women at the college level. It was quite clear that he did not consider women and men identical and interchangeable. He told me that the two sexes brought quite different skills and approaches to the student body. By the time he had finished his work at West Point, he believed that the academy had integrated the best qualities of women (the ability to form and motivate teams to collaborative effort) with those of men (a single-minded focus on analyzing the task at hand, devising a strategy for achieving a goal, and putting that strategy into place as quickly and economically as possible) into a new and enriched concept of what qualities were important for leadership.

Franklin's observations echo similar opinions about differences in the qualities of leadership in men and women. Luba Chliwniak of George Washington University Graduate School of Education and Human Development reminds us of the work of Carol Gilligan and Sally Helgesen, which holds that integrating masculine and feminine leadership skills would be to our advantage. Helgesen concludes that "women leaders place more emphasis on relationships, sharing, and process, while male CEOs, as per Mintzberg's studies, focus on completing tasks, achieving goals, hoarding of information, and winning."[10]

WHY BOYS DO WORSE ACADEMICALLY

The biology of the incontrovertible differences in male and female brains has been used to debate the suitability of existing educational systems for girls and boys. The claim that boys are "falling behind" is widespread, when in fact, the data to substantiate this are not very strong. Nor does inequality of achievement seem to be due to ignoring the sex-specific qualities and talents of boys. In the first place, equating anatomy—the amount and nature of neurotransmitters and even the functional systems activated in the brain—with aptitude is not appropriate. Our science is still too young and incomplete to warrant translating our data into recommendations for sweeping changes in the educational system to accommodate the unique needs of both sexes. Certainly by the time men and women are ready for college, they are developmentally similar enough to operate with equal effectiveness in the same educational institutions.

Nevertheless, there are some genuine differences in achievement between girls and boys in early education and at the high school level. The U.S. Department of Education, which surveys academic success in elementary and secondary school in the United States, points out several important gender-specific differences.[11]

- Reading performance declined between 1992 and 2005 for both twelfth-grade girls and boys; the percentage of students who had basic skills decreased from 80 to 73 percent, while those judged to be proficient declined from 40 to 35 percent. Female students outscored males.
- In mathematics, male students scored higher than female students, with some ethnic groups performing better than others (Asian/Pacific Islander students scored the highest, while black and Hispanic students achieved the lowest scores).
- Boys were more likely to be expelled from school (of those expelled, 42 percent are boys, 24 percent are girls) and more likely than girls to drop out of high school (65 percent of boys graduate from high school compared with 72 percent of girls).
- Regardless of gender, the most important determinant of academic success remained the socioeconomic status of the student; predictably, those from economically advantaged families in which one or both parents were college graduates did best.

In an excellent review of the issues, Sara Mead reaffirmed that the alleged crisis in boys' performance in school and their failure to go on to higher education in the numbers characteristic of women is not so much related to differences in brain biology as to striking differences in socioeconomic and racial cultures.[12] She questions the notion that our educational system is too female friendly and ignores the special needs and characteristics of boys. As she puts it, "The real story is not about boys doing worse; it's good news about girls doing better." She points out that poor, Hispanic, and black boys are performing most poorly and warns that focusing on gender differences will distract us from the steps that would most improve our educational system.

My daughter, who volunteered as a tutor for young children at a homeless shelter in Harlem some years ago, told me the story of Louis, a black eight-year-old boy who was clearly very bright but was not responding to her efforts to teach him how to diagram a sentence. He was clearly indifferent to "Mary has a new dog" but showed new interest when she substituted: "MC Hammer has a new disc." As she put it, "He then caught on immediately." She asked him where he wanted to go to college; he replied that he didn't even know the name of a college. Columbia University was ten blocks away from the shelter, and she suggested that they walk up there together to see what it was like. "Think about other colleges, too," she said, mentioning to him the names of Harvard, Yale, and Princeton. The cultural and economic deprivation of these boys, who do not even hear, much less dream, that college is an option for them, cannot be overlooked—nor its impact overemphasized.

ARE WE EQUIPPING OUR BOYS FOR NEW SOCIETAL ROLES?

The social evolution taking place in the workplace affects the roles of men and women. As work takes on new features, we need to prepare boys and young men for their changing roles in a changing society. J. P. Gee and his colleagues write:

> Young men have been expected to adapt to an increasingly unstable set of circumstances in the work sphere, threatening the conventional basis of both masculinity and its associated ideal of the male as breadwinner. . . . While schools challenged girls to adapt to new circumstances, young men were not offered similar possibilities to adapt to social and economic change, *even though the restructuring of the workplace and the family called for men with modern and more flexible approaches to their role in society.* New sets of values, aspirations and skills were being asked of men as workers, husbands and fathers. The failure in the last two decades of government, society and schools to address the prevailing forms of, and ideas about, masculinity, particularly in relation to changing work identities and challenges to the patriarchal dominance of the male breadwinner, has had negative repercussions on boys.[13]

In a brilliant essay, Marcus Weaver-Hightower explores the different concepts of what it means to be male in various segments of society.[14] He points out that many black males create a persona that adapts to "the realities of a racist, classist society, choosing to make trouble in school, appearing to be 'cool' and dissociated from the standards expected of them; they prefer and value manual as opposed to intellectual labor." Weaver-Hightower writes:

> The multiple versions of masculinity constantly struggle for dominance . . . and . . . some groups actually achieve dominance. Those that do not—typically but not always men of color, working-class men, gay men, and feminine men—are subject to varying degrees of oppression from the hegemonic group. . . . the masculinity created by and for African-American boys puts them in the double bind of being treated as either dangerous or

endangered, with extra surveillance by dominant groups as the result of either perception.[15]

A 1993 report on minorities in higher education summarized the data from the U.S. Bureau of the Census and the National Center for Education Statistics. It showed the impact of economic and social forces on achievement: Only 52 percent of male Hispanics (compared with 62.8 percent of Hispanic girls) graduated from high school. For African Americans, the completion rate in 1992 was 74.2 percent, down two percentage points since 1990. The figures for those going on to college are even more sobering: 33.8 percent of African American and 37.1 percent of Hispanic high school graduates continue on to college, compared with 42.2 percent of whites.[16]

The physical vulnerability of economically and socially disadvantaged children, particularly boys, is emphasized as a reason for their poor performance in the earliest grades of school by Byrd and Weitzman, from the Department of Pediatrics at the University of Rochester School of Medicine. They studied the data from the parent interviews of 9,996 children from the ages of 7 to 17 years who were the subjects of the Child Health Supplement to the 1988 National Health Interview Survey.[17] Nationwide, 7.8 percent of our children are required to repeat kindergarten or the first grade of school; 28.1 percent of 8-year-old boys and 21.7 percent of same-aged girls were below their modal grade. These children suffer excess illness, particularly deafness, enuresis, speech defects, asthma, and a history of low birth weight. Deafness, associated with repeated ear infections, was an important reason for producing more hyperactive behavior and increasing distractibility. Low maternal education, birth to a teenaged mother, poor comprehension of English, and male gender were specific risk factors for not progressing to the next grade.

An important 2006 Harvard University symposium looked at the fate of boys at the college level, pointing out that while there were 1.6 males for every female graduating from a U.S. four-year college in 1960, the ratios reversed by 2003, with 1.35 females for every male graduate.[18] The survey puts forward what happens to boys in the K–12 years as an important reason for this reversal. Boys have a higher incidence of behavioral problems and spend less time studying and doing homework. Even into the late 1990s, teenage boys had a higher incidence of arrests and school suspensions and a much higher incidence of the diagnosis of attention-deficit hyperactivity disorder.

If you're raising a boy, you know that boys can be difficult to manage, but you also know that one-on-one attention with them can be the most rewarding part of parenthood. Even if they seem difficult to access emotionally, boys are deeply sensitive creatures who need and want our attention. Adolescence and early adulthood is the best time that you can instill in young men the knowledge that their health and happiness matter.

CHAPTER FOUR

THE MALE ADOLESCENT

THE DANGEROUS GULF BETWEEN IMPULSE AND JUDGMENT

A recent paper on the behavior of adolescent male chimpanzees uncannily recalled the behavior of human male adolescents. The authors characterized the chimps as a noisy bunch who were not only hyperactive but also highly vocal—essential elements in what the authors called "intimidation displays." The youngsters "form close bonds with other males. . . . However, severe aggression resulting in serious wounds and even death can occur as they compete for dominance and limited resources." As very young chimps they spent most of their time grooming and playing with other animals in the group; as they grew older, they began to vie for control.[1] Young chimps in communities with just a single adult dominant male showed the highest levels of testosterone and were the most likely to vie for power with the adult. Where there were several adult males, testosterone levels were lower and challenging behavior was much less frequent. Apparently the probability of failure in targeting a number of adult males for defeat intimidated the younger chimps, and their testosterone levels fell accordingly.

The picture of young male behavior among the chimps is eerily similar in several respects to that among humans. Men who expect to prevail in combat have very high levels of testosterone; when they anticipate—or experience—defeat, levels decrease.

As a human adolescent, you were a work in progress. Even the definition of adolescence changes so rapidly that we are hard pressed to articulate it. One of the leading experts in the neurobiology of this crucially important period of development is Ronald Dahl, Staunton Professor of Psychiatry and Pediatrics at the University of Pittsburgh Medical Center. He defines adolescence in humans as "that awkward period between sexual maturation and the attainment of adult roles and responsibilities."[2] Not a very physiological definition, but it does tell us that adolescence begins with what some experts have characterized as the "shower of hormones" that puberty ushers in and culminates with the achievement of what are generally assumed to be the primary goals of adult life: marriage, owning a home, earning enough money to sustain oneself and a family. As Dahl puts it, "adolescence begins with the physical/biological changes related to puberty but ends in the domain of social roles. . . . it encompasses the transition from the social status of a child (who requires adult monitoring) to that of an adult (who is him- or herself responsible for behavior)."

The concept of adolescence is a new one. The period of transition from child to adult was much briefer in rural societies, when children were given adult responsibilities as soon as their physical size and strength permitted. In a survey of 187 different societies, A. Schlegel and H. Barry[3] found that in traditional cultures the interval between the onset of puberty and adulthood was short. In 63 percent of these societies, girls married within two years of the onset of menarche. Boys were married a little later (about four years after the onset of puberty) and only after they had achieved some rite of passage, like a major kill, or the achievement of a skill set that made them competent to care for families. In contrast, in the United States, the transition from menarche to marriage is almost 15 years for women.

You need only look at current data to be convinced that the most important risk factor for a violent or self-inflicted death is to be a male between the ages of 15 and 25. I have several young Wall Street traders in my practice; they are all beautifully dressed, impeccably groomed (brilliantly colored silk suspenders punctuated with amusing figures are a must for these young men), and wildly reckless. They drink huge amounts of alcohol, have a whole variety of sexual encounters—often without the benefit of condoms—and regard sleeping more than four hours a night as a sign of personal weakness. Their travel schedules are particularly punishing; they take pills to sleep and stimulants to wake up, and think nothing of changing environments and geographic locales several times a month. For many, drugs are accepted accessories for relaxing (marijuana) or for what they consider a focused, intense performance (cocaine). Many of them eat one (enormous) meal a day; the rest of the time they are fueled with black coffee and an occasional pastry. They are fiercely competitive and tolerate enormous risks in planning their strategies at work. Winning is the name of the game for these young men. And the size of their year-end bonuses is crucially important to their sense of their own value. They give new meaning to the word "swashbuckling."

Adolescence presents a unique and crucially important developmental paradox that is responsible for the reckless behavior, suicides, and accidental deaths that are such a striking feature of this period in human life. On all fronts, the hazards are worse for boys than for girls. These deaths are occasioned by what Dahl calls *difficulties in the control of behavior and emotion*. The problem is a disconnect between the abrupt increase in gonadal hormones, which produces intense emotional liability and high-intensity feelings, and the slower development of the parts of the brain necessary for judgment and impulse control. These passionate feelings of early adolescence are the impetus for seeking out risky activities that create a high-voltage environment packed with thrills and emotion. Unfortunately, the areas of the brain that are crucial for impulse control, judgment, and the consideration of consequences before acting are still far from finished. Dahl uses the metaphor of "turbo-charging the engines of a fully mature 'car' belonging to an unskilled driver, whose navigational skills are not yet fully in place." He calls this a time of life with *"the potential for internal dys-synchrony"*; it is that dys-synchrony that can have tragic consequences for the individual.

There are good data to suggest that the development of what Dahl calls the "driving skills" needed to modulate behavior come not from the actions of hormones on the brain but from an independent process of brain tailoring that is a function of age and experience. These changes are independent of the hormonal shower that characterizes adolescence and continue to develop long after puberty is over. They involve an increase of gray matter volumes in the frontal lobe at age 11 to 12 with a slow decline and selective pruning of neurons in the same area during adolescence. At the same time, myelination (which insulates individual cells from one another and improves the speed of impulse conduction) continues, and the volume of white matter increases in these areas. The frontal lobe functions to inhibit impulse behavior and regulate emotion and underlies capacity for planning and organization.[4] The cognitive development that proceeds in parallel with the impact of hormonal changes in adolescence proceeds completely independently of the latter; castrated boys have normal cognitive development, and children with precocious puberty have brain development that is completely consonant with their age. Experience is a crucial determinant of brain tailoring during this important period of life. It is known now that excessive alcohol intake and marijuana smoking impacts neural development and can have permanent negative effects on cognitive ability.

The fact that the adolescent male brain is a work in progress is attested to by the frequency of tics.

> Tics are an example of an impulse disorder that occurs in as many as 20 percent of boys. The natural course of the disability illustrates the importance of brain development in adolescence. Although tics begin in childhood and crescendo in severity at puberty, the development of the brain during adolescence coincides with an amelioration in symptoms and by the age of 18, 90 percent of patients are vastly improved and 40 percent are symptom free.

The importance of hormones in tic disorders is undisputed: Androgens can exacerbate tics,[5] and medications that block androgen receptors lessen the intensity and frequency of tics.[6] A fascinating study by Kerstin Plessen and her colleagues at Columbia University shows that girls with Tourette's syndrome "exhibited more gender dysphoria, had increased masculine play references and exhibited a more 'masculine' pattern of performance on spatial tasks than did female control subjects."[7]

Special survival risks characterize this time of life. The adolescent is convinced that he is immortal and protected from the vulnerability that other, older humans experience; this is a feature of his propensity for risky undertakings that cannot be underestimated. It is what sends 17 and 18 year olds to war; they assume that they will be immune from harm and, like all adolescents, have a passionate idealism that further fuels their willing acquiescence to accept—and even seek—dangerous assignments, particularly if they are perceived as important to the attainment of an idealistic goal. Consider the dedication, bravery in the face of certain death, and idealism of an all-black regiment of freed slaves led by Colonel Robert Gould, the scion of a prominent abolitionist Boston family, who himself was only 23 years old when he led his troops in a doomed attack on an impregnable Southern fort during the Civil War. He and over half of his men died in that effort. Thus, one might view young men as uniquely valuable to societies where great sacrifices are required for maintenance of the status quo and for defending territory and social systems. Indeed, it might be argued that the developmental explosion of intense emotion, idealism, and risk-taking behavior might make the adolescent one of the most important components of a successful society.

ABUSING CHILDREN: THE IMPACT ON ADULT EXISTENCE

The societal cost of adolescent abuse is graphically described in a study done on 169 former child soldiers who had been violently recruited by the armed forces in Africa's Great Lakes Region.[8] The average age of these children was 15; 83.4 percent were boys and 16.6 percent were girls. There are a number of different rating instruments and scales to quantify post-traumatic stress disorder severity. The instrument used in this study was the Child Posttraumatic Stress Disorder Reaction Index, in which 17 items, rated on a 0–4 scale, are assessed. A value higher than 35 classified a child as having clinically important post-traumatic stress disorder (PTSD). The median symptom score was 29 for these children, about 35 percent of whom had a score higher than 35. Interestingly, there was no significant association between the kinds of trauma these children had suffered and the presence of PTSD. However, children with high scores were significantly less likely to be open to reconciliation, less likely to renounce the desire for revenge, and less likely to integrate into postwar society—an ominous warning that the stability of such societies could be threatened by these individuals. PTSD obviously compounds the susceptibility of boys, who are often significantly depressed to begin with, to asocial behavior at the least and suicide at worst. The authors urged the United Nations Convention on the Rights of the Child to work diligently to promote the psychological recovery of these adolescents.[9]

THE IMPACT OF COUNSELING ON ADOLESCENT BEHAVIOR

If you're raising an adolescent, you know he needs surveillance, protection, and support at the very time when he is most likely to protest and rebel against them. Nevertheless, it is clear that counsel can be effective. At a reception for a major political figure, I was introduced to the CEO of an important international company. He had his three sons with him, and I told him I was researching a book on male health. He asked me to write about the vulnerability of adolescent males, whom he thought needed special supervision and guidance until they reached young adulthood. "Part of their brains just hasn't developed yet! If you can keep them from self-destruction until they are 20, they'll be fine." He is right: Parenting and input from concerned adults pays off. In one study, black male adolescents who received counseling about HIV risk reduction were more likely to use protective measures during sexual activity than those who had not.[10]

In a fascinating discussion of how adolescent boys are best prepared for adult life, William Pollack of Harvard Medical School points out that we all are painfully ignorant of the needs of young boys.[11] He describes a cultural tradition of pushing young men toward acts of false bravado and violence so as to prove themselves. He calls it a death-inducing model of what many psychologists depict as necessary for progress into masculinity. He says:

> Our research has demonstrated that adolescent males, as boys, are subjected to a . . . socialization model that is traumatic; this model is likely to lead to a continuum of difficulties that stretches from quiet desperation to academic failure to bullying and acts of overt violence. . . . [This treatment] leads to an early loss of inner connection from the vulnerable sides of the self, a psychic inner schism between vulnerable emotions of care and empathy which are forced underground or behind a "mask" and the only open common pathway of affect and the expression of affect: anger and anger-tinged expressions through action based activities.

He points out that "boys, much like the girls we cherish, frequently experience intense sadness, vulnerability, and a troubling sense of isolation, disconnection, and despair. While many of our boys are in deep emotional pain, their suffering often remains difficult to detect and is sometimes invisible."

Pollack deplores what he describes as our tendencies to force boys prematurely to separate from their mothers and "all things maternal," creating a traumatic separation for which boys are simply not ready. He believes that this is an important cause of adolescent suicide, so much more frequent in boys' lives than in girls'—and that our treatment of boys produces it.

WHAT ROLE DOES VIOLENCE IN THE MEDIA PLAY IN ADOLESCENT BEHAVIOR?

The role that violent elements in the media and video games play in creating maladaptive teenaged behavior has been widely debated.

Here are some important statistics: By the time they finish high school, American children will have watched 19,000 hours of television; by 18, they will have seen 200,000 acts of violence, including 40,000 murders.[12] Boys apparently enjoy watching violent programs and playing combat-laden video games more than girls. An Iowa State University study of 600 seventh- and eighth-graders at four schools in the Midwest showed that boys played 13 hours of games per week, and often named a game with very violent content as a favorite, whereas girls played only 5 hours a week, and only 20 percent of those girls named a favorite with "high violent content."[13]

A variety of similar studies suggests that neither the content of nor exposure to the games is a determinant of violent behavior: Children's behavior reflects parental monitoring and the interpretation of the content of such videos and programs. Children whose parents set limits on the frequency and type of video games used were less likely to defy teachers and disrupt classes with violent behavior.

What is the consequence of risk taking? Almost without exception, the risk-taking behavior is antisocial. In one study, 80 percent of 11- to 15-year-olds exhibited one or more problem behaviors, including substance abuse and even criminal activity like theft.[14] The use of drugs in adolescence is fraught with more intense penalties than at any other time in life. These individuals become addicted to alcohol more quickly than adults.[15] The earlier alcohol is used, the more dire the consequences: The rate of lifetime addiction in one study proved to be 40 percent when children began drinking at or before age 14, but only 10 percent when they waited until 20 years of age.[16] Similarly, adolescents who start to smoke are addicted to nicotine within a year.[17]

Traditional drug abuse programs that target people 30 years of age or older are less effective for adolescents; most drug abuse and drug dependence not only starts in adolescence, but peaks around age 19. Lynne Lamberg, a columnist for the *Journal of the*

American Medical Association, summarized some of the features of programs that succeed with adolescents.[18] The most effective allow participants to meet with others of the same age; the less effective fold adolescents into groups where members are usually over 40, discuss marriage, work, and children, and have a spiritual bent that may be foreign or irrelevant to the child. Smoking is an important first focus, since it is the gateway to alcohol and other drug use. It is also key to monitor the adolescent for the presence of a major depressive disorder. Such a disorder predicts a high degree of relapse in the addict and recommends the use of fluoxetine, the only antidepressant medication that has Food and Drug Administration (FDA) approval for the treatment of depression in adolescents.

As noted earlier, one of the most important issues of adolescence is the dramatic increase in suicide that occurs at puberty and continues to expand into the early twenties.

> At all ages, male suicides outnumber those of females. From the age of 15 to 19, 16 boys in 100,000 commit suicide, while only 3.6 girls do.[19] While females attempt suicide more frequently than males, males are four times more likely to succeed.[20]

The reasons for this discrepancy are various, none of them proven. Some authorities suggest that girls are encouraged to control angry feelings and withhold aggression, while boys are encouraged to operate in a proactive way and "to respond to problems with vigor and forthrightness, or at least stoicism."[21]

A new development in the pattern of adolescent suicide is the change in the vulnerability of African American boys, who had lower rates of suicide than whites in the past, but who over the last 20 years have become as likely as whites to kill themselves.[22] Again, explanations are only speculative, but some authorities contend that the diminishing (and previously strong) impact of stabilizing influences like family, religious organizations, and communities since the 1970s, and the migration of uneducated and economically disadvantaged children from rural to urban centers are among some of the reasons for this increase.

Occupational and work-related injuries are alarmingly frequent among adolescents. In a study of 14- to 18-year-olds, it was apparent that 37 percent of children under the age of 16 reported working after 7 P.M. on a school night, which is an employer violation of federal law.[23] Males were more likely than females to do physically challenging tasks that involved, for example, working at heights or lifting heavy objects. Fifty-two percent of boys (compared with 43 percent of girls) reported using dangerous equipment, prohibited for workers under the age of 18. Boys were more likely to work without supervision than girls. Working in retail trades is not necessarily protective: 13 percent of all deaths were in the retail trades and another 13 percent were in service industries. Homicides associated with robberies were the cause of between one-quarter and one-half of all youth fatalities in the retail trades,[24] and the potential for violent death in this and the service industries is greater than in other trades. Employment of underage children, lack of training and supervision, as well as exposure to potentially dangerous violence, then, are all elements in the high rates of adolescent injuries during this vulnerable period of life.

New and important emphasis on assessing the effects of adolescent bullying on both the perpetrator and the victim shows that society must make a significant effort to understand the elements that produce bullies and develop tactics for opposing them. A study by the National Institute of Child Health and Human Development that surveyed United States children in grades six through ten showed that bullying was more prevalent among boys than girls and occurred more frequently in middle school than in high school.[25] Of the children sampled, 10.6 percent reported bullying others "sometimes," and 8.8 percent admitted bullying others once weekly or more. The outcome for these children is grim: Former bullies have a fourfold increase in criminal behavior by the time they are 24, with 60 percent having at least one conviction and 30 to 35 percent having three or more convictions.[26] Their victims fared poorly as well: They were more likely to suffer depression and poor self-esteem at 23 years of age.

THE IMPRISONED ADOLESCENT

As a house officer on the Columbia University supervised teaching service at Bellevue Hospital, I had two unique experiences. In the first I was rotated through the famous Bellevue "prison ward," where ill prisoners were shackled to their beds while being treated for their illnesses. One of the many lessons about human behavior I learned at Bellevue was that these men seemed no different from those we cared for on the general medical service. I remember asking one quite pleasant and mild-mannered 20-something young man why he was in prison. "I killed my wife," he answered, just as I was preparing to draw his blood for lab tests.

The second unforgettable experience was my assignment to "ride the bus" (the city ambulance) to a Manhattan prison called the Tombs. There we were asked (as 25-year-old newly minted interns) to pronounce an inmate dead or, if he were still alive, to decide whether he was sick enough to take to Bellevue for care. The memory of those desperate prisoners, most of them African American, frightened, filthy, exhausted, and anxious to convince me that they deserved transport out of the prison to the relative safety of Bellevue, has never left me. The more savvy among them feigned seizure disorders. Some were so terrified that at times they screamed in panic. Some had attempted suicide. Without exception, they were visibly grateful to find themselves in the ambulance, escaping the Tombs for the relative safety of the hospital.

Prison populations are overwhelmingly male, and more than half of the inmates are younger than 34. Over 2 million people under the age of 18 are arrested each year in the United States; juvenile crime is being committed at younger ages and is marked by increasing reports of brutality and violence that seem to have no purpose. In the past 15 years, the number of juvenile criminals under the age of 15 increased by 94 percent. The most frequent crimes have to do with assault, carrying a weapon, and murder, which has increased 39 percent. Several explanations of these disturbing facts about juvenile criminality have been put forward:

- More crimes are committed by socioeconomically disadvantaged youths than more fortunate teenagers. Twenty-two percent of children under the age of 18 live in poverty, making them a very high risk group.
- Fewer families are headed by married couples: In 1996, 18 million children were being raised by single parents. Fifty percent of American marriages end in divorce—we have the highest rate of any civilized society.
- Thirty-three percent of American children are born out of wedlock.

The lack of a solid and supportive family structure has a profound impact on the emotional health of children. The broken family often cannot provide satisfactory oversight, guidance, or financial support for offspring. Many unwed mothers are little more than children themselves and have few emotional or educational resources to prepare them for parenting.

The question of whether an adolescent should be held responsible for criminal behavior as an adult, and punished as such, is an important issue. In 2004, eight medical and mental health organizations made the argument that, because the adolescent brain has not achieved its full adult potential, adolescents should not be put to death for their crimes.[27] The U.S. Supreme Court has abolished capital punishment for crimes committed when the perpetrator was younger than 18.

Prison is a much more common destination for men than it is for women, who account for only 6 percent of the incarcerated population. But criminal behavior by women is definitely on the increase, and it is predicted that many more women will be imprisoned in the coming decade. Over 2.4 million women were arrested in 2006—nearly a quarter of all arrests in the United States.[28] The increase in female crime, though, is almost completely explained by drug-related felonies; many fewer women than men were involved in violent crimes.

The vast majority of male prisoners are under the age of 34 and about 8.6 percent of those are under the age of 20. The causes of death among these men mirror those in the general population: Overall, heart disease and cancers lead the list. But while suicide claims only about 2 percent of men in the general population, male prisoners under the age of 18 have a suicide rate that is more than twice as high, almost 5 percent. Suicide rates become somewhat lower as inmates age, but until 35, more deaths are due to suicide than any other cause. Coronary artery disease (CAD) begins to take a grim harvest of men between the ages of 18 and 24, and by 45 to 54, the death rate from CAD has tripled over men ten years younger.

Adolescence is a dangerous and impulsive time—especially for males. We ignore young men's emotional and developmental realities at their risk.

CHAPTER FIVE

MALE DEPRESSION

ITS CAUSES, EXPRESSION, AND TREATMENT

Depression can shorten your life. It can be a lethal illness, not only directly, because it causes suicide, but indirectly, because it plays such a strong role in the production of other dangerous illnesses. In a study looking at the after-discharge survival of hospitalized male veterans, it became apparent that patients with depression were less likely to survive.[1] Moreover, symptoms of sadness during the hospitalizations predicted shorter survival times.

Men with coronary artery disease, hypertension, diabetes, strokes, and susceptibility to infection are often significantly depressed, and that depression plays a role in producing other physical illnesses that can kill them.

Often, my female patients are accompanied by their husbands, who sit patiently in the waiting room, sometimes for over an hour, until the consultation is over. Sometimes the wives ask the men to attend the final parts of the session, and I am able to ask them some relevant questions about what their wives have told me.

Characteristically, they have very little to say; they seem almost anxious not to disturb their spouses and are unwilling to share their thoughts with either of us. Even when they do venture an opinion, it is not unusual for their wives to simply interrupt, outtalk, and bury them in a torrent of words before the men have a chance to say very much. Many wives seem furious with their husbands, who remain meekly silent and have little to say about their own point of view. Discovering the female patient's emotional arousal and despondency is not hard; diagnosing an equally significant depression in the silent husband is not so easy.

> At a recent dinner party, I told a colleague I was writing a book about why men die first. Without a moment's pause, he looked me in the eye and answered, quite seriously: "Because women kill them."

While experts in depression maintain that the incidence of male depression is half that of women, the symptoms in men are such that diagnosis is often missed. Keith Hawton, editor of an important book on suicide, reminds us that suicide may not be easy to predict in men: Males are less likely than females to want to talk about their problems and have relatively less verbal ability to describe what they are feeling.[2] He emphasizes the importance of gender-specific treatment for men that depends not so much on exploring feelings as on constructing solutions for their apparently insoluble problems.

If you are out of work or have retired (even if you elected to do so), you have a particular vulnerability to depression. Men are taught early in their lives that their value depends on how successful they are at their jobs. A 42-year-old screenwriter who was out of work for the first time in a productive and successful career because of the long writers' strike found himself unable to sleep, losing interest in sex with his wife, and eating and drinking heavily. Despite having ample free time, he did not exercise and gained almost 30 pounds in six months.

Charlie, a 68-year-old man whose company had forced him to retire, tried in vain to fill up his empty hours with teaching engagements, but even those were drying up. His wife was threatening to leave him; she complained that he dogged her footsteps wherever she went, wanted to accompany her on even the simplest errand outside of the house, and found separation from her unbearable. Worse, sex became an issue, since he now turned to Viagra to jump-start their moribund love life, reversing a status quo with which his wife had been content. He had developed diabetes and hypertension that were almost impossible to control. His wife had spent most of her time alone at home raising her children while he traveled as a busy salesman, and she now had a hard time adjusting to his presence.

Another 40-something patient called me frantically one day to say that he had been fired from his job as the director of a new play and that he had started a relationship with a woman he found sexually irresistible. Although he loved his wife and their children, the disintegrative effect of losing his job had literally driven him into an affair that was so full of tension, danger, and sexuality that it drowned out his feelings of worthlessness and failure. With counseling, family support from his wise parents, and eventually a new position, the affair completely lost its appeal (and usefulness) and he resumed a life that was, once again, if not ecstatically happy, at least more peaceful.

Sometimes men complain of physical rather than emotional symptoms. A young hedge fund manager, who has wrestled most of his adult life with intense backaches that have defied a precise diagnosis, tells me that the only time he is pain-free is when he is drinking. Characteristically, depressed men become irritable and prone to easy rages. They increase their use of alcohol or other addictive substances, function less effectively at work, and have disturbed sleep patterns. Sexual activity may increase in an effort to suppress loneliness and grief. The basis for the famous seven-year itch is not so much that men tire of their lives—they are simply afraid that they are losing them. They sense the loss of their vitality, strength, and sexual prowess and they try to regain a sense of competence and mastery by seeking out new adventures.

> One charming 50-year-old told me that he had bought his two-seater red convertible Porsche because it was either that or a mistress—and he loved his wife.

Societal pressures on men can be lethal. One of my most heart-wrenching experiences was watching a young man live up to a standard of achievement that created unbearable pressure on him. He consistently earned admission to "the best schools," only to fail all of his courses and be threatened with expulsion. Miraculously, he would regroup, hit the books, and achieve such a brilliant result on his examinations that not only was all forgiven; he was accepted to the next exclusive school to which he applied. This continued in a series of self-engineered disasters and subsequent self-engineered rescues that expressed his profound ambiguity about the path his life was taking. Once, he had the wisdom to take a year off and was given the responsibility of managing a small restaurant. He was supremely successful—and happy—there, but driven by the internalized expectations of the society into which he was born, he went on to graduate school and now is struggling as a young member of a prestigious financial firm. He is valued for his brilliance but the high-pressure demands of his job keep him sleepless and anxious to the point of near exhaustion. He never admits to any distress; he simply keeps forging ahead. I am reminded of my father crossing that field of sunflowers and wonder why this young man cannot find the path to a way to life that will cause him less suffering.

THE ROLE OF TESTOSTERONE IN MALE BEHAVIOR

Imagine a board meeting of the Evolution Corporation chaired by president and CEO Charles Darwin, who is presiding over a discussion about how to design a human being ideally equipped both to perpetuate and to defend the race. They could do no better than create the current young adult male at the peak of his physical powers. Because of his sex and his age as he nears the third decade of his life, he has unique attributes. The high levels of testosterone (peaking during the late teens and early twenties) characteristic of this age support the fundamental role of the male: stabilizing, protecting, and expanding or improving the society in which he lives, even at the cost of his own survival, if necessary. As noted earlier, the young adult male is admirably equipped—and volunteers—for the most dangerous and hazardous jobs society has to offer. He does so with intense idealism, a lust for glory, and a passion for heroic deeds. Those qualities ensure that our society will have large armies in times of war and people who will defend the peace (police and firemen) or take significant risks to build better societies (entrepreneurs). These men are motivated initially by idealism and the pursuit of glory, but after experiencing the dangers, demands, and pressures of their occupations, they are sustained even in their most harrowing moments by an abiding sense of an indissoluble bond with the men with whom they work or fight. These characteristics depend on a testosterone-infused and organized brain working in tandem with an individual's genetic equipment, and they require a stead production of testosterone throughout the man's life.

WHAT CHANGES TESTOSTERONE LEVELS

Testosterone levels vary as a function of your experiences and your age. Free testosterone declines at a rate of about one percent per year throughout adult life. Total testosterone remains steady until about age 50, and then declines by less than one percent per year.[3] We scientists have traditionally thought of men as hormonally stable; we didn't study women directly for decades because we recognized that their hormonal levels fluctuated periodically and would impact the data from any experiment that included them. Testosterone can be tricky. Not only does its level decrease progressively after peaking in your early adult life, but there is a strong, transient impact of environmental conditions on testosterone levels, even in young men.

Marriage, the birth of a child, and competitive interactions can all change the amount of circulating hormone. Yet researchers seldom if ever measure testosterone levels during a clinical trial to see whether they are reasonably uniform in the men being studied. Men's testosterone levels fall after marriage or commitment to one woman. They dip even farther after the birth of a child. Daniel Farrelly and Daniel Nettle in Great Britain have shown that professional male tennis players performed significantly worse in the year after their marriage than in the year before; unmarried players showed no similar fluctuations from year to year.[4] The higher testosterone levels of single men presumably promote copulation with a number of females—or at least the search for them.

TESTOSTERONE AND MALE BONDING

High levels of testosterone promote male bonding and a strong sense of identity with a group. Men at war throw themselves onto live grenades to save the men whom they consistently refer to as brothers. For example, Colonel Jack Jacobs braved continuous, withering enemy fire to retrieve wounded men caught in an ambush in Vietnam, despite the fact that his face and skull were penetrated by shrapnel. Colonel Jacobs, who was awarded the Medal of Honor for his amazing courage, told me in a flat, matter-of-fact tone: "I simply realized there was no one to get those men to safety except me, so I did it. They would have come for me."[5] What drove him to put himself in such mortal danger was not a sense of heroics, but of devotion to the men under his command. After the birth of her fourth child, my mother successfully petitioned the Red Cross during the last year of World War II to negotiate the discharge from the Army of my father, then a captain. But he refused to leave his men, saying that they needed him and that any other demands on him were definitely secondary to that consideration. Male bonding is evident even during peaceful competitions; anyone who has watched a football game knows that successful teammates hug, pat, and embrace one another with enormous enthusiasm after making a good play or winning a game.

The young male wants to "make his bones," to prove his prowess and the ability to stand with other men as an equal, facing up to any task asked of him. His testosterone levels, which will never be higher at any other time in his life, guarantee him strong, thick bones and powerful muscles, physical endurance, a sense of optimism and vitality, and a pervasive, constant interest in sex. Testosterone mutes physical pain, promotes aggressive behavior, sharpens cognition, and guarantees an accurate sense of his relationship to the three-dimensional spaces through which he moves. He can get to a destination quickly and find his way home; he has a finely honed sense of how to aim a projectile so that it will hit its target.

The same high level of testosterone drives him to copulate with as many women as possible. His single Y chromosome provides a rich palate of mutations that ensure the creation of a diverse group of new humans, giving the group an enhanced possibility for survival in an environment that may be harsh and unforgiving. But those same qualities make him a prey to premature, violent death at the hands of bullets, machines, the elements, his fellow men, and suicide.

TESTOSTERONE, DOMINANCE, AND AGGRESSION

Testosterone promotes behavior of two types in males: dominance and aggression. They are quite different. Aggression is defined by scientists working in this field as an intent to inflict physical harm on another. While high levels of testosterone produce *aggressive* behavior in rodents, the hormone promotes *dominant* behavior in primates, including men. Dominance is an effort to achieve or maintain high status in a social system. This impulse, according to sociologists Allan Mazur and Alan Booth, explains antisocial behavior in young males: They maintain that societies like schools, prisons, the army, and family or work groups demand rigidly conscripted standards of behavior.[6] The testosterone-drenched male in a subordinate role within these systems is more likely to break these codes and is then labeled rebellious or even criminal.

When testosterone levels were tested in young male prison inmates, it was found that those with higher concentrations of the hormone were more likely to have been convicted of violent crimes; out of the 11 inmates with the lowest testosterone levels, 9 had committed nonviolent crimes. Those inmates with higher testosterone levels received longer terms before parole and suffered more punishments for disciplinary infractions.[7]

The techniques of achieving dominance include intimidating the opponent without physical confrontation. For example, social scientist Lee Ellis of Minot State University has found that young men with high levels of testosterone smile less than women[8]; it is well accepted that dominance is often achieved by an intimidating glare into the eyes of an opponent; the latter submits by failing to hold his own gaze steady. Smiling, obviously, interferes with the impact of such a stare.

Tony DellaVentura, a retired detective of the New York Police Department and a private investigator known for his ability to subdue enemies by the force of his gaze, describes the phenomenon of whole groups of threatening men "melting away" to let him pass without challenge simply on the basis of this technique. He believes that a cohesive and overwhelmingly powerful inner strength can be manifested by a "drill down" stare into the eyes of an enemy. It is an ancient strategy of warriors to cultivate a terrifying appearance to subdue the enemy, and, as Braudy points out,[9] many incorporate derivatives of fierce animals into their costumes to achieve this, like the lion headdress of Alexander or the tall, bearskin hat of the British soldier. The painted faces and heavily padded bodies of football players are not dissimilar; often teams have the names of bellicose, powerful animals: The Giants, the Bears, and—straight to the point—the Chargers.

Levels of testosterone rise before an anticipated confrontation as well as afterward. The frequency of rape in warfare once the population has been subdued may be related to the increased sexual appetite warfare produces. This phenomenon is possibly an evolutionary effort to replenish the population decimated by war; others think that primates threatened with destruction have an instinctive urge to copulate so that their genetic template will continue. In interviews with men and women cadets at West Point, both sexes mentioned the increase in sexual appetite that they experienced during field maneuvers: "When our sergeant began to look appealing, we knew we'd had enough time wet, dirty, and hungry on maneuvers," said one young female lieutenant recalling her experiences.[10]

MALE SUICIDE

There is no question that the testosterone shower that begins at puberty and reaches an all-time high in late adolescence and young adulthood fuels risk-taking behavior and the impulsivity that leads to violence of all kinds, including murder and suicide; this is the reason the rates of both are so high in the adolescent male and remain so until he has achieved relative maturity.

Suicide and lethal risk taking are the leading causes of male mortality in the teens and twenties. The most shocking events of my four years in medical school were the suicides of three fellow students. To add to the horror, two were "jumpers" who plummeted to their deaths from the windows of their dormitory rooms.

The Center for Disease Control, which records causes of death around the country, published a male mortality table for 2004 that should give us all pause.[11] Suicide was the third most common reason for death, accounting for almost 8 percent of all deaths in the 10 to 14 age group. Only "unintentional injury" (42 percent) and cancer (11 percent) claimed more lives. Homicide in this age group followed next, responsible for 6 percent of deaths. The prominence of homicide and suicide lasted until age 35: From age 15 through 34, homicide and suicide accounted for about 30 percent of deaths. (At age 35, heart disease took over after "unintentional injuries" as the chief cause of men's deaths; after middle age, the common chronic diseases that signal our waning strength and capacities take over—heart disease, cancer, chronic respiratory disease, diabetes, kidney disease and Alzheimer's/Parkinson's replace the violent circumstances of death at younger ages.)

The seriousness of suicide was reinforced by the World Health Organization, which reported in 2000 that 1.5 percent of all deaths worldwide were due to suicide *and that over a quarter of these occurred in young adult males (ages 15–44 years)*; these men were almost all compromised by mental disorders, particularly depression and alcohol addiction. In the Vietnam War years four times as many Americans died of suicide as died of combat.

What causes young men to take their lives? At ages 20–24, fully 15 percent of all deaths are self-inflicted. And the statistics for age groups just before and after this are almost as bad: 14 percent of 15- to 19-year-old boys and 13 percent of 20- to 24-year-olds die by their own hands. Suicide rates are higher in males than in females in most countries of the world (China is an exception).[12] While girls attempt suicide more often, boys excel at successful suicide because they are more likely to intend to actually end their lives (as opposed to simply making a plea for attention to their distress). They also have greater access to violent means of killing themselves and less concern about bodily disfigurement.

As we pointed out in Chapter 4, society itself produces much of the depression in young boys, particularly as they crest into puberty and are subjected to what can only be described as brutal rites of passage. William Pollack, director of the Centers for Men and Young Men at McLean Hospital in Boston, is particularly eloquent about the roots of sadness and isolation in men. He puts it this way:

> Behind their masks of pseudo-invulerability and the drama of action, the one full emotion boys are "allowed" to express within the narrow bandwidth of developing masculinity—*anger*—it is often hard to hear boys' stifled but genuine voices of pain and struggle, their clamoring for reconnection. Indeed . . . it is reasonable to suggest that *the same kind of shame* that silences girls from expressing their voice as adolescents *takes a toll on boys at a much earlier age.*[13]

Pollack believes that the lethal "boy code" we impose on male children intensifies when they begin school and sports; he says we shame boys into denying any feelings of pain and vulnerability and that we increase their distress by exposing them to adult males who have exactly the same responses as they themselves have been trained to exhibit: He quotes a young patient as saying: "My father gets blocked. Like if he's upset about something at work, he can't say anything and I have no idea what he's thinking. He just sits in front of the TV, spends all his time on the Internet, or goes off on his own. He's just totally blocked."

Substance abuse is often involved in male suicide.[14] Excessive alcohol use is perceived in many societies as consistent with gendered concepts of masculinity; refusal to share a drink with others often implies a lack of trust or respect among men. Drinking is also a coping strategy for depression in men. In Eastern Europe ten times as many men as women commit suicide, and the rates of alcoholism are astronomical. Schizophrenics who kill themselves are more likely to be men.[15] Occupational factors like unemployment and retirement also play an important role for men; society still calculates a man's worth in terms of what he does and how good he is at it: "Money is the report card of life," as a male CEO friend said to me.

Ninety percent of suicides are associated with mental illness, most commonly depression.[16] There is a strong genetic component to risk for suicide; the risk is estimated to be at 30–50 percent as a consequence of inheritance. Having a first degree relative who completed suicide increases the risk sixfold.

The link between testosterone and mood are complicated. Below-average levels of the hormone in men are associated with depression. Therapy to increase the levels can be a relief. On the other hand, higher levels (characteristic of the young male) are also

significantly associated with depression. Alan Booth of
Pennsylvania State University and his colleagues point out that
above-average levels are correlated with risk-taking and antisocial
behavior, low occupational success, and a tendency to not marry
or to divorce.[17] Marriage (which, as noted earlier, lowers testosterone levels in men) and employment are stabilizing factors that
lessen male depression.

DIAGNOSING DEPRESSION IN MEN

Although it is difficult for men to admit emotional pain—much
less its causes—they can be helped to understand that depression
is a complex, heterogeneous disorder and that it is the consequence of the interaction of genes, brain biology, and experiences, for most or all of which they are not at fault.

The chemistry of the male brain is different from that of
women: Serotonin synthesis in men's brains is 52 percent higher
than that in women's[18] and has often been cited as a reason for the
supposed lower rates of depression in men. I am personally
convinced that depression is much more frequent in men than we
physicians have realized; their symptoms are simply not those that
we have become accustomed to in women. At a dinner party a few
years ago, I proposed to the men at the table that males were more
frequently depressed than we were aware of: "Of course we are,"
one of them answered instantly. "That's why we die first."

Spotting depression in men becomes easier when we know
what to look for: Harry, a 62-year-old patient of mine, came to me
because his heartbeat had become wildly irregular. He was sweat-
ing profusely as he told me his story; he had chronic back pain,
drank so much alcohol his heart was failing, and was profoundly
alienated from his wife and children, who had stopped trying to
engage him in conversation. He spent most of his time at home in

silent isolation, watching television. His work had suffered; he told me his success as a salesman had diminished to the point where he feared being fired. When I suggested he talk to a psychiatrist about his obvious pain, he dismissed it out of hand: "I know what's wrong; talking about it won't help."

One of my colleagues has periods of communication shut-down that I find impossible to understand. Sometimes his inexplicable silences last for more than three weeks. When he resurfaced from one of these periods, I asked him the meaning of these ruptures in our conversations. He said: "When I get sad, I simply shut down and retreat into myself." To my regret, he didn't discuss the reasons for his periods of depression, nor could I succeed in getting him to discuss them, even though I pride myself on my ability to persuade others to tell me about their pain.

While women typically verbalize their sadness to others and reach out more readily for help with their disease, men isolate themselves in television, electronic games, or other hobbies or turn to drugs. As noted earlier, they become irritable and often uncharacteristically violent. As Dietmar Winkler, a psychiatrist at the Medical University of Vienna put it: "Aggression and especially anger attacks play an important role in the symptomatology of depression. . . . these symptoms are more prevalent in males than in females."[19]

A fascinating and perhaps underappreciated fact is that there is a high incidence of postpartum depression in fathers.[20] Not surprisingly, a father's depression will profoundly impact the family. Paul Ramchandani and his colleagues at the University of Oxford are authors of The Avon Longitudinal Study of Parents and Children (ALSPAC). In this work they point out that children of mothers who suffer postpartum depression have an increased risk of behavioral problems at ages three to five, even after any maternal depression has been addressed and accounted for.[21] The impact was more severe in boys than in girls. The importance of the influence of fathers in this crucial phase of child development has been underestimated, and *both* parents should be monitored for evidence of postpartum depression.

Once again, testosterone's role is center stage in men's vulnerabilities: In severe depression men have a decreased concentration of the hormone—particularly younger men (less than 55 years of age).[22] Cortisol, the stress hormone, on the other hand, is higher than in normal patients. The consequences of these hormonal shifts are crucially important. Lowered vitality, sexual dysfunction, and bone weakening all are features of severe depression in men and, furthermore, are risk factors for diabetes and heart attack.

War, as might be expected, produces a whole variety of mental and emotional illnesses. Seventeen percent of soldiers and Marines returning from Iraq showed twice the incidence of anxiety, post-traumatic stress disorder, or depression found among soldiers who were assessed before deployment.[23] The incidence of depression was highest in the personnel returning from Iraq (19 percent) compared with 11.3 percent after Afghanistan and 8.5 percent from other theaters of war. Clearly, the impact on the soldiers was directly related to the intensity of the conflict and the unpredictability of attack.

The study also showed that soldiers began to reach out for treatment within two months of coming home. Furthermore, over time, the numbers of depressed veterans increased: Veterans were twice as likely to report difficulty three to four months after their return. Because of this, the U.S. screening program was expanded to include a repeat inquiry and measure of depression at 90 to 180 days after the veterans' return.[24]

DEPRESSION IN THE OLDER PATIENT

Depression becomes more frequent as men age. Ten percent of adults 65 years of age or over who are seen in primary care settings have clinically significant depression.[25] At about the age of 50, testosterone levels begin to lessen, and 20 percent of men over the age of 65 have lower-than-normal levels.[26] Jurgen Unutzer, a psychiatrist from the University of Washington in Seattle, warns against assuming that depression is a normal part of aging.[27] He points out that late-life depression can last for years and has a serious, negative impact on health, worsening chronic medical disorders, intensifying pain, causing cognitive impairment, and leading to alcohol or drug dependence. He suggests several strategies for treatment:

- A combination of medication and psychotherapy, with care taken to reassure the patient that dependence on psychotropic medications does not occur;
- A new and favored form of psychotherapy called cognitive behavioral therapy; this avoids a prolonged exploration of the past and concentrates instead on current problems, emphasizing ways to address and solve them;
- Short-term (12-week) exercise programs; 45 to 65 percent of patients who participated in something as simple as a walking program reported improvement.

DEPRESSION AND DISEASE

Depression has a widespread and devastating impact on health. It is associated with disturbances in the endocrine, cardiovascular, and immune systems as well as affecting bone health.[28] The risk of coronary artery disease is three times higher among men with a diagnosis of depression; interestingly, there is no increased risk for women.[29] After they have had a heart attack, depressed patients have a 3.5 increase in cardiovascular mortality. Applying new criteria developed by the World Bank, Harvard

University, and the World Health Organization, researchers found that major depression is the leading cause of disability and lost days from work in developed countries, including the United States.

STRESS AND DEPRESSION

Many patients I counsel on a daily basis complain bitterly about stress; many are depressed—some of them profoundly so—by the challenges of their lives. Although some stress is beneficial (a challenge competently met often develops new competencies), emotional pain that doesn't end or a challenge to which a person is completely unequal eventually produces depression and some-times even suicide as the sufferer tries to escape the unendurable. A myriad of devastating illnesses assault the depressed individual and they must be treated along with the depression itself. Often, however, the uninformed physician will concentrate on the organic illness and remain unaware of the situational depression that lies at its heart. My patients often tell me they have lost their waistlines and accumulated fat in their midsection. They often have high blood pressure and diabetes; they complain that they cannot lose the weight, no matter how they try. Depression is at the root of the problem.

A real or perceived threat starts a well-studied cascade of events (in a process scientists call allostasis, literally, "same state") that begins in the brain and involves the secretion of two classes of hormones in the adrenal gland, glucocorticoids and catecholamines, which help us adapt and survive. Paradoxically, that same cascade can cause harm: The classic metaphor for this is water on a fire: The right amount puts out the flames, but too much causes more damage than the fire.[30]

We each have a different capacity to respond in a constructive way to stress and use unique adaptive mechanisms to cope with it. Mechiel Korte of Wageningen University in Holland and his colleagues use the image of the hawk and the dove to illustrate two major classes of responders.[31] The hawk, bold and aggressive, has a high testosterone and low corticosteroid level. He is a "hot reactor": When challenged, he attacks the foe and frequently conquers. The consequence for the hawk, though, might be wounding, depletion of energy stores, blood loss, and infection. The dove, who is more cautious when facing a threat, freezes in the presence of danger, reducing the likelihood of attack. Silent and wary, he is hyperalert. He gathers all the information his senses can collect and organizes it so that he can either avoid detection or escape. The trade-off for the immobile dove is a higher level of anxiety. Both strategies are useful for survival, but for both hawks and doves, enough stressors can be overwhelming and exceed even the most robust individual's ability to cope with them. In other words, when our allostatic load (as scientists call it) is more than our resources can handle, the body's attempts to cope, which include the secretion of cortisone, testosterone, and inflammatory agents called cytokines, end in illness. Even the production of new brain cells is inhibited.

Hawks react to threats with a surge of activity from the sympathetic nervous system: Their blood pressure and heart rates rise, their pupils dilate, their digestive processes stop, and blood is rerouted to muscles. Their immune system is activated to a high level; they are adapted to fight infection from the wounds they will sustain as part of their aggressive response to threats. As a result, hawks who are challenged too severely and too often run the risk of hypertension and disturbances in cardiac rhythm severe enough to be lethal. Ultimately, their efforts exhaust them, and they become chronically fatigued and depressed.

In doves, a challenge stimulates food intake in a powerful feed-back loop intended to mute anxiety. They store abdominal fat—a resource for survival in times when food is scarce, but, as in societies like ours, where food is virtually always available, those caloric depots are never metabolized. The dove develops insulin resistance, high blood pressure, and cardiovascular disease. Unlike the hawk, the dove's immune system is less competent in fighting off bacterial and viral infections; doves will be more vul-nerable to infections like the common cold. Wounds take longer to heal: The cascade of events with which the dove meets chronic challenges ultimately leads to melancholic depression and even psychosis.

A recently widowed patient of mine came in complaining of weight gain and a steady increase in her previously well-controlled hypertension. Her husband had died after years of a debilitating ill-ness, her financial situation required that she sell her home of 30 years, and she had been dealing with all of these losses and chal-lenges alone. I prescribed more medicines to control her blood pres-sure, then spent an hour explaining the impact of constant severe stress on her health. She had not thought of herself as depressed, but accepted the notion that finding her way alone through this thicket of sorrows and losses was making her seriously ill.

Men tend to suppress these negative feelings. They are reluc-tant to talk about them or even admit them to themselves, believ-ing that to do so is "unmanly."

A man I know, the head of a construction company that was on the verge of bankruptcy, was delivering supplies to a job site in a snowstorm when a tire blew out and sent the car skidding into a snowbank. He got out, surveyed the damage, vomited, and, strug-gling to regain his equilibrium, said aloud: "Well, at least I ain't dead." Marshaling his resources, he changed the tire, dug the car out of the snow, and pushed it back onto the road, completing his deliveries only three hours late. "That," said the man who told me the story, "is a man."

LEARNING HOW DEPRESSION WORKS

We are much more successful at treating depression than understanding what causes it. Thomas Insel and Dennis Charney of the National Institute of Mental Health have identified some of the most important priorities for much-needed research on the biology and successful therapy of depression.[32] These are their recommendations:

- Explore the identification of the genes that predispose to depression.
- Describe the systems of the brain involved in the regulation of mood; how the brain changes during the development of severe depression is unknown.
- Define the processes by which the brain recovers from depression, whether with the aid of psychotherapy or medication.
- Identify the experiences that put an individual at risk for depression. These include stress, loss, and abuse, whether in childhood or in adult life; often the impact of these experiences seems to be dormant for years but takes a dreadful toll later in life.
- Fill the need for new treatments: Existing medications take at least three to four weeks to reduce symptoms and require long-term administration to prevent relapse.
- Create better strategies for identifying the individuals at risk for suicide. Targeted, sex-specific methods of treatment are essential.
- Teach physicians that depression is a component or cause of wide-spread disability and that the treatment of cardiovascular disease, a compromised immune system, and diabetes, among other illnesses, must address depression as a cardinal component of illness.
- Significantly improve the treatment of the depressed patient by physicians: Only 25 percent of patients receive appropriate medicine or therapy.[33]

The first principle in combating depression is to acknowledge feelings of apathy, loss of pleasure, sadness, or even apparently baseless general feelings of irritability and easily provoked anger. Our usual patterns of behavior change too—sometimes in unanticipated directions. Changes in sleep patterns or appetite, an upswing or dip in sexual activity, are all signs that we "are not ourselves."

TREATMENT OF DEPRESSION

The treatment of depression is notoriously difficult in that most medications are prescribed on a trial-and-error basis: Often a patient will not respond at all to one class of drugs but will be improved by another. Roughly 20 medications have been approved for treatment. Many medications are available for the treatment of depression: Lithium; clozapine, an antipsychotic recognized by its commercial name of Clozaril; tricyclics such as Elavil, Tofranil; monamine oxidase inhibitors, such as Nardil, Parnate; and serotonin-reuptake inhibitors, or SSRIs, known by their brand names Paxil, Prozac, and Zoloft, are all effective. Men are more responsive to tricyclic medicines and younger patients to monamine oxidase inhibitors. The rate of synthesis of brain serotonin in normal men is 52 percent higher than that of females, perhaps explaining why SSRIs are more effective for women's depression than for men's. Electroconvulsive therapy should no longer evoke images from *One Flew over the Cuckoo's Nest*. Doses are much reduced, targeted more accurately to much smaller areas of the brain, and they no longer precipitate general seizures.

Only about two-thirds of depressed patients respond to medication at all; genomic analysis is beginning to elucidate at least some of the reasons why this is true. Psychiatrist Francis McMahon of the National Institute of Mental Health found that a specific gene predicts a response to one medication, citalopram (Celexa). Six percent of African Americans, who have a poorer response to antidepressants than Caucasians, have only one copy of the gene that predicts success; the allele was over six times more frequent in whites than blacks.[34] People with two copies (14 percent of whites) did much better on the medication. Genomic profiling will eventually occupy a prominent place in our decisions to treat this and other diseases with specific medications.

Between 30 and 70 percent of men suffer from sexual dysfunction (SD), including erectile dysfunction, delayed orgasm, and diminished libido, after taking antidepressants.[35] The result is often that they discontinue the medication, all too often suffering a relapse. Nearly half have a relapse within 2 to 12 months after prematurely stopping their medicine. Sildenafil (Viagra) was an effective treatment for the sexual dysfunction associated with antidepressants in almost 60 percent of patients studied, except that it did not enhance libido. Lifestyle risk factors such as smoking, drinking, obesity, and stress, and a reaction to other drugs (notably medicines used to treat high blood pressure) may contribute to the failure of some men to respond to Viagra.

Some principles of the treatment of depressed patients with medications include:

- Serotonin-norepinephrine-reuptake inhibitors (SSNIs) should be the first choice in older patients even though tricyclic medications are more effective in younger men. There is a greater likelihood of troublesome side effects with the tricyclics in older patients.
- It may take up to three months of treatment to gain the full effect of medication; two-thirds of patients improve somewhat, however, within four weeks. Only about half will respond to medication.

- Continuing medication after an episode of depression lowers the risk of a relapse. But even patients who continue their medicines can have a recurrence, and the doses of medications often have to be adjusted. Often, entirely new drugs or combinations of drugs are prescribed. Some depressions are chronic and recovery is never complete; 30 percent of the affected people fall into this category, and of those who recover, 60 percent have a relapse within five years. The concept of depression as a chronic condition for some sufferers is a valid one, and new research is focused on determining whether the treatment of persistent depression should be different than for the first episode of illness. The production or use of at least nine of the chemicals that transmit messages between neurons in the brain are disturbed in this illness; recent research is concentrating on developing new drugs to target these entities.

- Electroconvulsive therapy (ECT) is an excellent choice for those patients who fail other modalities. The side effects are much less dramatic now than in the past, but headaches and temporary memory impairment do occur, though both disappear over time. The effect of ECT diminishes, however, and pharmacologic agents should follow the treatment in an effort to maintain stability.

I think the cause of the reportedly higher incidence of suicide in young patients treated with certain antidepressants may have been misinterpreted. I do not believe that the medication per se has been proven to be the cause of suicidal behavior. The observations of my physician father about depression are still very pertinent. He pointed out to me that a depressed person is debilitated. He cannot motivate himself enough to be self-destructive. "Be careful," my father said, "because it is *when they begin to recover that the likelihood of suicide increases.* They feel enough energy, ironically, as their depression lifts, to create and plan and carry it out." He also warned me that sudden improvement in the mood of a depressed patient should be monitored with extreme care; he felt that patients who had made a decision to end their lives found peace and a certain contentment in knowing that their pain would soon be ended.

Depression can strike at any time in a man's life. As an adolescent and young adult, your feelings are acute and raw, and it helps to have an adult who can offer support, such as a therapist. In your adult and middle years, it is equally important to have someone to confide in. Checking in with yourself emotionally is an ongoing project in life and will ease the stress of the many challenges you will face.

Things to do if you are feeling pressured, anxious, or stressed:

- **Check your testosterone level.** This dominant male hormone changes in response to age and the environment. Both high and low levels can produce depression. Testosterone levels decline from age 50 onward; feelings of sadness and increasing anxiety, common as men age, can be corrected with treatment.
- **If you do feel sad or hopeless, resist the impulse to avoid contact with others.** Talk to someone you trust and ask for help. Emotional turmoil affects everyone at some time and it's not a sign of weakness or a lack of masculinity. It takes real courage and resourcefulness to ask for help.
- **Ask your doctor about treatment.** Untreated depression leaves you vulnerable to other illnesses, particularly coronary artery disease, and it can lead to suicide. Depression

weakens the immune system. Wounds heal more slowly and infections increase in frequency. A whole spectrum of useful medications is now available, as well as a new "talking cure" called cognitive behavioral therapy. These brief, practical conversations with a therapist define your problems, help you understand why you are upset, and develop solutions for ways out of seemingly insoluble dilemmas and pressures.

CHAPTER SIX

THE MALE LIBIDO

MEN AND SEX

Men tell me they think about sex all the time: Every one of them says the same thing. Sex and hunger are probably the two most fundamental driving forces in our nature. We have to procreate and eat in order to survive. Everything else is an add-on.

Biologically, men's role is to inseminate women and they are equipped accordingly. Most men possess an unquenchable sexual appetite (particularly when they are adolescents and young adults), an enormous number of sperm (albeit hastily and sometimes haphazardly assembled), and a drive to copulate with as many women as possible. As much as we women resist this truth, many men agree to sustained monogamy for the most part only under pressure from a particularly compelling—and rewarding—mate, and then only because of a unique set of circumstances. This invariably leads to a fundamental divide between the sexes: Women are interested in securing an ally to protect themselves and their offspring and have a laserlike focus on keeping their mate to themselves—at least until their children are old enough to be on their own. One newly minted widow said to me at her husband's funeral that she planned to remarry as soon as possible: "Unmarried women are dead in the water socially." She's right. Nothing is more threatening to a married woman than having an attractive or interesting single woman at her dinner table. Generally, women like to have other women safely paired up with men of their own. If they're not, those singletons should plan on hosting their own dinner parties!

Physically, men in their prime are hard-wired to be in a state of near-perpetual readiness to couple with any female in their environment who is likely to be able to conceive and bear children. Watch a man who is not being monitored by his wife stare at a nubile female—or watch his gaze immediately—and dismissively—slide off the face of a woman clearly past child-bearing age. Accordingly, men joust with other males for control over as many females as possible and discourage invading competitors with every resource at their command. The reward for winning is a further boost to their testosterone levels (just as the penalty for losing is a dip in levels). They compete for first place just as their counterparts in the animal kingdom do: They offer women gifts as a sign of their material resources (read: power over the environment), don dazzling raiment, and mount exotic displays of strength, intelligence, and charm. The displays vary with the environment: One of my favorite activities is watching people in the gym. Women quietly go about using their treadmills or bikes, often plugged into their iPods and pretty much oblivious to everyone else in the room. If they have trainers, the exchanges are almost inaudible and brief between the client and the professional. Most men, though, strut up and down the exercise floor, making a whole variety of sounds as they grind through their exercises, talking extensively with their trainers about every maneuver. They take up so much space! Some of their exercises carry them, grunting and leaping sideways, up the whole extent of corridors. It is impossible to ignore them and I've seldom seen one listening to his iPod; most are very much plugged into the environment and aware of their impact on it.

Once the conquest of a female is achieved, it's not uncommon for a man's interest to disappear. Some of the most relentless womanizers I've met in my career are notorious for their ability to treat women like used Kleenex. They operate at full throttle to achieve the successful seduction of the partners they target but never copulate with the same woman twice unless they have no other alternative. Winning—keeping—the interest and, more relevant, the exclusive allegiance of a man is no easy task. And the odds are even worse for negotiating a long-term monogamous relationship. Unlike most women, most men can—and often do—easily dissociate sex from affection.

Lovemaking produces a bath of the bonding hormone oxytocin, which encourages and deepens devotion to your sexual partner. But while estrogen intensifies the action of oxytocin, testosterone blocks its effect.

Listen to the dry voice of science on the subject of monogamy:

Monogamous pair bonds are relatively rare among mammalian species . . . only about 3 percent of mammalian species display such bonds, and even fewer appear to exhibit obligate monogamy.[1]

And this:

Monogamy is one of the most puzzling of mammalian mating systems, for it is not clear why males should confine themselves to breeding with a single female.[2]

For most scientists who think about the reason for monogamy, the most persuasive explanations for it are practical ones: Males stay with one female when the cost of more than one is too expensive.

That translates into contemporary life: One of my patients, in love with a woman to whom he wasn't married, told me that divorce was too expensive to contemplate—despite the attraction of the idea of changing spouses! Environmental resources may be so scarce that competing for them is the overwhelmingly important priority; many men are consumed by a 14-hour workday that they then continue on their ever-active BlackBerrys.

Scarcity of women is another factor in compelling male commitment: Females may hold control of such a large territory that males cannot defend more than one from interlopers, and reproductive success depends on an investment not only in the female, but in helping her raise the offspring successfully. This was true in the early days of the Wild West, where men hotly competed for the occasional woman hardy enough to venture into the untamed world of that time.

So monogamy ultimately turns out to be an eminently practical decision. The increase in the number of house husbands in the current climate of women's ever-greater success in the marketplace attests to the practicality of monogamy in a world where women have tremendous earning power and command a greater investment in child-rearing (and nest maintenance) from their spouses. At a recent conference of powerful women at Harvard I met a managing director who was as remarkable for her obvious intelligence as for her personal beauty. She had married one man who had stayed at home while she pursued her successful career, only to lose him to cancer. Within a year she had met and married a second man, who also was content to remain at home while she traveled into the marketplace and around the world, earning the family income. She loved both men dearly and had chosen wisely for her purposes. As had each of her husbands.

Adolescent males present a unique problem with commitment: The problem of promiscuity in adolescent males (and its attendant epidemic of sexually transmitted disease) is compounded by the issues discussed earlier in this book, such as risk taking.

Adolescents often intellectually acknowledge their vulnerability to risk—talking about it quite rationally but believing (illogically) that they will never experience any adverse consequences of such behavior.

One of my patients, a stunning African American male who is a superlative athlete, has a whole bevy of women competing for his attention. I asked him if he had one favorite; predictably he answered that he slept with many young women. "Do you use a condom?" I asked. "Not always," he answered. "Why not?" I countered. "Because it feels better without one" was the immediate answer. He reassured himself that testing annually for HIV infection was enough to monitor his sexual activity. Denial, I often remind myself, is an essential part of young male behavior. Unfortunately for them, evolution has fashioned young males at the peak of their physical powers to believe they are immortal. They enthusiastically take the enormous risks needed to perpetuate—and defend—the tribe, emotionally shielded from the painful awareness that they are vulnerable, and often engage in mortally dangerous behavior.

Testosterone's fueling of sexual desire isn't restricted to one sex. Many studies of testosterone treatment of women with low libido document its impact.

In a study led by investigators from the prestigious Massachusetts General Hospital in Boston, a testosterone patch in 75 women produced spectacular results: The percent of women having sexual fantasies at least once a week doubled[3] and the number of women who had intercourse at least once a week went from 23 percent to 41 percent. Desire, the intensity of arousal, and the enjoyment and intensity of orgasm all increased significantly. Women reported less depression and an improved sense of well-being on the hormone.

YOU SMELL SO GOOD:
WHAT MAKES US MONOGAMOUS

Practicality doesn't seem to explain the whole mystery of why some people pair with unique devotion. Scientists have long been fascinated with the prairie vole, an animal that lives in contented bliss in pairs that mutually care for the young and show no impulse to copulate with any other than their chosen mate. The chemistry underlying this amazing fidelity is multifaceted, but it seems to depend in an essential way on a hormone called vaso-pressin. Vasopressin finds its way to the pleasure centers of the male's brain; the release of vasopressin is prompted, experts think, by the smell of a beloved, a unique odor by which he recognizes and bonds to her.[4] His cousin, the rapacious mountain vole, has many fewer receptors for vasopressin in his brain and is a notorious philanderer.

The prairie vole isn't the only species whose nose guides him to romance and commitment: Pheromones, those sex-specific chemicals that send erotic messages to the brain, include a sub-stance in male sweat and another in female urine; both are processed in the brain differently from ordinary odors. Heterosexual women respond to the male odor and heterosexual men to the female scent in their hypothalamus, a part of the brain involved in sexual arousal, rather than in the olfactory center of the brain, where all other odors are processed.[5]

Women also use men's odor as a signal of good or compatible genes: When scientists asked women to rank the appeal of the scent of T-shirts worn for two days by various men, the women chose shirts worn by males who were least similar to themselves; in this way, evolution has equipped women to increase the diversity of their offspring's genes.[6]

HANGING ON: WHY WE DO IT

Nevertheless, both men and women are hardwired to stay with their lovers at least until offspring are born and weaned. Helen Fisher, an anthropologist who has made the physiology of falling in love her life's work, says that there is a predictable biochemistry in the brain that underlies the temporary (about 18 months) but delightful phenomenon of infatuation. At no other time in their lives are the brains of men and women more similar in their activation and chemistry than during an infatuation.

It's the product of a sequence of changes that involves an increase in brain dopamine (the "reward" chemical that's released when we do something pleasant and that underlies addictive behavior). Infatuation also produces an increase in epinephrine and norepinephrine, hormones that fast-forward the metabolic rate, reducing appetite (the best way to lose weight fast is to fall into infatuation), and producing sleepless nights (which the French call "white nights"). The third component in infatuation is a decrease in brain serotonin, which produces the obsessive behavior ("I can't stop thinking about him/her") that blots out everything except thoughts of the beloved. It also serves to blot out any attraction to a third party, at least as long as the infatuation lasts. Interestingly, cocaine addiction involves the same areas of the brain as are involved in infatuation: Both stimuli produce euphoria!

Dr. Fisher points out the close relationship between infatuation and rage in the brain. The rejected lover often is aroused to intense anger against the beloved. Fisher believes that this anger enables people to move away from these intense relationships when they are no longer viable so that the rejected partner can start new relationships.[7]

The toll that loss and rage take on the human heart is not trivial: People literally die of broken hearts, succumbing to heart attacks and strokes as a result of their depression. Fisher believes that the sadness of the rejected, mourning individual might have been conserved during evolution because it is useful in enlisting others to help the abandoned lover to recover, to protect him from harm while he is profoundly sad, and allow him to survive so that he can go on to new beginnings. As Fisher puts it:

> [W]e are built to suffer terribly when love fails—first to protest the departure and try to win the beloved back and later to give up utterly, dust ourselves off and redirect our energy to fall in love again. We are likely to find evidence of any combination of these myriad motivations and emotions as we examine the rejected brain in love.

If a romantic relationship does continue, it transitions into commitment; this longer-lasting, steadier state triggers the release of nature's painkillers, the endorphins, in the brain. Reasonably happy, enduring relationships between two people produce feelings of safety, comfort, and satisfaction in both partners. Men in particular become very dependent on the comfort and advantages of such a pairing: "My wife is my rock," says one man; "I would die for her." And I know he means it.

ERECTILE DYSFUNCTION

Erectile dysfunction is as old as man, and has preoccupied physicians who lived as long ago as Hippocrates. A popular ancient remedy (versions of which still exist) is Spanish fly, which is prepared from the wings of a green beetle and yields a compound that, when ingested, irritates the urinary tract and produces an erection. It's no wonder that a drug such as Viagra has proven to be one of the most successful drugs in the history of the pharmaceutical industry.

Pfizer's sales of it are $1.5 billion a year, and 16 million men have taken it as of September 2001.

> Erectile dysfunction, formally defined as "the inability to achieve and maintain an erection sufficient to permit satisfactory sexual intercourse,"[8] affects 20 to 30 million men in the United States.[9]

And they are not all old men: There are so many things that can impair male sexual performance that it's a challenge just to pinpoint the major problem in any one case. Often it's a lack of confidence: One couple I counseled, both in their midthirties, had been anticipating being alone for the first time for weeks. Both were tremendously eager for the encounter, but inexplicably, once they got to bed, the man found himself unable to achieve any erection at all. He was simply too anxious about whether or not his performance would be adequate. Happily, this never happened again during any of their subsequent enthusiastic and frequent couplings: After the first successful sexual encounter, anxiety about sexual performance was never a hindrance again.

An erection depends on an increase in blood flow to the penis and a simultaneous block to the outflow of blood from the organ. In other words, at the peak of a rigid erection, the penis contains a maximum volume of blood, which is trapped there. The pressure inside the penis reaches several hundred millimeters of mercury. (Remember that we like to keep the body's blood pressure below 140 mm of mercury, so the pressure in the penis is inordinately high by comparison.) There's a whole array of sequential processes that have to go right to produce an erection: First and foremost, the brain has to send the right messages to the penis. Anxiety about performance, a stressful relationship, anger, or fatigue can all dampen or eliminate an erection. Other causes are organic: Diseases of the nervous system like Parkinson's or Alzheimer's disease or some types of spinal cord injury impair erection. Testosterone deficiency is only responsible for some of the problems: A lack of the hormone can diminish libido and decrease nocturnal erection. But erection in response to visual sexual stimulation (a very important factor in male arousal) is unaffected. Other reasons for the dysfunction include hypertension, high levels of serum fats, cigarette smoking, diabetes (about 50 percent of men with diabetes mellitus have erectile dysfunction), and injury of the blood vessels carrying blood to the penis. Cyclists beware: Scarring and narrowing of the penile artery can occur in men who have hit either their penis or the whole lower pelvic area.

It's inevitable that sexual function diminishes with age, even in healthy men. Finally, many drugs produce erectile dysfunction as a side effect, and a careful review of the medications you are taking is essential to unravel the cause of erectile dysfunction: Antipsychotic, antidepressant, and some antihypertensive drugs can all work against adequate sexual performance.

Some of the epidemiologic facts about erectile dysfunction suggest that self-esteem or lack of it may play an essential role in sexuality. For example, a careful survey found that erectile dysfunction is almost twice as frequent in men of lower socioeconomic status and less education than in other men.[10] I asked a few men about this; one suggested that the more advantaged members of society had better health profiles and didn't have as high an incidence of diabetes and high blood pressure as other men. I wonder, however, if men who believe they are inadequate to support their families aren't less confident than the men my daughter and her friends call the Masters of the Universe: One investigator found that a drop in family income produced a doubling of erectile dysfunction.[11]

So what will your doctor do to decide the cause of your erectile dysfunction? It's a rather elaborate process that starts with a *careful interview* that takes an inventory of any emotional or social issues you might be facing. For example, the discovery that your partner has been unfaithful or a reversal in your financial situation might be the sole cause of the problem. A medical history and physical examination are the next essential steps. Erectile dysfunction is often the signal that you are suffering a wider and more serious illness, like atherosclerosis or diabetes. Your doctor should evaluate your breast tissue, the distribution and amount of your body hair, the condition of your penis and testes, the strength of all your pulses, and finally, the sensation of your perineal and genital tissue. A complete panel of laboratory tests that assess, among other markers of health, your levels of testosterone, prolactin, and luteinizing hormone are also necessary. Treatment of erectile dysfunction will, of course, depend on what you and your doctor establish as the reason for it.

There are, happily, new medications and devices that eliminate erectile dysfunction and that have largely replaced older interventions like vacuum constriction devices. They include:

- Androgens, which may correct erectile dysfunction *only if a man has abnormally low levels of testosterone*. In men with normal levels of the hormone, there is no effect of additional testosterone on erectile function. If testosterone is given, it's best administered in a skin patch; this ensures even absorption. Your doctor must monitor your liver function, your blood count, cholesterol levels, and, most important, the state of your prostate gland.

- Medications such as Viagra, the commercial name for a drug called sildenafil, inhibit the degradation of cyclic GMP, the substance released during sexual stimulation that allows the penis to fill with blood. Happily, you must be aroused to achieve an erection with sildenafil; without sexual excitement, an erection won't occur. Sildenafil and similar medications have to be avoided in men who are using arterial-dilating drugs like nitroglycerine, because the combined effect can lead to cardiovascular collapse. Minor side effects include nasal congestion, headache, hot flashes, and abnormal vision.

- Older medicines that combat erectile dysfunction include drugs like Yohimbine, which works in the brain and corrects dysfunction that is not due to organic causes like arterial disease. In fact, it has little if any effect on men with an organic cause of their erectile dysfunction. It sometimes produces unwelcome side effects like anxiety, tremors, and palpitations.

- Penile injection with various substances (such as Papaverine) is effective in up to 80 percent of men with psychogenic and neurogenic erectile dysfunction but is less effective in men with arterial disease. Combining Papaverine with phentolamine increases the success rate. Alprostadil (Caverject or Prostin) is the only drug approved for injection in the United States, and it is superior to Papaverine and phentolamine; it produces erections in more than 70 percent of men.[12] Unfortunately, a persistent erection (priapism) and scarring are two not infrequent side effects of these injections.

THE PRICE MEN PAY: UNSAFE SEX AND ITS CONSEQUENCES

As compelling as sexual activity is for men, the consequences of indiscriminate coupling without protection and with multiple partners can be fatal. The following paragraphs provide some common-sense information about sexually transmitted diseases (STDs).

Discharge from the urethra first thing in the morning is a common sign of infection. It is often accompanied by pain. The most likely causes are gonorrhea, which usually develops a few days after exposure, and chlamydia, which takes somewhat longer to appear. Diagnosis depends on an examination of fluid from the urethra. Both illnesses are curable with antibiotics. Some people contract both infections at the same time, so your doctor may give you more than one medicine. Your sexual partners should be told about your own infection so they can be examined and treated as well. While chlamydial and gonorrheal infections are common causes, other bacteria can also inflame the scrotal contents.

Another signal of infection is pelvic pain that extends to the lower back. It is usually a sign of prostatic infection. Gonorrhea, chlamydia, and trichomonas can all affect the prostate, but other organisms can also be the culprit. Your doctor should test you for STDs but may also do an ultrasound examination in some cases. Happily, the long-established custom of prostatic massage to express prostatic fluid for examination has been eliminated.

Pain in the anus and the urge to defecate, bleeding, and discharge all can signal a sexually transmitted illness. Men who are recipients of anal intercourse often experience tears in the anal skin, anal itching, hemorrhoids, or hematomas, which are collections of blood under the skin due to injury.

Genital warts, caused by the human papilloma virus, also require treatment. Gonorrhea, chlamydia, herpes, and syphilis can also express themselves with lesions in and around the mouth. The most serious of these is the primary lesion of syphilis, called a chancre. It is painless but should prompt an immediate visit to your doctor for assessment and, if necessary, treatment.

SYPHILIS: THE "GREAT IMITATOR"

Syphilis deserves special mention. Once essentially vanquished through penicillin, the disease is again on the increase. Syphilis was rampant in the pre-antibiotic era, and was an important cause of premature death. It was as pervasive and terrifying as the AIDS epidemic in our own time—and it was inevitably fatal. It spared no one who was sexually active and some authorities have suggested that some of the most famous names in history were infected, including Friedrich Nietzsche, Isak Dinesen, and Franz Schubert (apparently, Nietzsche was infected by smoking a contaminated cigar when he was an ambulance driver tending to wounded troops).[13] Many instances of so-called inspiration were, in fact, a result of the insanity often manifested in the third stage of syphilis.

Chancre sores appear in the first stage of the infection. The chancre appears ten days to three months after contact and lasts from three to six weeks. If these lesions are not treated, the second stage of syphilis begins, about 6 to 12 weeks after contact. Symptoms during this time are general aches, sore throat, fatigue, and headache. Hair loss in clumps and a red, bumpy, scaling skin rash that involves the soles of the feet or palms of the hands (locations that are usually spared by other skin rashes) are important clues to this second, invasive stage of the illness. Often this second stage passes away, and the illness can lie dormant for up to 30 years, until it explodes again in the final, third stage. The physician William Osler called it the great imitator, because the scope and diversity of symptoms are legion and characteristic of many other illnesses. Ultimately, untreated syphilis leads to fatal damage of the nervous and cardiovascular systems.

Some unexpected consequences of other sexually transmitted diseases deserve mention.

- Chlamydia is an infection caused by an organism called Chlamydia tracomatis. It is particularly dangerous because it can exist without symptoms. It can cause infertility and is an important cause of prostatitis.
- Gonorrhea is important to detect because it makes the body vulnerable to syphilis, and patients should be treated for both

diseases. Infection can involve the mouth and eyes as well as the penis. Untreated gonorrhea is an important cause of scarring of the urethra, which allows urine to exit the body. Testicular infection is another complication; it results in infertility, if not treated. All your sexual partners for the three months prior to your own infection should also be notified and treated.

- Hepatitis B is a serious viral infection of the liver that is transmitted by sharing needles for drug injection or having unprotected sex with an infected person. Infection can also result from getting a body piercing or permanent tattoo with inadequately sterilized equipment. Treatment if the illness becomes chronic is difficult and sometimes ineffective. Drinking alcohol makes liver function deteriorate further. Vaccination against hepatitis B is an essential step for health care workers, those who work with drug addicts, personnel at homeless shelters, and male homosexuals.

- Although most people think that the human papilloma virus infection is confined to women because it causes cervical cancer, it is an important cause of oral and inner throat cancers, particularly among men younger than 45, who are three times more likely to be affected than women. Worse, more than half of the diagnoses are missed until they are so advanced that the patient can't be saved. Early detection is essential to survival. It is possible to get vaccinated, and the option should be considered seriously by both men *and* women.

- HIV, the virus that causes AIDS, is the most famous infection in recent history. This deadly infection has lost some of its menace because if it is diagnosed early, modern therapy has transformed it for most patients from a fatal to a chronic illness.

There is an important debate about whether or not circumcision limits HIV infection or its transmission to a partner. A recent review of 35 studies of the subject suggests that the recommendation to mandate circumcision as a means of preventing infection is not scientifically sound.[14] Its author points out that most studies don't consider the incidence of factors that might increase the danger of infection, including exposure to and extensive contact with infected prostitutes and penile ulcers. Other authorities point out the extensive innervation of the human prepuce that enhances sexual pleasure and stress its important function in preventing disease.[15] The foreskin also manufactures natural lubricants that facilitate penetration during intercourse and generate an immune response to invading organisms.

The best defense against STDs is the use of the male latex condom. Condoms are the *only* contraceptive method proven to reduce the risk of all STDs, including HIV infection. Even when the condom is stretched or stressed, viruses cannot pass through it. In countries where its use is promoted, such as Thailand, condom use by sex workers reduced the number of cases of bacterially caused STDs from 410,406 cases in 1994 to 27,362 cases in 1997. As a result, condom use grew from 14 percent in 1990 to 94 percent in 1994 in Thailand among sex workers.[16]

So the message is clear:

- Restrict your sexual activity to as few partners as possible, and ask them to be thoroughly tested if you are going to embark on a prolonged relationship.
- Use latex condoms until freedom from infection *for both partners* has been clearly demonstrated through proper testing. With some diseases there is a six-month latent period between infection and the appearance of antibody in the blood; you must wait for six months after a sexual contact to be certain you haven't been infected.
- If you do develop signs of infection, consult your doctor immediately. If an STD is diagnosed, accept your responsibility and inform your partner(s).

OTHER CAUSES OF TESTICULAR DISCOMFORT

Some problems aren't from infection. One emergency is the twisting of the testicle on its suspending cord. This usually occurs in adolescence and produces intense pain, enough to make the sufferer vomit. Immediate help from a physician is necessary in order to save the testicle. Children between the ages of three and seven may actually have their appendix in the scrotum; this is an important cause of sudden scrotal pain in a child of this age. Some medications, including amiodarone, given to control cardiac rhythm, can cause scrotal swelling and pain. Herniation of the intestine into the scrotum is another important cause of this symptom.

Other causes of scrotal swelling, particularly if it is painless, include cysts (which are usually benign and require no treatment), tuberculosis, syphilis, or a malignancy; ultrasound examination of the scrotum is important for an accurate diagnosis. Varicoceles, which feel like a collection of worms suspending the testicle, can be a cause of infertility in men and should be investigated by a urologist.

A man should be taught to examine his scrotum regularly, just as women are encouraged to monitor their breasts for lumps. An important cancer in young men between the ages of 20 and 30 is a seminoma of the testicle; it is fatal if not diagnosed and treated early. A second peak of seminomas occurs in men between 50 and 60.

MEN ALSO GET HEADACHES FROM SEX

One of the least well understood of all headaches is the one that occurs after sexual intercourse, and it affects predominantly men.

Called "coital cephalgia" it can be mild, lasting a few minutes, or it can start suddenly at the moment of orgasm and last about 20 minutes. Late coital cephalgia lasts hours to days: Some neurologists think this is related to a tear in the covering of the membranes that cover the brain and spinal cord, the meninges, and that a small amount of spinal fluid escapes, causing the pain. The actual mechanism of this peculiar malady is unknown, though. Among the risk factors for it are hypertension, psychological stress, and a history of migraine headaches. It is usually a harmless condition, and may lie latent for many years and then appear. Patients are most often middle-aged men in relatively poor physical shape who are overweight and have mild to moderately high blood pressure. Anyone suffering from this should have a careful initial evaluation that includes an examination of the vessels supplying the brain to rule out any abnormal dilatation of an artery or a hemorrhage following coitus.

It is difficult for men to admit to problems involving their sexual organs. Society defines men by their virility. The truth is that your genitals are just another part of your anatomy and require the same dispassionate medical attention as your lungs. But because the gonads reside outside the body they are more vulnerable to external factors such as heat and pressure. The more you can think of them as body parts that require clinical upkeep the safer you'll be.

Things to keep in mind about sexual activity:

- **Unless your partner and you have tested negative for HIV infection, never have sex without a latex condom.** If an accident happens (the condom breaks or comes off), get tested immediately and again in six months. Early and increasingly more effective treatment for HIV infection has changed what was once a death sentence into a chronic illness.

- **Erectile dysfunction can be caused by one of many factors.** It can have either psychic or physical causes. If you are exhausted, distracted by crises, or angry with your spouse, an erection may be difficult to achieve. But ED for no apparent cause can be the signal that you may have a significant illness like coronary artery disease or diabetes; see your doctor to rule these out.

- **See your doctor if you experience any unusual pelvic or genital pain.** Sexually transmitted diseases are treatable. Make sure, if you have one, that both you *and your* partners are treated.

- **Remember that fertility issues aren't just the result of women's problems;** undetected infection, low sperm count, varicocele, or exposure to substances like pesticides that attack the integrity of sperm are all possible factors in a failure to conceive.

CHAPTER SEVEN

HITTING 40

NEW CHALLENGES

CORONARY ARTERY DISEASE

I was once buying an evening bag in a small shop when a sixty-year-old friend of mine came in. I showed her the purchase I was considering. "I can't imagine buying something like that anymore," she said. "All the men with whom I would have gone out wearing it are dead now." That comment was inexpressibly sad to me and I've never forgotten it.

When I told a male friend who'd been recently discharged from the hospital after months of struggling with a complicated infection that I was writing a book on why men die first, he said, "Oh. I thought that was a given and that there was nothing we could do about it." That few people realize there is hope is an earsplitting alarm bell to me: Certainly there's a great deal we can and *should* be doing! The first step is to understand the scope and nature of the unique weaknesses of men so that we can support targeted research to erase the survival gap.

If I had to focus on one illness that claimed men too early, it would be coronary artery disease (CAD). While it's true that cardiovascular disease is the chief killer of both sexes, it claims them at very different ages.

D.J. Kruger and R.M. Nesse of the Prevention Research Center and Institute for Social Research at the University of Michigan have said: "If you could make male mortality rates the same as female rates, you would do more good than curing cancer." They think that men's vulnerability to disease may be linked to their natural competitiveness for mates.[1] They point out that the primary role of men is to procreate and that they have been selected across millennia for their ability to do so successfully. Paradoxically, the very traits that enable them to succeed at capturing and impregnating females result in both physical and behavioral vulnerabilities that can lead to illness and early death.

Successful mating in our society entails competition with other males as well as the ability to accumulate considerable resources to provide for and share with that mate and her offspring. This success operates to ensure the continuation of the race, but is developed at the personal cost of injury, susceptibility to illness, and death.

As Darwin pointed out, evolution operates to promote the propagation of the most successful genes, but often takes a toll on the well-being and survival of the individual: "Males in many species have been shaped by trade-offs that increase competitive abilities and risk-taking, which in turn increase male reproductive success at the expense of health and longevity."[2] Deer and elk with long antlers have more reproductive success. The same is true of a male peacock with a spectacularly beautiful tail. But oversized antlers and long, heavy tail feathers are unwieldy and heavy, and thus are often a handicap in combat. Similarly, the high testosterone levels of mating season create ideal conditions for parasites to multiply in courting males. And in our own society, the relentless pressure on men to provide more and more resources for their families creates a whole variety of illnesses, including coronary artery disease, hypertension, and diabetes.

Kruger and Nesse write, "The variation and skew in male reproductive success is still substantially higher than that for females. In humans, displays of wealth and social status may literally be a costly signal analogue to the peacock's tail. Cross-culturally, men are evaluated by potential partners in terms of social status and economic power."[3]

Society doesn't help the plight of men. There is no question that life's terrible impact on them is related to societal attitudes about the nature of masculinity. Cultural pressure frequently requires men to minimize vulnerability, pain, and negative emotions such as shame and anxiety. From a young age, boys are taught to dismiss misfortune or discomfort, to press on no matter the situation, often to the point of refusing medical help even in life-threatening situations. But while it is clear that many of the grim deaths of younger men are due largely to their penchant for injudicious, ill-considered, and risky behavior, the reasons men into their forties continue to die in greater numbers than same-aged women are more related to differences in men's internal physiology and susceptibility to disease.

One of my patients is a wealthy man who has not achieved any level of satisfaction with his success in the business world. Timothy drinks six to eight glasses of wine a day, smokes at least two packs of cigarettes, and long ago gave up the physical exercise that had kept him trim as a young man. He is intensely competitive even in social situations, but has a profound sense that he has not achieved the success level that his colleagues and friends have. He strives to "keep up" with them by arranging elaborate parties, and he thrives in social situations laced with alcohol and camaraderie. He is an expert skier and often risks life and limb in aggressively pursuing the sport. (He's had so many fractures that he's now lost count.) Our exchanges are really not exchanges at all: He listens to my suggestions and then rejects any idea of changing his stress level or talking about his emotional state. I have no idea why he comes to see me, and I close his chart in frustration every time he leaves the office. I can only assume that he keeps coming because, in the event that he does have a heart attack, he may actually need me!

The stress that men feel to succeed in contemporary society is an important factor in their vulnerability to CAD. The ability to successfully compete for women in contemporary societies implies economic and social success. An important British study showed that higher socioeconomic positions were directly associated with less coronary heart disease.[4] Men in the least prestigious positions in society had disease rates four times higher than those who held the highest status. Such differences in health have been consistently linked to social class differences since data first became available in 1921. An even more interesting finding is that the rates of CAD are initially higher in people who can best be described as "strivers," such as new immigrants. As strivers prosper, the rates fall, presumably due at least in part to the adoption of healthier lifestyles, but also to the satisfaction that accompanies a sense of achievement and control. The question of whether healthier individuals achieve greater socioeconomic success is a good one: Does achievement lead to health or does health guarantee higher levels of achievement?

CORONARY ARTERY DISEASE, HORMONES AND THE "X" FACTOR

Other factors that make men vulnerable are not attitudinal but genetic, the consequences of their very different hormonal status compared with women. Having only one X chromosome and thus only one copy of any deleterious genes means that men cannot depend on its correcting impact (as can females) by accessing a copy from a second X chromosome.[5] Males also lack the pre-menopausal female's higher estrogen levels, which protect against CAD. In addition, high levels of testosterone are a health hazard: "There is accumulating evidence that prolonged high levels of circulating testosterone may incur costs that may potentially reduce lifetime fitness. These include interference with paternal care, exposure to predators, increased risk of injury, loss of fat stores and possibly impaired immune system function and oncogenic effects."[6]

A 50-something construction engineer came into my office recently, looking gray and haggard. He complained about a symptom that seemed so trivial I didn't understand why it had prompted a visit. "I have some tingling in my back," he said. "It lasts only a few seconds, but it's new and I'm worried about it." I asked what he suspected was causing it: "Heart disease," he answered. "I'm afraid it's angina." His tests indicated that he might well have been right, and I was grateful that he hadn't, like so many of my male patients, simply ignored it.

Saddest of all was a call I had from one of my patients, who sobbed into the telephone receiver that her 42-year-old husband had collapsed at the dinner table and died of a heart attack. He had passed his physical the month before with flying colors and his death horrified everyone, including his doctor.

CAD looms larger than any other illness on the horizon of diseases that threaten men in the prime of their lives. In both sexes it claims more lives every year than any other ailment, but it begins at least a decade earlier in men. Estrogen seems to protect women from the illness until they are well into midlife, but it is not uncommon for the symptoms to begin in men by the age of 35. It is only at the age of 60 that women's risk of suffering the death of part of the heart muscle (called a heart attack or a myocardial infarction) as a result of CAD becomes equal to men's. The vulnerability of men is further evidenced by the fact that between 70 and 89 percent of sudden cardiac events occur in men.[7]

Surveys of the CAD epidemic in men in the British Isles during the twentieth century show a much higher mortality rate in men than women between the years of 1921 to 1998. At the peak of the CAD epidemic in the late 1970s, there were four times as many male deaths as female deaths per 100,000 of the population.[8] Even by 1996, men were dying of the disease three times more frequently than women. Of great importance is the sudden peak in death rates of men of all ages that occurred in 1948.

The most dramatically high incidence was in men between the ages of 35 and 44. Some suggest that the two great wars of the twentieth century claimed the fittest men, leaving the more vulnerable ones to die of CAD years later. War leads to more depression in men and women, and this may also have been a factor.[9]

The reason for this unique vulnerability of men is one of the most important questions in medicine. Since estrogen is known for its protective qualities in women, a clinical trial was set up in the 1970s to test its efficacy in men. The doses administered were so ridiculously high that the patients who received them were dying and the trial was stopped.[10] We have never taken a look at the impact of lower doses, or of an estrogen-like compound that could be effective in postponing the average age of CAD onset in males.

We do know, though, that men have estrogen, although less, of course, than women. If young men become estrogen deficient, levels of good cholesterol (HDL), which acts to keep CAD at bay, decrease. Glucose levels in the blood rise too.

An important source of estrogen for men is aromatase, an enzyme that converts testosterone to estrogen. Men who have no aromatase have the same problems as those who lack estrogen sensitivity in their tissues. They also grow very tall because their bones never stop growing (their epiphyseal plates, which make new bone cells, don't close) and develop early CAD and insulin resistance. Another less well known factor related to men's estrogen levels is obesity; androgens are converted to estrogen in fat cells and very overweight men can develop high voices and grow breasts. Excessive alcohol intake depresses testosterone levels in men and a striking feature of alcoholic males is reddened palms, which exactly resemble those of a pregnant woman. The effects of alcohol abuse are much more pronounced in men than in women; this is also true of their use of tobacco and other drugs.[11]

As its name implies, coronary artery disease assaults the great vessels that carry blood to the heart muscle itself. The resulting arterial lesions are accumulations of cholesterol, inflammatory cells, calcium, and other substances in the wall of the vessel; the older accumulations are capped by a smooth capsule of tissue and are called "hard plaque"; this is the kind of lesion that changes the blood vessels from soft, pliant tubes to hard, rigid, and narrowed channels (hence the term "hardening of the arteries"). Soft plaque is more recent and unstable; it is more likely to rupture, attracting a fresh clot that forms to cover the damage, often with the result that the lumen of the artery is critically narrowed. Blood supply to the heart muscle is interrupted, with disastrous results.

The flow of blood through a narrowed coronary artery can be sufficient when we don't cause the heart muscle to contract rapidly and vigorously. It is only when the heart is called upon to meet the demands of exercise or emotional stress that a problem arises; the stream of blood through the affected artery is insufficient to supply the needs of the working muscle (this is called *coronary insufficiency*). The pain that results is called *angina pectoris*, which literally means "a strangling in the breast." William Osler, whose clear and trenchant prose is as captivating and accurate in 2007 as it was in 1910 when he delivered a lecture on CAD to the Royal College of Physicians in London, describes the patient who is likely to be afflicted by this disease:

> It is not the delicate neurotic person who is prone to angina, but the robust, the vigorous in mind and body, the keen and ambitious man, the indicator of whose engines is always "at full speed ahead." There is, indeed, a frame and facies at once suggestive of angina—the well "set" man of from 45 to 55 years of age, with military bearing, iron grey hair and florid complexion. More than once as such a man entered my consulting room the suggested diagnosis of angina has flashed through my mind.[12]

The unfortunate thing about CAD is that by the time physical symptoms are apparent, it has probably been present for years, and the arterial occlusions (and their precursory lesions) have begun silently accumulating and expanding in the susceptible host, probably beginning in childhood. Genes, lifestyle, and certain other diseases all come together in the susceptible individual to make it likely that he will develop CAD. These are called "risk factors." Preventing the high casualty rate of CAD demands that we know the risk factors for the disease and either eliminate them or, in the case of predisposing conditions or disease, treat them.

RISK FACTORS FOR CORONARY ARTERY DISEASE

One of the best studies of what makes us vulnerable to coronary artery disease is the famous Framingham project, which carefully observed and analyzed what happened to an entire community of people who experienced the illness in a small town in Massachusetts. The observations began in 1948 and continue to the present day. The Framingham scientists studied all the risk factors for having CAD and developed a tool to calculate our individual likelihood of having a heart attack within the next decade of our lives. Keep in mind, however, that the Framingham assessment is based on an almost exclusively white population and likely will not represent the impact of ethnicity on risk. (To assess your own vulnerability, visit The American Heart Association website.[13] It's a useful way to choose the parts of this chapter of particular importance for you.)

Risk factors are situations or conditions that increase the likelihood of our developing a specific disease. The risk factors for CAD are the same for men and women, but they have a different impact depending on the sex of the patient. One of the most important for men is *age*. As discussed earlier, men are about 10 years younger than women when the disease first causes symptoms, and 20 years younger when they have their first heart attack.

The other risk factor that no one can change is genetic vulnerability to disease. *Family history* is an important factor in whether or not you have a genetic susceptibility for CAD. If the disease was diagnosed before age 55 in a first-degree male relative or before age 65 in a mother or sister, your own risk increases. Such a history should prompt a special urgency to modify the lifestyle factors that predispose you to CAD and to treat the specific conditions that further increase risk.

There are several diseases that increase the risk of developing CAD: high blood pressure (referred to as hypertension), diabetes, increased serum cholesterol and/or triglycerides (dyslipidemia), and obesity. The other important risk factors are lifestyle issues: excessive alcohol intake, lack of exercise, smoking, and stress. One of the most important, though, is depression.

Heart Disease and Emotion

As a young doctor, I remember sitting in the office of a senior physician who had suffered his first heart attack in his late forties. I had come to ask about some administrative matter, but I found him in an unexpectedly conversational mode. This was unusual for him; he usually growled out the briefest answers possible to any questions I asked. Overweight and florid-faced, he paced his office as he smoked the cigarette he was seldom without, and to my astonishment, began to open up about personal issues that were weighing on his mind. He told me his concern for his daughter, whom he feared was an alcoholic. I remember thinking that his disclosure reminded me of patients who, anticipating their death, lay bare their memories and worries about unfinished business. At the end of our conversation, he commented on how physically tired he felt and I hesitated uneasily at the door, wondering if I should ask more about what he was feeling. I was very young at the time, and he was a much older, accomplished, and senior physician; I felt it would have been intrusive and even presumptuous to ask him any personal questions. I still regret that I didn't. I left and, the next day, learned that he did indeed lay down on the couch in his office and died at 58 of his last heart attack. I was the last person who ever saw him alive and I still wonder if I could have at least postponed that tragedy had I not been so timid. He never complained, as far as any of us knew, about pain or fatigue. He died alone in his office at the hospital, late in the afternoon of what for him had been an ordinary day of work, ending a life of service to medicine that few have equaled. He was a brave, uncomplaining man whose heart and mind were preoccupied with the sadness of his personal life.

Without a doubt, we pay for emotional pain with heart disease: The old adage of an aching or a broken heart in response to what happens in our lives is exactly on target.

A new condition called Takotsubo's disease has been identified to describe cases where a perfectly good heart fails after sustaining a great emotional shock. There is a measurable death of part of the heart muscle after such emotional trauma, and, although most sufferers repair the damage and recover without ill effect, there is no question that the heart pays a significant price for emotional pain.[14]

I have often found it to be true that the great clinicians of a century ago knew all about what we now rediscover under the guise of a "controlled clinical trial." They often provided us with vivid and accurate descriptions and explanations of the relationship between emotional pain and health. Walter Cannon was one of these: He wrote about the swift death of healthy men condemned to death by voodoo "medicine men." The men succumbed to the conviction that they had been bewitched and would surely die as a result of a curse put upon them. Cannon attributed their subsequent deaths to the devastating effect of the aroused nervous system on the heart's rhythm. Cannon explains the death of a person on whom a spell has been cast this way:[15]

He is now viewed as one who is more nearly in the realm of the sacred and tabu than in the world of the ordinary. . . . The organization of his social life has collapsed and, no longer a member of a group, he is alone and isolated. The doomed man is in a situation from which the only escape is by death. During the death illness, which ensues, the group acts with all the outreach and complexities of its organization and with countless stimuli to suggest death positively to the victim, who is in a highly suggestible state. In addition to the social pressure upon him the victim himself, as a rule, not only makes no effort to live and to stay a part of his group but actually, through the multiple suggestions which he receives, cooperates in the withdrawal from it. He

becomes what the attitude of his fellow tribesmen wills him to
be. Thus he assists in committing a kind of suicide.

The emotional component of vulnerability to CAD has been studied
extensively, and there is strong evidence that depression is not only
causally related to heart disease, but also impacts whether or not
the patient is likely to survive a heart attack: There is a three- to five-
fold CAD increase in patients who suffer from major depression,
and, in fact, the causal association is as important for smoking.

It was once believed that the "Type A" personality was associated with CAD. These individuals were described as people who
were "rushed, ambitious, and competitive and who exhibited
impatience, hostility, and intolerance." In fact, there is no good
association between such personality traits and CAD; it is much
more likely that depression and social isolation are the important
features that cause disease.[16]

"Stress" is qualitatively different from depression: Stress may
impose a welcome or completely acceptable challenge to the
patient and even prompt him to achieve goals he wouldn't otherwise have been able to master. Some patients structure their lives
to be heavily spiced with challenge and what we call "stress."
They like the excitement and shun the humdrum existences that
others term peaceful. My practice sees a wide array of high-
achieving men for whom no goal, once met, is enough; they are
always planning the next promotion, the next merger, the next
"big deal." In fact, they seek out these challenges; they love—and
create—the excitement, and thrive on it. Biochemically, these
men live on adrenaline.

Depression, on the other hand, is a deflator. It is a malignant
emotion. Basically, it is the loss of hope about being able to solve
painful issues that seem to go on without remedy no matter how
hard one tries to address them.

The link between depression and CAD is incontrovertible.
British investigators point out that in a study of 188 men with CAD,

there were three times as many depressed men among the victims. Interestingly, depression was not associated with an increased risk for CAD in the women in this study. The explanation for this remarkably strong association between depression and CAD in men may have many factors. Men smoke more, exercise less, and take medication for their emotional illnesses that further enhances their risk. Depressed patients with established heart disease have more disturbances in their cardiac rhythm due to changes in the balance between their sympathetic (excitatory) and parasympathetic (muting) nervous systems. The persistent elevation of the stress hormone cortisol, which is characteristic of depression and impairs glucose metabolism, lowers levels of good cholesterol (HDL), elevates triglycerides, and can eventually produce diabetes, which itself doubles the risk of CAD in men. The British group writes:

> None of the above factors has so far explained why depressed men seem to be at a higher risk of ischaemic heart disease than women. . . . Men's higher risk might result from a difference in *general practitioners' ability or opportunity to make diagnoses of depression in men.* . . . It might reflect differences in severity of depression and illness behavior between the sexes—for example, men may be diagnosed with depression only if it is of a certain severity. [Italics added.]

Other experts suggest that failure to follow medical recommendations is a key reason for the vulnerability of depressed patients to developing, and dying of, CAD. Depression was found to be the only factor significantly associated with such failures,[17] and there is a two- to threefold increase in risk of death for such patients in the year following a heart attack.[18]

The devastation depression wreaks on both the sufferer and his family is vividly depicted in an account by Alexandra Styron, the daughter of novelist William Styron. She depicts her famous father's depression:

> At times querulous and taciturn, cutting and remote, melancholy when he was sober and rageful when he was drinking, my father inspired fear and loathing in his children more often than it is comfortable to admit. His turbulent moods—mitigated by a good day's work, medicated by a good long drink—were the weather in our ecosystem. The capriciousness of his anger was astonishing. I once watched him curse, chew apart and then hurl across the kitchen a pencil that had had the gall to lose its graphite point. In the time it took to sweep up the remains of a toy left foolishly in his line of vision, your day could turn as splintery as a thousand shards of bright-colored plastic.[19]

A robust study of 1,190 male medical students, followed since enrollment in medical school (from 1948 to 1964), showed that depression is a risk factor for coronary artery disease, which develops within twenty years of the depression diagnosis.

Those who were significantly depressed (12 percent of the cohort) had a doubled risk for coronary artery disease and heart attack.[20] About a third of these men used antidepressant medication, but a quarter of them reported no treatment for their illness. The usual period between the onset of depression and the first cardiac event was 15 years. That means that 24-year-olds had a mean onset age of 39 years of age for their heart attacks. Because of the early onset of coronary artery disease in men, three quarters of men with CAD are dead before they reach 65 years of age.

There was no increase of strokes in depressed men, but their risk for suicide was much higher. The authors of this study believed that clinical depression had a direct impact on the pathology that occluded coronary arteries: They believed the accentuated sympathetic nervous system activity, which is increased by depression, played a role as well.

The risk for CAD was twice that of non-depressed men in the group, even when the data were corrected for body mass index, premature death of a family member from CAD, smoking, alcohol use, and coffee drinking. The profile of affected men included the fact that 98 percent of the population studied was white. The median age of the first onset of depression was 46 and 23 percent of these men reported no treatment for their depression. The survival rates of men who developed major depression *after* a heart attack were lower than those who did not. Interestingly, other studies support the observation that depression is *not* an independent risk factor for CAD in women: In a study of 5,623 patients in England, men diagnosed with depression were three times more likely than same-aged men without depression to develop CAD.[21] No such vulnerability was found for the women in the study, although women who had heart attacks had twice the risk of developing depression after the attack as same-aged women without CAD. The reasons for the greater vulnerability of depressed men to CAD are unclear; some suggestions include the notion that they may smoke more and avoid exercise compared with healthy men.

Hypertension

My patient, Richard, a 40-year-old overweight African American entrepreneur who runs several businesses, interrupted our visit to listen to an urgent message on his cell phone, which he refuses to turn off, even in my office, lest he miss some crucial matter needing his immediate attention. He has dangerously high blood pressure. When he hung up the phone, I asked him if he was taking his medication. "No," he answered. "I took my blood pressure last month and it was normal. I figured I was cured." I looked at him in disbelief. He had just admitted that his headaches, which are a red flag alert of rising blood pressure, had returned.

With very few exceptions, there is no cure for high blood pressure; it's a disease that has to be treated on a chronic basis once it's discovered. Yet one of the things patients ask me most often when we begin treatment is: "Will I have to take this medicine for the rest of my life?" The answer with this illness is always: "Most likely, yes." To ignore it and the damage it will do to vision, kidney function, the brain, and heart can be lethal.

Many of my patients resist taking medicine for any indication except insomnia, severe pain, or an obvious infection. Ironically, they will beg me for an antibiotic for a simple cold (when it will have no effect at all) but refuse treatment for what I call the "silent" diseases—illnesses that don't cause them any obvious discomfort but may do significant, even deadly, damage. Hypertension is one such condition. The most frequent objection to my prescription for medication is: "I only get high blood pressure in your office. When I take it myself at home, it's always normal." My answer is to explain that I am not the only challenge they face in life. If they measured it in other provocative situations (a missed deadline at work, a quarrel with a spouse) they would find elevated values as well.

Most quit because of side effects: One type of medication, the beta-blockers, cause fatigue, depression, and even sexual dysfunction. Angiotension-converting enzyme inhibitors invoke chest discomfort, such as coughing. An attentive physician can find a medication or combination of medications that eliminate the most troublesome side effects.

Doctors are much more aggressive now than they were a decade ago about treating high blood pressure. We used to accept values of 140/90 millimeters of mercury (mmHg). (The first number is created in the blood vessels when they are filled with blood, the second when they are empty and waiting for the next burst of fluid.) We now try to lower the figure to at least 130/80 mmHg in both sexes. Our bodies are sensitive to the slightest increase. Increasing the first number, called systolic blood pressure, to even 120–129 mmHg produces a 13 percent rise in risk of CAD. At pressures between 140 and 159 mmHg, the risk goes up by 51 percent and nearly doubles for values over 160 mmHg.[22] If the second number (called diastolic blood pressure) is over 90, the risk rises by 33 percent.

Frequent monitoring of blood pressure is always important. Many patients initially control their blood pressure on simple medication for about three months, but then "escape" and need another drug added to their regimen. Often a combination of two or more medicines is required. There are many useful monitoring machines that patients can buy to document their own blood pressures during the day. Your physician may order their own 24-hour monitoring test of your blood pressure, to be accompanied by a detailed diary you keep about what you are doing as the time progresses. Often I order this when an individual believes it is only when he sees me that blood pressure soars; it's important that we both look at the actual readings we record over a 24-hour period in order to convince him to take medicine.

Henry is an 83-year-old, very slender, and vigorous man who comes to see me once a year to make sure everything is in working order. He brings in his list of questions on a sheet of paper; his writing is the precise calligraphy of another era. We go over his diet, discuss what he does for exercise, and catch up on his extended family, with whom he has a warm relationship. His physical examination is usually perfect, but on a recent check of his blood pressure, I found it to be 190 over 78. His top number, which was a reflection of how hard his heart had to pump blood to perfuse his stiffened, narrowed arteries, was very high, but his bottom number was reasonably low. Henry had "isolated systolic hypertension" (ISH), which needed treatment. Usually a simple water pill (a diuretic) will bring the top number down to an acceptable level.

Doctors were once reluctant to treat this condition for fear that they would lower blood pressure to the point where organs would not get enough oxygen because the heart was not pumping blood with enough force to compensate for the stiff, narrow arteries of elderly patients. Nevertheless, researchers found that controlling ISH reduced the incidence of stroke by 36 percent and heart attack by 27 percent. Congestive heart failure was decreased by 55 percent.[23]

Know your numbers, no matter what your age, and be aware of the fact that even elderly patients need supervision. There is an unfortunate tendency of many physicians to say: "What do you expect?" about the health issues of older patients and to accept rather than treat many conditions that should be corrected. As human lifespans grow longer, this practice becomes even less acceptable and patients and their families should advocate for appropriately aggressive care at all ages.

"High Cholesterol" (Dyslipidemia)

In the process of metabolizing the food that we eat, several fats (or lipids) are produced that, if they reach higher-than-optimal levels, increase the danger for developing coronary artery disease. The most important values everyone should have tested are total cholesterol (TC), low-density lipoprotein cholesterol (LDL-C, the so-called "bad cholesterol" that helps deposit deadly plaque in our blood vessels), high-density lipoprotein cholesterol (HDL-C, called "good cholesterol" because it seizes cholesterol from blood vessel linings and returns it to the liver for elimination from the body); and triglycerides (TGs, a type of fat particularly important in the diabetic patient, who has a problem with either utilizing it or producing enough insulin to utilize it).

There are other varieties of fats that can be measured in some circumstances, but these are the four that are most important. The guidelines have changed, and doctors now believe aggressive lowering of an elevated TC is an important measure for preventing CAD. The upper limits of each of the four elements that we recommend for patients are: Total cholesterol (TC) of 200 mg/dL or less, low density cholesterol (LDL-C) of 100 mg/dL or less, and triglycerides (TG) of 150 mg/dL or less.

> One of the most important features of men's lipid profile that puts them at increased risk for CAD is a low value for high density lipoprotein cholesterol. As we've explained, HDL-C protects against the disease: It harvests cholesterol from the body's blood vessels and takes it back to the liver, where it is destroyed and eliminated from the body.

The average HDL value in U.S. men is 45 mg/dL.[24] The impact of a suboptimal level of HDL is unique and not changed by lowering LDL levels to 70 mg/dL or below.[25] Unfortunately, there are only a few ways to raise HDL levels: One of them is by vigorous exercise on a daily basis, and the good news is that it works well for men. Another way is treatment with niacin (nicotinic acid, a B vitamin). It can increase HDL-C by 15–35 percent; maintaining an optimal level of HDL-C does, in fact, decrease mortality from CAD.[26] Unfortunately, niacin has unpleasant and even intolerable side effects for many patients: Flushing and unacceptably rapid heart rates can make patients discontinue the medicine. We urgently need a new drug that will raise HDL-C levels in both sexes, because statins, the powerful, relatively new medicines we use to lower TC and LDL-C, have very little impact on HDL-C levels. Recently, Pfizer invested huge sums of money on a new drug that raised HDL-C levels, which would have been a tremendous boon to preventing CAD. Unfortunately, the drug failed clinical trials, and we are still looking for a medication that will selectively raise this important element of serum fats.

Once a patient has coronary artery disease, it becomes urgent to drive down total cholesterol and "bad" LDL cholesterol levels as much as possible; values of 130 mg/dL for TC and 60 or less for LDL-C are not unusual if we use the newer, powerful statin drugs. Many of my male cardiology colleagues who don't even have the disease take statins on a daily basis. I can still remember being in the audience when the results of the famous Scandinavian Simvastatin Survival Study were announced: After studying the effect of the drug on 4,444 participants with CAD, the researchers found that the lowered cholesterol in men increased survival by 43 percent. In patients who have all the signs of CAD, I now order a computed tomography (CT) coronary angiogram, a noninvasive test, to assess the amount of old (hard) plaque and newer (soft) plaque in their coronary arteries. In expert hands, the pictures of the arterial tree that result are very helpful in establishing the extent of disease in the blood vessels as well as monitoring the results of vigorous treatment for the prevention—and even reversal—of coronary artery soft plaque.

Men at risk because of their family history of CAD should be tested in adolescence for dyslipidemia, particularly because of the increase in obesity rates afflicting our population. Even 20- to 30-year-old men with abnormal lipid profiles who cannot or will not control their levels with exercise and diet should consider medical treatment. A reduction of 1 mg/dL of LDL-C is associated with a 1 to 2 percent reduction in risk for CAD.[27]

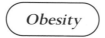

Obesity

We live in a world where food is abundant and physical exercise is not an obligatory or essential part of life. Unfortunately, our genes haven't caught up with the changes in our environment! We are still hard-wired to take in as many calories as possible when food is available and deposit the excess in fat depots to use when food is scarce. And the caloric demands of sitting at a desk for most of the day are significantly less than what are required in agricultural societies. So we are the victims of our own success: There is a troubling epidemic of obesity that is even affecting our children in this country. Between 1980 and 2000, there was a tenfold increase in the rate of obesity in the U.S. population; by 2000, 31 percent of us were obese.[28] Even more concerning was the fact that while the prevalence doubled in adults, it *tripled* in children during that 20-year period.[29]

The epidemic character of obesity in this country has led to speculation that it may be due to infectious causes—specifically one or more viruses.[30] Certainly this happens in animals that have had a viral infection of the central nervous system. There is even a virus found in humans that is associated with obesity.

The way men and women lay down fat is gender specific. Men deposit fat in the abdomen, packing it around their internal organs, where it is easily mobilized and produces high levels of harmful serum lipids. Estrogen helps women keep their waists small and their hips and buttocks sizable. After menopause, when estrogen levels drift downward, women, also accumulate poundage around the midriff.

Doctors measure optimal body size in two ways (height and weight aren't enough): They calculate the body mass index (BMI) by dividing the body weight in kilograms by the square of the height in meters. You are officially obese if your BMI is over 30. In men, BMI plateaus at about age 50; women are not so fortunate, and continue to develop increasing BMIs as they age. The most important impact of increased weight is that it increases risk for hypertension and lowers HDL-C.[31]

A good way to assess your body shape is to calculate your waist-hip ratio (WHR). Divide the circumference of your waist by that of your hips: If the value is greater than 1.0, you're at high risk for CAD; it is a reflection of harmful fat deposition around your midsection. Even values over 0.95 increase risk.

Obesity has a negative impact on blood pressure, cholesterol levels, and responsiveness to the crucially important hormone insulin, which facilitates the entry of glucose into our cells so it can be metabolized for energy. Most of my patients know this, but what is newer and not so well appreciated is that blood is more likely to clot in obese patients, and the susceptibility to inflammation is greater: Both have a negative long-term impact on risk for CAD.

Frank is an anxious, hyperactive man who perspires a lot. I see him at regular intervals and each time he is heavier. His knees hurt, his back bothers him, and he loses his breath going up just one flight of stairs. Whenever we weigh him, he rationalizes away the new ten pounds; he explains that it was the holidays, he was under stress, his mother was visiting and cooked all his favorite foods . . . nothing seems to work for him. Another very heavy young patient of mine never eats a meal with anyone else in the family present and refuses any invitations to dine out in a restaurant. He is a secret eater, and hides the enormous trays of doughnuts and the boxes of pizza he consumes after work.

Some men maintain an optimal weight during college because they are heavily involved in sports, but put on a significant number of pounds when they begin their adult working life. While physical activity falls by the wayside, their eating habits don't change much. One colleague of mine, a ruddy-faced cardiologist who puffed his way up and down the stairs at our medical center, suddenly lost close to 80 pounds. "I just stopped eating as though I were still playing football!" he explained.

Sustained weight reduction is one of the hardest things for any patient to achieve. It requires not only a strategy for immediate, short-term weight loss, but a genuine restructuring of eating habits to maintain the lower weight. I always start my overweight patients out by pairing them with a skilled nutritionist who will take a detailed history not only of what patients eat, but how much, when and *why* they overeat. I've listened to several interviews that these talented individuals have conducted with my patients. They are excellent psychologists as well as weight-loss therapists. Their observations richly enhance my own, and help me to formulate an individualized action plan that really works on a given patient. Many of my overweight men—Frank is one of them—tell me they can't eat during the day, but consume giant meals at night; these start late and last for hours. It's a way for them to relax and reduce tension after a long workday. A careful analysis of what men are feeling as they reach home and shed at least the immediate stresses of the day can be very helpful to structuring a therapeutic program to aid weight loss. Another important strategy involves not leaving any decisions about what to eat—and how big a portion size should be—to the patient. Asking your nutritionist to plan a daily menu and ordering from a food service is very effective.

Some rather bizarre—and potentially dangerous—schemes do melt away the pounds. Patients come up with these on their own. I remember one whippet-thin man who loved bagels. He started out at over 300 pounds and restricted his *entire diet* to one bagel a day, which he ate slowly at lunchtime. How he kept his hair and teeth intact, I'll never understand! I don't recommend a strategy like this for many reasons. A good nutritionist will take into account foods you love when creating your regimens, albeit perhaps in smaller quantities than you're used to.

Lack of Exercise

Here's a useful rule of thumb: Active people have half the risk for CAD as sedentary individuals.[32] Sadly, most of us do far less than the 30 minutes of moderate-intensity activity a day that the U.S. surgeon general recommends. Fully 35 percent of men do not do any leisure-time physical activity at all.[33]

Why exercise? The quantitative impact of physical exercise on risk for CAD is uncertain, but it definitely lessens the likelihood of other risk factors for the disease: It reduces blood pressure, lowers cholesterol, and enhances our sensitivity to insulin, reducing blood sugar levels. It also helps keeps weight down and, without a doubt, relieves anxiety and depression. I still remember dining with a lawyer friend who told me that running two miles a day kept him sane during the course of a painful divorce. Another patient told me he found it hard to grieve over his recently deceased daughter when he was playing a furious game of tennis against a skilled opponent. It was the only relief he had from the pervasive sadness he felt.

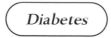

Diabetes

Diabetes mellitus is a complex disorder with a broad negative impact on human health. When high levels of blood sugar form a resistance to insulin or when there is inadequate insulin secretion in the blood stream, the body loses its ability to break down complex sugars. There are two kinds of diabetes. The first, called Type 1, occurs when cells in the pancreas that produce insulin are destroyed. Type 2 is due to a complex combination of abnormalities in the production and effectiveness of insulin secretion. Not only does diabetes confer high short-term risk for CAD, but once they have the disease, diabetics have a worse outcome than those who are not diabetic.[34] We have recently surveyed the literature about the unique features of the disease in men and women; each sex experiences it differently.[35] Interestingly, the risk for CAD in diabetic men doubles, while there is a four- to sixfold increase in risk for women. No one understands this sex difference, but it is at least in part related to the lower-than-usual levels of HDL-C that are characteristic of the disease in both genders; women with diabetes are more likely than men to have lower levels of HDL-C and higher levels of triglycerides. The chief cause of death for diabetic men is arteriosclerosis, including stroke and CAD. Regrettably, tightly regulating blood sugar levels does not decrease the increased risk for CAD in the diabetic; we must rely on eliminating other risk factors for the disease to reduce coronary events and increase chances for survival.

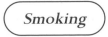

Smoking

One of the most prominent epidemiologists of cardiovascular disease alive today, JoAnn Manson, Professor of Medicine at Harvard, put it this way: "Cigarette smoking is the leading preventable cause of death among both women and men in the United States. . . . Smoking more than doubles CAD incidence and increases CAD mortality by approximately 70 percent."[36]

It's worth the effort to quit smoking. Risk begins to decline within months and falls to the level of nonsmokers in three to five years—regardless of how much or how long you smoked or how old you were when you stopped.[37] Besides being a risk factor for CAD, smoking is a risk for stroke; it constricts brain blood vessels, limiting the supply of blood to the brain. The risk for stroke in current smokers is 2.58 times that of normal nonsmokers.[38] Happily, the number of men who smoke has decreased over the past 30 years. It dropped significantly between 1965, when 52 percent of the population smoked, and 1990, when that number was down to 28 percent.[39]

In fact, smoking rates decreased among men aged 35 to 64, but increased in women in the same age range.[40] Watching the provocative new series *Madmen* on AMC, many viewers remarked on the pervasive cigarette smoking by both sexes in this story of life on Madison Avenue in the 1960s; we've forgotten how many of us smoked routinely only 40 years ago. When faced with such history, the success of New York's Mayor Bloomberg in eliminating cigarette smoking in public places is almost unbelievable.

Drinking and Cardiovascular Disease

Whether or not drinking helps or hurts patients in terms of their developing cardiovascular disease depends on two things: how much alcohol they drink and the pattern of drinking. Moderate drinking, about two and a half "typical" drinks per day, reduces the risk of CAD.[41] More good news: There is also evidence that for those who already have CAD, moderate drinking can reduce the progression of the disease and the risk for subsequent cardiovascular events. And perhaps the best news of all for the enthusiastic drinker: Almost all studies show that the more frequently an individual drinks, including on a daily basis, the lower the risk for many diseases, including CAD. Some, though, have raised objections to the studies that establish these guidelines, because the "control" group (those who don't drink) might include sick people who have decreased or stopped their drinking altogether; their increased vulnerability to illness might have to do more with illness than with simply the absence of alcohol. Interestingly, moderate drinkers tend to have healthier habits than the rest of the population, and these may contribute to their relative freedom from CAD rather than the fact that they take in moderate quantities of alcohol on a daily basis. The major impact of alcohol on CAD risk is that it elevates the level of good cholesterol (HDL-C).

TESTING FOR CORONARY ARTERY DISEASE

Screening tests for coronary artery disease should begin in men in their twenties. A baseline electrocardiogram and blood test for serum lipids should accompany a careful assessment of risk factors in every individual. These should be repeated, depending on the likelihood of the patient's developing CAD, at regular intervals; if there are no risk factors, retesting in five years is appropriate.

After the age of 30, a baseline stress-echocardiogram should be done. This test looks at the function of the cardiac muscle at rest and at peak exercise. Further testing of myocardial blood flow with radioactive markers that trace the adequacy of blood supply to the heart muscle at rest and during exertion should follow any abnormal result. This method of viewing blood supply to the heart muscle is called myocardial perfusion scintigraphy. It involves injecting a radioactive substance into the blood stream that is taken up by the heart tissue or that labels the blood cells flowing through the coronary vessels so that we can see how well the muscle is supplied with blood. This is a very useful test because it helps predict which patients should go on to cardiac catheterization and rescue maneuvers for an occluded coronary artery. It is a very sensitive and specific way to label heart muscle at risk. Patients who have only mild to moderate abnormalities will do as well with conservative management—that is, medication—as those who have angiography. Patients with severely abnormal perfusion scans, though, should be referred on to further intervention.

In men who have abnormalities, an imaging of the coronary arteries is now possible through the CT angiogram, which allows doctors to see the location and extent of coronary artery obstruction; this is a newer and very valuable study that in many cases obviates the need for a coronary angiogram. The CT angiogram is very useful for following the impact of treatment on the extent of coronary artery obstruction: "Soft" plaque in the coronary arteries can often be reversed by intensive medical treatment. Cardiac catheterization, which is done by threading a catheter into the point of origin of the coronary arteries themselves and injecting them with dye to see their structure, is still the "gold standard" of coronary artery assessment. The actual degree of obstruction at any point in the arteries can be measured quite precisely with intracoronary ultrasound.

TREATMENT FOR CORONARY ARTERY DISEASE

The initial treatment for coronary artery disease is medical and con- sists of a variety of medications, including drugs that mute the activ- ity of the sympathetic nervous system, daily aspirin to minimize the likelihood of clot formation in the coronary arteries, and intensive attention to lowering the levels of cholesterol in the blood. This can be achieved with niacin (which raises the levels of HDL-C), or drugs that lower the concentration of total cholesterol and LDL-C: These include drugs that inhibit cholesterol absorption from the intestine and the statins, which lowers levels in the bloodstream. A combi- nation of several medications is usually prescribed.

When the arteries are so packed as to make it difficult for blood to squeeze through, an inflated catheter is inserted into the diseased artery. The balloon catheter relieves the obstruction at the site of the plaque. A tiny wire cage called a "stent" can be inserted within the artery to keep it open; some of these are drug-coated so that the like- lihood of clot formation is reduced. Recent studies indicating that drug-coated stents themselves increase the likelihood of a cardiac incident are now being resolved by other investigations that show they are safe and appropriate for treatment. Finally, coronary artery bypass surgery, which involves bypassing the points of obstruction with venous or arterial grafts implanted into the arterial tree as accessory pathways for blood, is another treatment; it remains effec- tive for a decade or more.

STROKE

The coronaries aren't the only arteries affected by atherosclerosis. Plaque builds up in the arteries that supply the brain, and stroke (the death of a portion of the brain when its blood supply is interrupted) is the third leading cause of death in the United States. The mechanism of tissue death is exactly like that of a heart attack.

A stroke is often called a "brain attack." More than two-thirds of strokes occur in people over 65, and after the age of 55, the risk of having a stroke doubles in the ensuing decade.

There are two kinds of strokes; the most common is an ischemic stroke, caused by the blockage of one of the blood vessels to the brain. About 20 percent of strokes are hemorrhagic, which occur when a blood vessel in the brain suddenly ruptures. This can happen between the covering of the brain and the skull (a subarachnoid bleed) or deep within the brain itself.

Immediate treatment of a stroke is essential; brain cells begin to die within minutes and every second that is lost getting to a hospital kills additional neurons. If the cause of the stroke is high blood pressure, medications are used to lower the blood pressure; brain swelling can also be treated with special medicines. Clot-busting drugs can be used to dissolve a clot if the incident happened less than three hours before the patient arrived for treatment. Surgical treatments are sometimes useful: An aneurysm, or weakened spot in a blood vessel, can be clipped to prevent further leakage.

The most memorable patient I ever treated for a hemorrhagic stroke was my best friend's mother. She collapsed while visiting her hometown down South. She later recalled noticing that a "shade had come down over her vision" before losing consciousness. When she regained consciousness, she reported that she had one of the worst headaches of her life but in spite of extensive investigation, no evidence of an aneurysm was found. After weeks in Southern hospitals, she was diagnosed as simply depressed. We transferred her back for more investigation to Columbia Presbyterian. One of the best neurologists on our faculty, Linda

Lewis, told me that the patient's symptoms were classic for a stroke in the visual part of the brain. When her CT scans were analyzed, sure enough, there was an aneurysm deep in the back of her brain. In a six-hour operation, the aneurysm was clipped, and the patient's only residual defect was paroxysmal attacks of coughing that she suffered for the rest of her life. She lived decades more to enjoy the lives of her family, and I heard her daughter tell the story many times of how her mother's aneurysm was almost missed. Another very important case of mine is that of a friend whose sister died suddenly of a massive stroke caused by aneurysm at the age of 32. Since there is a genetic component to strokes, and there is a 20 percent increased incidence of undetected aneurysms in the family members of people who suffer them, I nagged my friend to get an MRA (magnetic resonance imaging, a picture of the blood vessels) of his cerebral arteries. Lo and behold! He, too, had an aneurysm that was significant but had not yet bled. His own lesion was successfully clipped, and he believes (correctly) that doing this examination saved him from a stroke of his own, and possibly saved his life. If you have had any family member who has suffered a cerebral bleed from a bleeding aneurysm, you should have an MRA of your brain's blood supply to rule out such a complication in your own anatomy.

Some bleeding is from unusual, congenital, unruly accumulations of blood vessels called arteriovenous (AV) malformations; to prevent rupture, many of these can be removed, sometimes using focused beams of radiation directed at the lesion. Sometimes a coil or small particles are inserted into the AV malformation to reduce its size so that it can be treated. Probably the most important single test that you can do to monitor your vulnerability to a stroke is to have a painless and noninvasive sound-wave picture of your carotid arteries, which bring a substantial amount of blood to the brain. (The vertebral arteries, in the back of the brain, supply the rest of the tissue.)

A baseline carotid Doppler ultrasound test is a must at the age of 30 for anyone with a risk factor for stroke (namely hypertensives, patients with a strong family history of high blood pressure or stroke), and certainly by the age of 40, men should have a picture of their carotids on file. The plaque in the carotid can actually be removed in a process called a carotid endarterectomy. Instead of opening the artery, another tactic is to put a catheter is put into the vessel to dilate the area of obstruction. Drugs to dissolve clots can also be injected through a carotid artery catheter.

Things to keep in mind about heart disease:

- **Review your risk factors for coronary artery disease with your doctor.** Ask for a stress test and an analysis of your serum lipid levels. Identify personal habits that need correction, such as smoking, excessive alcohol intake, or lack of exercise.
- By age 40, even if you have no symptoms, your doctor should **do an ultrasound examination of the carotid arteries,** which supply blood to the brain. Any abnormality should be monitored and, if your serum lipids need correction, medication prescribed.
- If you experience unusual shortness of breath, pain involving your chest, neck, jaw, and/or arm, or dizziness, report to your doctor. **Early treatment is a life saver.** Remember that this disease can appear much earlier in men than in women; symptoms in your mid-30s are not unusual.

CHAPTER EIGHT

MEN AND CANCER

CANCERS

My 59-year-old patient, so anemic his skin looked ivory, wept as he told me that he was too weak to stand for more than a few minutes at a time. He was breathless from the effort of talking. He had undergone surgery and radiation treatment for prostate cancer and knew neither had cured him. His wife sat wordlessly by his side, exhausted from grief and the work of caring for him. There was no need for many words; it was enough just to be with him and his wife. These are hard moments for doctors. We know there is little we can do clinically, and even comforting the patient is almost impossible. I was struck with the sense of profound isolation my patient seemed to express; like many terminally ill who are staring death in the face, he was in another place and no longer accessible to ordinary overtures.

Another beloved patient of mine is now 12 years in remission from colon cancer, which was cured successfully by surgery and chemotherapy. He is just now beginning to believe that he has conquered the malignancy, and on every anniversary of his operation we rejoice together that he has not only lived, but has had a full and productive life since his recovery.

Only heart disease rivals cancer as the chief killer of men in middle and older age. Cancer is the second most frequent cause of death for men aged 45 to 54, accounting for 23 percent of all fatalities. For men between the ages of 55 and 74, it is the chief cause of death, at 33.4 percent; at this age, heart disease as a killer drops to second place. Only after age 75 is cancer's toll surpassed by that of heart disease. The three most common cancers—and the most deadly—are malignancies of the prostate, lung, and colon.[1]

Prostate Cancer

My male patients don't exactly beat a path to my door for their annual prostate examination. To put it mildly, they are infused with palpable dread at the prospect of a rectal examination, and postpone coming until it nearly becomes a biennial event.

I remind them that a woman's gynecological examination is not pleasant either, but this is little consolation. "It's embarrassing," said a good friend, who is also a patient. I hope it helps to point out that we doctors don't find body parts emotionally loaded in the consulting room: breast examination by a male doctor—as much as a rectal examination by a female doctor—concentrates only on the physical features of the anatomic parts of interest. Nevertheless, patients resist them as intrusive, and colonoscopies are very hard to "sell" for this reason. One psychotherapist told me that any entry into an orifice, even the mouth, threatens a patient because of the vulnerability the individual feels when he surrenders the usual protection provided these orifices. This very understandable apprehension is one reason we all dread the dentist.

The prostate is a walnut-sized gland that wraps around the urethra, the short tube that carries urine from the urinary bladder to the outside world, and is located just in front of the rectum. It produces the fluid that helps carry the sperm from the testicles. As men age, the prostate enlarges and narrows the urethra; this produces the hesitancy men feel in starting their urinary stream and makes it difficult to empty their bladders.

Prostate cancer is the most important malignancy men face. In 2007, one man out of six was diagnosed with it in the United States (the average age of these patients was 68) and one out of 34 died from it.[2] It gets an early start: At autopsy, up to 29 percent of men 30 to 40 years old have small prostatic cancers, and by the time they are 60 to 70 the number climbs to 64 percent.[3] In 2002, 189,000 men were diagnosed with prostate cancer and there were 30,200 deaths from the illness.[4] Happily, because of early detection and widespread screening, death rates have begun to decrease.

There are several risk factors that increase your chances of developing prostate cancer. First, there are inherited prostate cancer *susceptibility* genes. There are many mutations that help produce the disordered growth; some of them are acquired as the cancer progresses. Others have to do with alterations in the genes that suppress tumors. If your father or brother had prostate cancer, your own vulnerability to the disease increases. In fact, men with prostate cancer were more likely to report having an affected brother or father. One family member with the illness increases your risk by a factor of 2; if 2 are affected, by 2.5, and if you have 3 affected family members your own risk increases 11-fold.[5]

Race is another important factor. In the United States, both the incidence of prostate cancer and death from it are highest in black men—[6] and death rates were more than twice as high for blacks as for whites in the 1990s. During this same period, death rates for whites and Asians were half of that for blacks and Hispanics. Although the incidence of prostate cancer is lower in Asia than elsewhere, once Asian men immigrate to the United States, their susceptibility increases, suggesting that environmental factors, such as nutrition and the stress of immigration, play key roles.

A diet rich in meat and fat has been implicated in causing prostate cancer, but this is not certain. Vegetables do protect against it.[7] Vasectomy (an operation designed to block the flow of sperm into the urethra) does *not* increase the risk for prostate cancer. Inflammation, however, may start the cascade of changes that turns into prostate cancer; chronic or recurrent inflammation of the prostate, particularly when it is associated with sexually transmitted diseases, has been implicated.[8]

The first step is going to your physician for a manual examination of your prostate to assess its shape, size, and hardness. A blood test for elevated levels of prostate specific antigen (PSA) is another survey instrument that can alert your physician to the possibility of cancer, although inflammation of the prostate is often the cause of an elevated PSA. Obese men may have a deceptively low PSA because they have a greater circulating blood volume that may dilute the concentration of hormones, so a physician should add on a supplemental value to adjust for their weight.[9] Men with an elevated PSA are treated with an antibiotic to see if inflammation is, in fact, the cause, before further investigations are planned. These next steps may include an imaging of the prostate with ultrasound, a cystoscopy (inserting a thin tube into the urinary tract to examine the urethra and bladder), or a biopsy of the prostate (inserting a thin needle through the rectum into the gland).

The symptoms of prostate cancer are exactly the same as those of an enlarged prostate: They include erectile dysfunction and urinary problems, including difficulty starting the urinary stream, difficulty stopping the stream, a weakened flow of urine, urinating during the night, or discomfort during urination. Lower back pain, hip pain, or upper thigh pain may also be warning signs. Some men with the disease, however, have no symptoms and those who do have them may simply have a benign enlargement of the gland. If a diagnosis of cancer is made, the extent of the cancer is assessed by classifying its "stage." We've all heard of the dreaded stage four of a cancer, which means that it has metastasized to other parts of the body. In truth, there are other values factored into the overall picture.

> We calculate a diagnosed patient's likelihood of survival with three tests. The first is the "Gleason score," which measures the size and cellular characteristics of the tumor and the likelihood that it will metastasize. The second is the degree to which the cancer has spread. The third is the value for PSA. If you are told you have prostate cancer, ask your doctor for your Gleason score and find out what stage of the disease you are in.

Treatment is planned according to the aggressiveness and spread of the cancer and can include removal of the prostate and/or radiation treatment (both external and internal radiation, which comes from radioactive seeds implanted in the tissue). It's important to know that doctors may recommend that older patients do nothing about the disease if it is still in the early stages, because they are more likely to die from other causes before the malignancy becomes a threat. Prostate surgery would save the life of only 1 of 300 men age 65 or older within ten years of the diagnosis.[10] Some carefully selected older patients whose cancers are not progressing significantly—with a Gleason score of less than 7—will simply be monitored. These patients should have serum PSA tests and digital rectal exams every six months, with biopsies at frequent intervals. In a large series of patients treated this way, after eight years less than 1 percent had died from cancer.[11]

When treatment is necessary, hormone therapy is sometimes recommended to prevent male hormones (androgens) from stimulating cancer cells to grow. Some therapies prevent the manufacture of testosterone (luteinizing hormone-releasing hormones), and others block the action of male hormones (anti-androgens). There are also medications aimed at preventing the adrenal gland from making testosterone. Finally, surgery to remove the testicles, which are the body's main source of testosterone, is offered to some men.

Unexpectedly, one of my best friends told me at dinner that he had prostate cancer and was in the process of a treatment that eliminated most if not all of his testosterone in an effort to prevent the malignant cells from multiplying. His description of his symptoms made me feel as though men and women in the later years of their lives were more similar than different: His hot flashes, loss of mental sharpness, and tendency to feel depressed and vulnerable mirrored exactly the symptoms of menopausal women. There are other side effects from blocking testosterone production as a way to contain prostate cancer: Loss of libido and thinning of the bones are two of the more troublesome. Remember to ask your doctor whether treatment is necessary at all, as some prostate cancers grow very slowly and metastasize very late. Depending on your age, you and your physician might elect to simply monitor your situation. The data suggest that if this is the course you take, there is a 25 to 40 percent risk of progression, requiring definitive treatment within five years.

Lung Cancer

There are two types of lung cancer: One, called a "small-cell" lung cancer, makes up about 13 percent of tumors and is very aggressive, spreading quickly. Non-small-cell lung cancers are less often lethal and spread more slowly. Lung cancer kills more men than any other cancer, accounting for 28 percent of all cancer-related deaths in the 1990s.[12] Rates were higher for black and white men than for other races. It's important to *prevent* the disease by eliminating tobacco smoking—the most frequent cause by far of this terrible illness.

Radon is a little-known radioactive gas, but it is extremely common in the environment and is a leading cause of lung cancer. Radon may be inhaled by coal miners in some parts of the country, and it can be present in houses built on soil that contains the gas. Any purchase of a new house should include a survey for radon gas. Men exposed to asbestos (such as shipyard workers during World War II or men who work in construction where exposure is inevitable) are at risk, particularly after years of inhaling the material. One of my good friends had spent the years during World War II in a naval shipyard and had extensive exposure to asbestos. He accepted the fact that he would likely die of the malignancy associated with this situation. Forty years later, I met him walking along a New York street one evening, alone and looking quite sad. I can still see his face as he told me that he had indeed developed the cancer that would shortly kill him. Like so many men, he was very brave: Although obviously upset, he accepted his fate without protest, and remarked that thousands of others had died at much younger ages as a consequence of that war.

Aside from environmental factors, a family history of lung cancer slightly increases your risk for developing the disease. Having other chronic diseases of the lung, like tuberculosis or bronchitis, however, does not increase the risk for malignancy.

Symptoms of lung cancer include a persistent cough—particularly when accompanied by bloody phlegm—shortness of breath, chest pain, hoarseness, frequent lung infections, fatigue, and unexplained weight loss. While other illnesses might well be the reason for any or even all of these symptoms, you should bring them to the attention of your physician. He will investigate with a physical examination, chest film, and a CT scan of your chest. He may check your sputum for cancer cells and, if you have fluid in your chest, will withdraw some for an examination. A bronchoscopy may also be ordered. In this procedure, a thin tube is placed into the breathing tubes so that any visible cancer can be identified and samples of cells taken for analysis. Ultimately, your physician may recommend an operation to remove a suspicious mass for further testing.

As in the case of any cancer, determining how far the cancer has spread is crucial. In addition to the CT scan, a bone scan and a magnetic resonance imaging (MRI) examination may be ordered. Another way to find errant cancer cells in the body is through at PET (positive emission tomography) scan, in which radioactive sugars, which cancer cells absorb at a higher rate than normal tissue, are located in the body. Treatment depends on the nature of your cancer and the degree to which it has spread; your oncologist may advise local therapy (surgery and local radiation) or systemic therapy with chemicals (usually more than one), which enter the bloodstream and kill cancer cells wherever they are in the body.

Cancer of the Colon and Rectum

Most cases of colon cancer begin as polyps, small masses of cells that appear in the colon. There are three kinds of polyps. The first is called an adenoma, which can become cancers and are removed during testing maneuvers such as a colonoscopy. The second type is called a hyperplastic polyp; these almost never become malignant. Inflammatory polyps, the third type, may occur in patients with inflammatory bowel diseases such as ulcerative colitis; they indicate a higher risk of developing colon cancer.

Cancer of the colon is slightly more prevalent in women (1.2 to 1) but cancer of the rectum is more common in men (1.7 to 1).[13] These are the cancers we can prevent most easily because we can examine the intestine regularly and visualize any cancer or pre-cancerous growth before the cells turn errant. *All patients who are 50 or older should have a colonoscopy and if no pathology is detected it should be repeated at a minimum of every ten years.*

Blacks have the highest death rate for colorectal cancer, and death rates for black men and women have declined half as much as for whites. Risk factors for this disease are better known than for lung cancer: There are known genetic mutations that carry vulnerability to the disease. The most common, responsible for 2 percent of colonic cancers, produces the disease at an average age of 44. The second is rare and inherited, caused by a specific gene mutation called the ademonatosis polyposis coli (APC). It produces hundreds of polyps in the colon that almost always turn cancerous by age 40. Doctors usually recommend a removal of the patient's colon. Current wisdom dictates that people who have a family history of ten or more colon polyps should have genetic testing to see if they are vulnerable to developing the disease and thus need careful and frequent testing.

Patients with chronic inflammatory diseases of the colon (Crohn's disease or ulcerative colitis) are more likely to develop colon cancer, as are patients older than 50 (the average age at diagnosis is 72). The polyps (called adenomas) that degenerate after years into cancer can be found by colonoscopy and removed before they become malignant.

A word about the dreaded colonoscopy: My colleague, Dr. Louis Schneider, with whom I work closely in diagnosing and treating gastrointestinal disease, agrees with me that the *preparation* for the colonoscopy is far more uncomfortable than the procedure itself. It involves drinking a large quantity of salty liquid that draws water into the intestinal tract and produces diarrhea in order to clean out the colon. I once complained to him about how much

I hated the preparation; he answered coolly: "It's a lot less uncomfortable than intra-arterial chemotherapy for a colon cancer." I never complained again, and I've used his comment with any patient who refuses the first baseline colonoscopy we recommend for all patients at age 50, or who delays or avoids re-examination every five years. It's comforting to know that colonoscopies every two years for high-risk patients are covered by most health insurance companies.

Screening for colon cancer is not restricted to colonoscopy. In cases of one or more instances of colon cancer in a family, I do a test for blood in the stool no matter what the patient's age. Only recently we tested a 37-year-old man who had a family history of the disease. His test was positive, even after eliminating any factors that would produce a false positive. When we sent him for colonoscopy, his adenoma was discovered and removed.

The risk factors for colon cancer are well known. They include a sedentary life style, diabetes, obesity, smoking (which not only increases your chances of developing the disease, but makes it more likely that it will kill you), heavy use of alcohol, and a prior bout of radiation to the abdomen to treat a previous cancer. One colon cancer also increases the likelihood that you will develop a second cancer.

The symptoms of colon cancer include a change in bowel habits (either diarrhea or constipation), a feeling of incomplete emptying of the rectum after a bowel movement, finding blood in your stool, a narrowing of stool caliber, bloating or painful gas, weight loss, nausea and vomiting, and unusual fatigue. Your primary care physician should certainly be testing your stool for blood by means of a rectal examination every year if you are 50 or over. If she or he isn't, ask why not!

As in the case of all cancers, your doctor will examine your whole body for signs that the malignancy has spread. Local therapy (surgery and radiation) may be the only treatment recommended, but most oncologists now advise systemic chemotherapy as well, to guard against recurrence of the disease, particularly if the cancer has escaped the colon and invaded adjacent tissue. Follow-up surveillance of the patient after the cancer has been treated involves monitoring carcinoembryonic antigen (CEA) levels in the bloodstream. CEA is a substance produced by some cancers, and it is useful particularly in screening patients who have had colon cancer to detect a recurrence early. In patients whose cancer hasn't been completely vanquished, it's a good way to follow the extent of the disease. CEA is not used as a general screening test in all patients. It can be elevated in smokers and in patients with some kinds of inflammation, cirrhosis of the liver, or peptic ulcer disease (erosion in the stomach lining).

Chemotherapy involves the use of a chemical agent that will kill cancer cells and/or prevent them from growing. Patients are given a combination of chemicals coupled with medications that will help them finish the required treatment in a timely fashion. Unfortunately, the chemotherapeutic agents target and vanquish the most rapidly reproducing cells in the body—including many normal cells—causing hair loss, nail damage, and a dip in the numbers of blood cells produced. A delay or reduction in treatment can be harmful; most of these side effects occur as a result of the chemotherapy and can be avoided or corrected with the proper attention and care.

Radiation therapy can be used on almost any solid tumor, including colon cancer. For some types of cancer, radiation may include tissue that is near but is not yet invaded by the malignancy; this is called prophylactic radiation therapy. Some radiation therapy is also used to eliminate pain from the spread of cancer to other parts of the body. The treatment can be given *systemically*; the radioactive substance is injected into blood vessels that carry the material everywhere in the body. External radiation therapy is localized to the affected part of the body from a machine outside the body. Sometimes doctors will place radioactive material *within* the body, near or in the site of the tumor. Some types of radiation therapy actually make the patient radioactive, and precautionary measures have to be taken during certain periods of the treatment.

Testicular Cancer

When I was still in medical school, I got my first look at cancer in a young person: It was the brother of a man I was dating. Tom was beautiful to look at, delightfully charming, and only 21 years old. He was the son of a distinguished surgeon. His family was optimistic because, if caught early, recovery from this cancer, which accounts for 1 percent of cancers in men, is almost guaranteed. Unfortunately, his cancer was diagnosed only after it had spread to his lungs and caused him to develop a relentless cough. Every adolescent boy should be taught how to self-examine his testicles for the presence of an irregularity in the smooth, bean-shaped organs; the failure of many physicians to do this irritates me beyond belief. We certainly teach adolescent girls to watch for cysts in their breasts. We produce shower cards and mockups of breast tissue that include a mass like a cancer for them to learn from, but to my knowledge there is no such concentrated effort made for men. The peak period for the occurrence of a testicular malignancy, called a seminoma, occurs between ages 15 and 34; there is a second peak between ages 50 and 60. The cancer is usually completely asymptomatic when it arises in the testis: A 50-something patient of mine was urged by his wife to investigate a lump in his scrotum of which he had been completely unaware. Unlike Tom, who died in his father's arms despite all the doctors could do to help him, my 50-year-old patient recovered from his seminoma and, in fact, owes his life to his wife's alertness. In some patients, though, symptoms occur: There may be a feeling of heaviness in the scrotum, a dull ache there or in the groin, a sudden increase in scrotal size and/or, interestingly, breast enlargement and/or tenderness.

Non-seminomatous tumors are a much more aggressive type of testicular cancer and occur at younger ages. They are not as sensitive to radiation therapy but chemotherapy is often very effective.

An important cause of testicular cancer is the failure of one of the testes to descend from the abdomen into the scrotal sac after birth. Another risk factor is a history of testicular cancer in a father or brother. Finally, it's one of the cancers that is more prevalent in white than in black men.

Your doctor will do several things to diagnose the presence of a problem. The first is to create a picture using sound waves of the scrotum and its contents. Blood tests are taken in order to monitor for tumor markers. If malignant tumors are present, the affected testis is then surgically removed. Biopsy is usually reserved for people with only one testis. Other tests are important to decide what stage the cancer is in: A computed tomography (CT) scan of the abdomen to detect malignant lymph nodes, an X-ray of your chest, and blood tests are all indicated.

The complications of treatment don't necessarily include infertility or erectile function if you only lose one testis. However, if you have extensive surgery that interrupts some of the nerves to the area you may have some problems with ejaculation. Radiation therapy does often interfere with sperm production and can cause infertility, which may be either temporary (disappearing after one or two years) or permanent. The effect of chemotherapy depends on the drugs used. You may want to bank sperm before any treatment, *even if you think you'll never want more children.*

In a world where we wear pink ribbons for breast cancer and participate in several walkathons a year, we should be equally vigilant in mobilizing effective screening and treatment for men, who have their own unique and equally deadly issues. Prostate cancer is eminently curable if detected early and there is even hope for a permanent cure for some lung cancers; our efforts to curb smoking, particularly by the young, should be a point of special focus. Finally, again, it is baffling to me that we are not teaching men of all ages to examine their own testicles. The aggressive approach we've taken to guard women from cancer should be extended to men. Not to do so is indefensible.

What symptoms should lead you to ask your doctor about cancer?

- **Tell your doctor** about any change in the strength of your urinary stream or if you have difficulty starting or stopping the flow of urine. The urge to urinate during the night is another signal that you need a prostate examination. An evaluation of prostate anatomy with ultrasound and, if necessary, biopsy, should follow.
- **If you smoke or have smoked in the past ask your doctor for a baseline chest X-ray.** Such X-rays are no longer routine, but patients at risk should have one. Report any persistent cough, particularly if you see blood in the mucus, at once. Most lung cancers announce themselves earlier in men than in women, and early intervention can be life saving.
- **Your first colonoscopy should be planned for the age of 50**; almost twice as many men as women will experience colon cancer. A good examination will reveal any precancerous lesions that can be removed on the spot. The preparation for the test is disagreeable, but the treatment for colon cancer is much worse.

CHAPTER NINE

SPORTS

THE PRICE MEN PAY

WHY MEN LOVE SPORTS

I understand men's fascination with sports completely: They are a metaphor for combat, and both the players and audience enjoy the game. Athletic games produce a rise in testosterone levels before *and*, for the winner, after a competitive match. The elevated level before the match[1] promotes willingness to take risks and improves the speed and clarity of thinking, concentration,[2] and muscle coordination. The phenomenon has been reported in physical contests like wrestling, martial arts, golf, chess, and even coin flip games of chance. Allan Mazur of Syracuse University argues that heightened levels of the hormone give participants an edge. Equally fascinating, a drop in testosterone levels accompanies a continuous streak of losses and therefore reduces the likelihood of success in future contests, possibly explaining otherwise inexplicable "losing streaks"—one loss begetting a string of others.[3] Testosterone also improves mood. Men with high levels exhibit enhanced self-esteem, invincibility, and an ability to handle whatever the future holds.

The passion men have to *watch* sports may be at least partially explained by the fact that testosterone levels also rise in spectators if their team wins: In the 1994 World Cup soccer tournament in which Brazil defeated Italy, levels of the hormone rose in Brazilians watching the match on television but fell in Italian viewers.[4] The fascination of men with athletic games reflects their own response to their team's success: P.C. Bernhardt and his colleagues at the University of Utah summarize the response of fans to a win:

> When a sports team wins or loses an athletic contest, its fans respond much as the team athletes do: they bask in its glory and suffer in its defeat. If their team wins, they wear team colors the next day, talk about how "we" won, feel stronger and more optimistic, and are prouder of themselves. If their team loses, the opposite happens and fans feel defeated, depressed and angry.

The higher levels of testosterone in spectators who back a winning team is a key factor in the violence that often follows intensely competitive matches.

Men can and often do pay a terrible price for their dedication to sports. In a series of interviews with professional soccer players, British sociologist Martin Roderick notes that players minimize their pain and downplay their injuries. Men are encouraged to "play through" their injuries and ignore the possible consequence of further injury. Many players who are injured, particularly those who are most frequently hurt, are mocked by their teammates. Such jokes, Roderick points out, "often deliver unpalatable messages with a softened impact. . . . they are a type of social control to minimize perceived malingering."[5] In other words, the athlete is encouraged *not* to complain and to continue playing no matter what the cost. There is a sense of having let the team down after an injury: "You want to tell them what they want to hear, so you are always optimistic. . . . when you are not, you feel as if you have let everybody down."

SUDDEN CARDIAC DEATH

One of the most startling and unexpected events in sports is the sudden death during play of a young athlete. Herodotus recorded the death of the Athenian's fleetest runner, Pheidippides, who had been sent to seek help from Sparta during the Persian invasion; he ran 167 miles to reach the Spartans, then raced back to the Athenians with the news that the Spartans had refused to help. He then fought in the Battle of Marathon, in which the Greeks triumphed over the Persians. As soon as the victory was secured, he ran 26 miles at top speed to bring the Athenians the wonderful news. On arriving, he gasped out his message, "We have won!" and fell down dead—but his feat inspired the 26.2-mile footrace we call the marathon today.

Young male athletes are particularly vulnerable to cardiac arrest as a consequence of several kinds of congenital heart diseases, which produce fatal arrhythmias during games. A congenital abnormality in the heart's electrical system (which produces a regular heartbeat and an orderly excitation of the heart muscle) predisposes them to disturbances in cardiac rhythm. These patients can experience sudden death, particularly during competitive sports. Other fatalities are due to a disorderly growth of the heart muscle itself. For example, some parts of the heart's septum, which separates the right from the left pumping chamber, may grow disproportionately large and actually prevent blood from leaving the chamber when the heart contracts. There is also an illness called Marfan's syndrome, in which patients are unusually tall and have weaknesses in the wall of their aorta, which can rupture when blood pressure rises during a game.

Some players who are victims of sudden death during sports events have undiagnosed inflammation of the heart muscle due to a viral illness called myocarditis. Myocarditis was present in 6 to 7 percent of competitive athletes[6] and 20 percent of military recruits who had sudden cardiac deaths.[7] An article by Paul Gardner, who reported on the deaths of three soccer players between the ages of 16 and 26 in September 2007, points out that about 1,000 players a year die from sudden cardiac death. Exhaustion due to the increased rate of speed of play as well as the higher number of games played by each competitor also can end in a fatal outcome. Gardner quotes the assertion of former French soccer star Michel Platini that soccer is characterized by "a relentless drive to play more games. . . . 'we all want to play less but . . . the system is made so that the players play more and more.'" Body contact is now more severe; size and weight of players has increased over the past 40 years.

Unfortunately, young and superbly trained athletes continue to die suddenly and unexpectedly, and not always during a game: Soccer player Antonio Puerta died at the age of 22, three days after he collapsed on a soccer field in Spain. Another devotee of the sport, Chaswe Nsofwa, 26, died during practice with his Israeli team, and 16-year-old Anton Reid died during a warm-up session with his British team. Soccer seems a particularly hazardous sport: The modern player covers five to six miles during a 90-minute game. This, coupled with the dangers of sudden bursts of speed and body contact with ever-heavier, larger players compounds the risk. The cause of these sudden deaths is almost always cardiac, but not always for the same kind of disorder.

At the very least, between 125 and 200 young athletes die every year in the United States.[8] In fact, Dr. Barry Maron, who has tabulated over 1,900 sudden cardiac deaths in young, competitive athletes over the past 27 years, believes that this is a significant underestimate of the true number. There are usually no warning signs. Some experience palpitations, fainting, or episodes of chest pain. Exercise training changes the electrical and mechanical behavior of the heart: The mass of the great pumping chamber of the heart, the left ventricle, increases, and the resting heart rate goes down, often well into the low forties or even the high thirties. Emotion and competition put additional strain on the heart: The release of hormones from the adrenal gland increases heart rate and the force of heart muscle contraction and raises blood pressure.

What can we do to save the lives of these athletes? First of all, any team member who collapses on the field should be presumed to have a lethal cardiac arrhythmia and be defibrillated or resuscitated with CPR until help arrives. Still, most attempts at saving the victim are unsuccessful, so adequate screening ahead of time is crucial. In Italy, the only country where screening of athletes is mandatory, deaths per 100,000 athletes has dropped to 0.4 from 4 since the screening was introduced.[9] However, it is still difficult to spell out an effective routine for screening these young people; even a careful history and physical examination can be unrevealing. So can an electrocardiogram, a picture of the heart created by sound waves reflected from the organ itself. Even echocardiography is not inevitably helpful.

The cost of screening all athletes for vulnerability would be prohibitive, even if more sophisticated tests such as echocardiograms were universally available. In 1996, the American Heart Association developed the following guidelines for assessing vulnerability:[10]

- A family history of premature or sudden death in a relative should trigger a fuller investigation.
- Personal history of heart murmur, high blood pressure, excessive fatigue, chest pain or fainting on exertion, or excessive shortness of breath should be investigated. This should be verified by parental affirmation that the details are all present and correct.
- Physical examination for a heart murmur, pulse strength in the legs, and any stigmata of Marfan's syndrome should be carried out.

CONCUSSION

One of my colleagues commented recently that if women died routinely in athletic competition, the sport would be banned. Somehow, he remarked, we tolerate death and incapacitating injuries in men as a result of the games they play. Boxing and football are cardinal examples of dangerous sports that require careful surveillance and training of players, coaches, and managers. Unfortunately, the drive in men to forge ahead in spite of significant pain or compromised abilities is so powerful that they often suffer irremediable damage by continuing to play. The problem is not rare in men's competitive games: The National Football League reports about 160 concussions a year and the National Hockey League 70 annually.[11] In high school football alone, there are as many as 250,000 concussions a year,[12] and 20 percent of players suffer head injuries.[13] The likelihood of injury isn't just confined to football: Concussions are sustained in boxing, ice hockey, wrestling, gymnastics, lacrosse, soccer, and basketball.

Concussion is one of the most treacherous injuries in sports: It can easily go unrecognized and, with repeated injury, create lasting and incapacitating damage and even death. The term is defined as "an immediate and transient loss of consciousness accompanied by a brief period of amnesia after a blow to the head."[14] The definition has been expanded to include a sensation of being "starstruck" or dazed momentarily, even without loss of consciousness. The trivializing term "dinged" should be abandoned; it makes little of the incident and encourages the victim to brush off any injury—and its consequences. Interestingly, convulsive movements may follow the injury; when these victims are televised immediately after trauma, several types of involuntary muscular behavior are documented and aid the observer in making a diagnosis. The snapping or jerking of the brain where it joins the stalk-like brain stem interrupts the function of neurons that maintain alertness; it is this that causes the brief loss of consciousness and, in more serious cases, the sleep that follows injury. Amnesia, both for events before the injury and after, is another feature of concussion, but the neurological basis for this is unknown.

Even when the neurological examination finds nothing out of the ordinary, significant brain bleeding can occur; 10 percent of patients have this as a complication of their injury and 2 percent need surgery to correct it.[15] The only way to detect this is by a CT scan of the brain; unfortunately, this is expensive and, in some rural areas, not readily available. Some guidelines have been published for who should get the test; they include being over 60 years of age and experiencing headache, vomiting, and persistent amnesia.[16] The onset of new symptoms after a concussion is a powerful indication for a head CT, because a delayed bleed is often the reason. Another complication may be a stroke from a tear in the carotid artery of the neck, which is a major supplier of blood to the brain.

One of the most troubling consequences of a concussion is what happens after the blow. It is not widely acknowledged that a hit to the head can alter a person's personality. We understand physical injury but have a harder time when a friend or relative begins to act differently. The post-concussion syndrome is a real phenomenon and can last days, weeks, months, or the rest of one's life. Memory problems, headache, and trouble concentrating are cardinal features of the illness. Often the frightened, misunderstood patient, incorrectly labeled neurotic, suffers from a range of problems such as aphasia, anxiety, and obsessive self-involvement that leads to an inability to empathize with others. The patient is profoundly aware that something is wrong and the refusal of health care professionals to confirm this compounds his sense of isolation, depression, and panic.

I know a young litigator who was hit by a truck and sustained a head injury. He was taken to the emergency room, where he was agitated and irritable. He told me later that he couldn't process what he had heard and, even worse, had to search for words to express himself. He was clearly shaken up by having his sense of himself as an intelligent and articulate man compromised. It took several months after the injury for his brain to repair the damage.

If a second concussion occurs before the first one is healed, the effects on the body and brain can be disastrous. There have been reports of massive brain swelling as a result of a second trauma. The American Orthopaedic Society for Sports Medicine explains that after a brain injury, cells that are traumatized but still alive are in a vulnerable state. A second injury disrupts the processes that repair these neurons.[17] Repeated, even mild, injuries can cause cumulative damage that lasts a lifetime; old boxers are referred to as "punch drunk," a result of repeated brain trauma.

Various guidelines for training and protocols for determining when a return to play is appropriate have been published. The most exhaustive and thoughtful is by the National Athletic Trainers' Association.[18] The manual explains the mechanism of brain injury under various conditions and defines a concussion, including its telltale signs. It provides criteria for when to refer the athlete to a physician after the injury. The reasons for disqualifying an athlete are spelled out, emphasizing the vulnerability of players who have suffered repeated injury. These men are at increased risk for new injury and have a significantly slowed recovery. The association cautions: "In athletes with a history of 3 or more concussions and experiencing slowed recovery, temporary or permanent disqualification from contact sports may be indicated." The guidelines include a useful graded symptom checklist, the timing of symptoms after injury, and a physician referral checklist.

THE COST OF ANABOLIC STEROIDS

It is not only external factors or physiological abnormalities that threaten men in sports. Sometimes the competitive fire itself—win at all costs—can wreak havoc as athletes try to improve their performances by using drug and hormones. Even the most accomplished athletes do it: Dick Pound, chairman of the World Anti-Doping Agency, says that the use of performance-enhancing drugs by Major League Baseball players was "out of control,"[19] an opinion reiterated by the recent Mitchell Report.[20] Barry Bonds faces permanent disgrace for allegedly lying about his use of anabolic steroids. Baseball is not the only sport affected: Floyd Landis, winner of the 2006 Tour de France cycling race, was stripped of his title for using synthetic testosterone during the competition. But amateur use of anabolic steroids is increasing, too: Incredibly, the 2005 Monitoring the Future study reported that 1.7 percent of eighth graders, 2 percent of tenth graders, and 2.6 percent of twelfth graders are using them![21] The cost is staggering: In 1990, the illicit steroid market was estimated to be 400 million dollars.[22]

Anabolic steroids are variations on the hormone testosterone: Athletes take them to build muscle mass, promote aggressive behavior, and increase body weight. Stimulants and painkillers are often added to the mix; this is called "stacking." These drugs increase blood rate and serum cholesterol, impair liver function, accelerate baldness, and promote fluid retention. The psychological bill is high: mood swings, violent behavior, depression, and even psychotic episodes. Anabolic steroids depress the natural production of testosterone, causing breast and prostate enlargement, temporary infertility and altered sex drive. Abnormal sperm production and painful erections are other side effects. Loss of bone mass in both males and females is also common, and some of the impact on women's reproductive capacity is not reversible.[23]

Pumping steroids into their systems also predisposes young athletes to tendon rupture, enlargement of their breasts and, importantly, reduction in levels of good cholesterol (HDL-C); the Framingham study pointed out in 1983 that men with HDL-C levels of 25 mgm/dL were three times more likely to develop coronary artery disease than those with 50 mg/dL.[24]

The World Anti-Doping Agency, in an international effort to spell out guidelines and prohibitions for the use of performance-enhancing drugs, has just published its World Anti-Doping Code.[25]

THE WEEKEND WARRIOR

Amateur athletes suffer too, mostly of them as a result of paroxysms of violent exertion for which they are unprepared by any regular exercise regime. On my annual summer trip to Bermuda, I was called on at least once a week to tend to athletic casualties among the guests. It became a family joke, and my son suggested I ask for a retainer from the hotel management while we were there! Frequently, an injured warrior, sometimes in his thirties, had played singles tennis so enthusiastically in the blazing mid-day sun that he suffered from heat exhaustion and fainted at the dinner table. I resuscitated one 60-something male who had a cardiac arrest on the beach after a half-mile swim in rough water. (I still have the tiny purse his grateful wife knit for my four-year-old daughter!) Back spasms on the golf course, caused by swinging heavy clubs, are very common and render otherwise healthy men immobile for days. One overweight young man herniated a lumbar disc doing just that; he spent all of his vacation on the floor of his cabin, unable to move, and barely managed the plane ride home in agony. Others tear the rotator cuff that enables them to move their shoulders; some injuries are so severe that they need reparative surgery. An enthusiastic scuba diver went so deep exploring a coral reef that he ruptured both ear drums; another ignored the warnings on the beach of jelly fish–infested waters and sustained a painful sting that warranted a visit to the local hospital. Injudicious exposure to hot tropical sun is another frequent issue: Some patients actually develop generalized, maddening itching after a severe sunburn that requires steroid cream for relief.

A little common sense would go a long way to avoiding what the Center For Disease Control euphemistically calls "unintentional injuries." Important principles include paying attention to the hazards of exercising in the dry climates that promote excessive fluid loss; dehydration can lower blood pressure to a near-lethal degree, and drinking enough water and taking in enough salt to compensate for fluid and sodium loss during exercise is crucially important. Stretching tight muscles before running, bike riding, or tennis avoids injury; I have seen more than one Achilles tendon rupture that could have been avoided as one of our Bermuda tennis stars lunged for a backhand.

Trainers emphasize what they call "core strength" and teach their pupils how to strengthen hip, knee, and lower leg muscles that help them balance and give them protection against sprained and fractured ankles. Try standing on one leg for a minute or more; it's not easy for the man who spends most of his life at a computer, I can assure you. If you can't do it, seek out a trainer who will help you develop essential strength for balance! Wearing improper shoes is another health hazard for the unprepared athlete; foot fractures and/or inflammation of the connective tissue that protects the heel—a painful condition known as plantar fasciitis—can be avoided by investing time in choosing a pair of athletic shoes that cushion the foot against harsh impacts and provide proper support with laces that can be tightened to ensure a snug fit.

Another sensible recommendation is to start any unaccustomed activity *slowly*, allowing your body to accommodate to the new demands and develop the strength and cardiac reserve that will let you meet the challenge without hazard. You'll be amazed what progress you can make with just three days of gradual increase in exertion rather than lurching into exercise at full tilt. If you do something for which you are absolutely untrained, like riding a horse for the first time, make sure you tell the stable personnel you are inexperienced and take a competent person with you to help manage the challenges of even the smoothest trot! One of my patients "discovered" the joy of horseback riding on a dude ranch, only to come home practically crippled with a slipped cervical disc that required weeks of major pain killers and physiotherapy to remedy.

And a note to those spa visitors who seek out vigorous massages when they have barely recovered from low back pain or some other muscle injury. A patient of mine had just begun ambulating after a low back spasm that had reduced him to immobility; he went for a "massage" because he thought it might help and found two hours later that he had lost all progress and was once again immobilized.

Beware of the challenges of high altitudes; some people can actually decompensate to the point of heart failure if they are exposed to the low concentrations of oxygen that prevail in popular vacation spots like Santa Fe, for example. Your doctor can give you a medication (diamox) that will mitigate the difficulty you feel on a trip to such places; if you have suffered from a cardiac condition, be sure to get your doctor's approval. Finally, if you have trouble "keeping up" with your companions, don't be shy: say so, and if they can't or won't slow down, let them go on without you. You can join them on another day, when you are more fit.

A word to patients on chronic medication: Review your prescriptions with your doctor before a trip. For example, some of them (called beta blockers) may impair your ability to increase your heart rate in response to the challenge of unaccustomed exercise. If you have a seizure disorder and are injured on vacation, remember to warn the local doctors not to give you meperidine (Demerol) or tramadol (Ultram), because those medications lower the seizure threshold. Make sure you carry a list of any medications *and their doses* in your wallet when you travel.

There is nothing more satisfying than the high of physical exercise. Endurance sports put you into a zone where your body and mind are in complete peace. The endorphins produced after a long run, a hard game of basketball, or an afternoon golfing provide relief from day-to-day anxiety. You will want to continue exercising throughout your life, and therefore you must exercise wisely. Diversify your sports activities in order to condition your entire body. And pay attention to pain. It is your body's way of telling you something inside is wrong and needs attention.

What should you know about sports injuries?

- **Make sure you are physically fit enough for vigorous competitive sports**, even at an amateur level. Report any history of an irregular heartbeat and ask your doctor if you need an echocardiogram before he clears you for play.

- **Don't minimize a head injury**. Concussion, particularly repeated concussions, can have life-long consequences. Ensuing symptoms include severe headaches, mood changes and problems with cognition. Dropping out of the game until you are completely well is worth the time out.

- **Taking steroids for performance enhancement can have disastrous consequences** including tendon rupture, breast enlargement, impotence, and a significantly increased risk for coronary artery disease. Don't even think of doing it.

- If you are a weekend warrior, **warm up before competitive play**. Particularly in hot, dry climates, monitor your hydration and level of exertion so you avoid heart exhaustion. Make sure you have the proper footwear. If you are out of shape, consider building regular strengthening and conditioning exercises into your routine.

CHAPTER TEN

MEN'S WORK

WHAT ARE THE HAZARDS?

Without question, we ask men—and they volunteer—to do the most dangerous jobs we need done. Men are still the great majority of the soldiers who fight our wars, but this is not the only hazardous role men fill. Some professions carry guaranteed health risks, and often a dramatically increased probability of premature death. In a masterpiece of understatement, one team of investigators observed: "Women and men tend to work in different occupations. . . . women choose safer jobs than men."[1]

MEN WHO SAIL THE SEAS

Whenever I find myself growing grim about the mouth; whenever it is a damp, drizzly November in my soul; whenever I find myself involuntarily pausing before coffin warehouses, and bringing up the rear of every funeral I meet; and especially whenever my hypos get such an upper hand of me that it requires a strong moral principle to prevent me from deliberately stepping into the street and methodically knocking people's hats off—then I account it high time to get to sea as soon as I can. This is my substitute for pistol and ball.

—Herman Melville, *Moby Dick*

Prolonged solitude, hazardous work conditions, and absence of medical treatment combine to make a sailor's job one of the most perilous. Extremes of weather, toxic and inflammable cargoes, and all the deathtraps on board a vessel—what Roberts and Hansen at the University of Oxford have called "the harsh architectural structure of ships"—threaten the sailor's health. A century ago, they were six times less likely to return from sea than coal miners to emerge from the mines. Their chances of dying on the job nine times more likely than that for railway workers and *146 times* those for factory and shop workers.[2] Since then their survival chances haven't risen by much: Swedish seamen had a four-fold increase in mortality compared with other men of working age in the decade 1945–1955.[3] Danish seafarers in the 1990s had an eleven-fold increase risk for death compared to land-based workers.[4]

Perhaps the most underappreciated risk factors for sailors are the consequences of prolonged isolation; a ship's captain once told me that depression and alcoholism are rampant. One of the most challenging problems for a commander is how to keep the men entertained.[5] Even on cruise ships, where trips are shorter and the ambience livelier, it is a little-known fact that most of a sailor's time is occupied painting the ship. It's a striking feature of life at sea; some of the work is necessary, but much of it is designed to keep the men occupied and out of trouble during long voyages. "As soon as we're finished painting the whole ship, we start all over again," one sailor confided to me.

Suicide levels are higher in seamen than in shore-based populations.[6] Alcoholic intoxication was a factor in the deaths of most seamen who drowned while the ship was docked, but attempts to board their vessels were handicapped even for the sober by fluctuations in the tide, icy gangways, poor visibility, and the absence of safety nets. In a major survey of the causes of death of British merchant ship seafarers between 1986 and 1995, S.E. Roberts and H. L. Hansen of Oxford University established that 42 percent were due to illness, and 93 percent of these were due to cardiovascular disease. The mean age of death was 54 years. Only 5 of those who died were taken to the hospital. Some of the findings at post-mortem examination bear mention: Many of the victims were obese, and tobacco in various forms was found in their personal effects. The doctors on board were clearly inadequate to deal with critical situations such as heart attacks. The researchers found that most of the eventual victims should have failed the physical examinations and not have been allowed on board to begin with. Many had had illnesses such as epilepsy, schizophrenia, and general mental instability that dated back many years. The men not killed by illness, were claimed by accidental death—fires, explosions, and collisions as well as occupational accidents like being swept overboard by heavy waves or falling overboard. Alaska's commercial fishermen often fall overboard while crab fishing far offshore in winter. Their vessels frequently capsize and sink.[7]

FIREMEN

Firefighting is a high-hazard job, and the work is at times extremely physically demanding. It involves heavy lifting and maneuvering in sometimes awkward and unstable positions while wearing heavy clothing and protective gear in a hot environment.

In addition, exposure to carbon monoxide and particulate matter in the air is routine, and there is a highly variable risk of exposure to a broad array of other toxic chemicals generated from the smoke of burning materials.[8]

How do we explain, given these facts, that neither burns nor smoke inhalation claim most firemen? Firemen, it turns out, die disproportionately from heart disease. Almost exclusively due to coronary artery disease (CAD), cardiovascular events account for 45 percent of all deaths of firemen on duty.[9] In an interesting survey of all deaths among firefighters between 1994 and 2004, Harvard researchers Stefanos Kales and his colleagues sought to identify the tasks that were most dangerous for these men. In their survey of 1,144 deaths, 39 percent were due to CAD; 32 percent of those occurred during fire suppression, and 31 percent during the alarm response *or return to the firehouse.* The remaining 37 percent occurred during other non-emergency duties.[10]

The actual time firemen spend fighting fires is very small— about 1 to 5 percent of the average fireman's professional time. As other observers have commented after reading these data, some of the increased mortality is due to carbon monoxide exposure: Even mild carbon monoxide intoxication produces a compromise of myocardial blood supply, and firefighters who don't smoke and who don't use their self-contained breathing apparatus correctly may show levels as high as 14 percent.[11]

Another very interesting comment was offered by Lawrence Raymond and Thomas Barringer at the Carolinas Medical Center, who suggested that even when firemen had stress testing to screen for the presence of underlying cardiac disease, they probably had not had heat stress testing: Stress imposed not only by the fire, but by thermally restrictive protective gear.[12] Yet another study found, however, that 40 percent of firemen who died from CAD were smokers.[13] Flaws in the criteria for acceptance of recruits as firefighters include inadequate screening for underlying risk factors for cardiovascular disease, including obesity.

The vulnerability of firemen to sudden death is probably almost exclusively due to periodic demands for extremely intense physical exertion; thermal, chemical, and emotional stress, obviously, further intensify their risk. Overeating, lack of exercise, and tobacco are important risk factors for CAD. While most career firefighters retire at 50 years of age, those who do remain active should have annual physical examinations, and it should be routine to have regular fitness and preventive health programs in place for these vulnerable workers.

POLICEMEN

Tony della Ventura, a celebrated and respected NYPD detective (retired), is a completely self-contained man whose stillness is more formidable than any hostile gesture could be. He is an eloquent testimonial to how the most effective police officers maintain control, even in the most threatening situations. First, he says, successful police work depends on meticulous planning: "I always have a backup plan," he confides. "If the first gun doesn't fire, I always have a second in reserve." In Tony's case, it also depends on the icy fearlessness that is a cardinal feature of his persona: He believes that a compelling stare straight into the eyes of a perpetrator can quell even the most vicious enemy—without firing a shot. Men who have worked with him say that he can walk through the most dangerous neighborhoods and that gangs of even the most fiercely threatening men simply pull back and let him pass. He told me that at the moment of confrontation, he feels no fear at all, but only a concentration of inner strength that allows him to quell even the fiercest adversary—without using anything except words and the fixed intensity of his expression. He says that one of his shortcomings is that he has no deep personal attachments. Listening to him, I don't know what strikes me more: the integrated and unmistakable power of his personality or the sense I have that he is completely impervious to any impact from those around him.

Police work takes a high toll. Policemen frequently succumb to cancer and alcoholism or to suicide, driven in large part by on-the-job stress. According to Tessa Tate, founder of Survivors of Law Enforcement Suicide, police are "incredibly adept at masking their emotions," distrust mental health professionals, and are often suffering from untreated depression.[14]

John M. Violanti, one of the foremost experts on police health and a professor at the University of Oregon, has conducted a 40-year retrospective study on the causes of death of 623,000 policemen.[15] The mean age of death was 66—scarcely an advanced age. This and several other surveys report that police officers' mortality is higher than that of the general U.S. white male population, and is highest for those who've been in the force anywhere from one to two decades.

More policemen died of cancers and diseases of the digestive tract compared with non-policemen. Possible reasons include inhaling carbon monoxide from cars and fumes from gun-cleaning solvents and fingerprint kits, particularly in the case of blood and lymphatic cancers. Brain cancers occurred more frequently in policemen compared with the general population. This may be related to their higher exposure to electromagnetic frequency fields in radio and radar frequencies in vehicles and police stations. They also have an increased rate of testicular cancer.[16] Prostate cancer is commonly associated with policemen who used handheld radar units inside their patrol cars. A higher-than-expected rate of esophageal cancer is attributable to the fact that about 40 percent of police officers smoke. Statistically, police had an only slightly elevated risk for coronary artery disease compared to the general population, but it appeared most frequently during the first few years of service. Warren Franke and his colleagues at

Iowa State University had similar findings, affirming that police officers were no more likely to have CAD than men in the general population, and that they had a lower incidence of diabetes and physical inactivity. However, they found a higher prevalence of some risk factors such as hypertension, high cholesterol, obesity, and tobacco use.[17]

Stress levels are naturally high, and peak at year 13 of employment.[18] Such stress predisposes police to coronary artery disease, and weakens the immune system, possibly leaving the door open to cancer. The specter of retirement hangs over the officers: Chances of suicide increase ten-fold in retirees. The reasons for this are complex, but experts attribute them to the availability of firearms; 95 percent of all police suicides involve a gun.[19] Fifty-eight percent of these occurred in the victims' own homes. Many officers deal with stress by drinking: A full quarter were alcohol dependent, and drinking was a factor in 60 percent of suicides.[20]

In analyzing the data he collected, Violanti blames the nature of the work: As is the case with the military, he says, the experience of these workers is "hours of mind-numbing boredom punctuated by brief periods of intense, unpredictable, life-threatening action."[21] Many officers are not physically fit for those brief periods of intense action: They can maintain readiness, though, by as little as three hours of training a week, according to the Law Enforcement Wellness Association. Violanti believes that maintaining physical fitness, avoiding excessive use of alcohol, and giving up tobacco would increase policemen's longevity to levels approaching that of the general population.

CONSTRUCTION WORKERS

The young men renovating my Manhattan apartment include plumbers, electricians, and painters. They are there to transfer the architect's plans into the walls, floors, and closets that will be my new home. A fine, grey dust is everywhere. Some workers are wearing masks that recall hospital interns and residents, their rough contemporaries also masked for protection from the hazards of very different work. Each group of workers pays a special price for the demanding jobs they do. The construction workers endure exposure to lead, dust, asbestos, paints, and solvents. They work in extremes of heat or cold, often in confined spaces, suffer falls, and work with heavy tools in repetitive patterns that injure muscles and tendons. And they do it all amid the mind-numbing noise of heavy machinery and powered gear that are the tools of their trade.

Construction workers are predominantly young—their average age is 39—and 90 percent are male and white.[22] They suffer the highest rate of fatalities and injuries of any occupational group, most of which are sustained by those in the older age range of 35 to 44.

Iron workers are well-educated. Many have completed high school courses in mathematics, mechanical drawing, English, and welding. Some contractors have extensive training programs for their iron workers; on-the-job trainees learn informally, assisting on simple jobs like carrying various materials and gradually assuming responsibility for more complicated tasks like fitting and assembling the different material components that go into the construction on which they are working. They must be in good physical condition and possess agility, balance, and indifference to heights.

In spite of meticulous and often prolonged apprenticeships and training, iron workers (still called that in spite of the fact that they work with steel) are the most vulnerable of all construction workers. They erect steel frames, assemble the cranes and derricks that move the components of the project, and unload and stack the prefabricated parts as they arrive at the workplace. Then they face the challenging job of connecting the pieces according to blueprinted instructions, often at dizzying heights. Their mortality figures for 2001 showed a twelve-fold greater injury rate for these men than those at lowest risk: 76 per 100,000 full-time iron workers died compared with 6 per 100,000 dry wall installers in that year. Their rates of nonfatal injuries and illnesses made up 37 percent of all those in the construction trades—a figure that is even more remarkable because there are fewer of them than in any other trade involved in building: only 0.6 percent of all workers. Not surprisingly, most of them die in falls. They also have the highest rate of nonfatal occupational injury and illness. The next four most common causes of death among construction workers are being involved in highway accidents, coming into contact with an electrical current, being struck by an object, and being killed by a vehicle or mobile equipment.

Natural and man-made disasters carry their own penalties: Skin conditions made up a quarter of all diseases treated in construction workers involved in the rebuilding following Hurricane Katrina.[23] Well over half of skin rashes were due to an allergic reaction to insect bites, probably from spiders in flooded homes.

STAYING SAFE

Men agree to do the most dangerous jobs in society. The costs are significant; many of them die or are injured as a direct result of the hazardous work they perform. Protecting themselves involves several basic principles, the first of which is to stay physically fit. Physical fitness doesn't take hours a day at a gym with a professional trainer; cardiovascular fitness is within the reach of any man who spends at least three days a week in 30 minutes of aerobic exercise. Portion control and sensible dietary principles keep weight down; this is a particularly important survival technique. Obesity is not only a risk factor for cardiovascular disease, which claims men's lives prematurely and is the chief cause of death by the age of 45, it is also a significant burden for the musculoskeletal system. A basic principle of orthopedics is that one pound of body weight is equivalent to a ten-pound burden on the hips and lower back; many men battle the pain of low back injury on a daily basis, and some of them take potent drugs to combat the pain. The ability to do even brief periods of intense physical work requires a reasonable level of cardiovascular and musculoskeletal readiness. It is significant that heart attacks happen to firemen, for example, almost exclusively during or just after combating a blaze.

Paying close attention to the safety rules of your particular trade is essential; learning how to work at heights, enter and exit confined spaces, obey the principles of electrical safety, handle heavy machinery, and stay current with how to combat possible chemical hazards at a worksite are all essential. Finally, common sense dictates that you keep a clean, uncluttered, and well-lit workplace.

From their early years, men are socialized to take risks, and this continues into their careers. Whether you perform dangerous physical labor such as construction, potentially life threatening work such as law enforcement, or even an emotionally demanding job such as finance, you are often asked to overlook your personal safety in favor of the greater benefit you bring to society. The good news is that many of the ill effects of risky behavior are avoidable. As a society we should pay more attention to the risks men take and develop on-the-job regulations and guidelines so that you can be respected and rewarded for the work you do without penalty to your health.

What to keep in mind about men's work:

- **Pay attention to the safety rules for any job you undertake.** This includes on-the-job manual labor or weekend carpentry around the house. If you are untrained, make sure you are apprenticed to a more experienced worker so that you can learn how to do the job you're assigned.

- **Fitness is essential** for work that demands short bursts of intense physical activity; the overweight, out of shape policeman or fireman who faces sudden challenges is particularly at risk for sudden cardiac death. If you are experiencing depression or negative thoughts as you approach retirement, consult your doctor and alert him to your problems. One of the most useful things you can do is to construct a reasonable plan for how you'll spend your time after you stop working. A second—or third—career may be just the thing that will prove most helpful.

CHAPTER ELEVEN

ANDROPAUSE AND THE AGING MALE

AGING, SOCIETY, AND THE FAMILY

Let's face it: We all have to deal with the fact that there is no escape from aging. It generally involves a progressive loss of many of our faculties and abilities and an acknowledgment that, ultimately, no matter how hard we try to deny and avoid it, our lifespan has a finite limit. The philosopher Kierkegaard said that the most anxious and neurotic of us were actually the only normal members of the human race. The rest live in blissful denial of our mortality. The few people I know who are open to discussing death at all say that they want to go suddenly, in their nineties, with undiminished powers, doing something they really love. (A popular alternative is to hope one dies in one's sleep—my personal favorite!)

Accepting the fact that life is not eternal and rather is sharply limited to a finite number of years is a central and difficult task for many older people. Tremendous progress in medical science over the past century is helping us remain functional even at advanced ages. "Let's face it," said a 60-something friend of mine recently, adopting a metaphor from golf, "we're on the back nine." "But we're still in the game!" I answered.

The demographics of aging have changed profoundly with improvements in health care. Over three hundred baby boomers are turning 60 every hour.[1] They comprise 28 percent of the adult U.S. population and are not taking aging sitting down. They are expected to live longer than any previous generation of Americans; of the 3.4 million born in 1946 (including Bill Clinton, George and Laura Bush, Donald Trump, Susan Sarandon, Steven Spielberg, and Sylvester Stallone), 2.8 million are still alive. The surviving men can expect to live another 22 years. By 2030, more than 20 percent of the population will be over 65, and more than 35 percent will be over 50. In the United States, by age 85 women outnumber men 2.2 to 1,[2] and by their nineties, 3 to 1.

How do we age? The United States is peculiar in that we don't regard old people with the reverence that is customary in more traditional societies. This is to the detriment of both our young and old alike, I might add. We are wasting the value of elderly parents and grandparents. In our insistence on nuclear families we've lost the knack of utilizing the unique talents of each generation and integrating them into an effective whole. The incidence of female depression throughout the world is said to be twice that of men— except for India, where there are whole networks of relatives folded into common households, sharing chores and child rearing. Those of us who are younger have an unfortunate disconnect with the growing population of older people: The modern family tends to warehouse older relatives. Society encourages them to live apart from the nuclear family in separate, often supervised living facilities with paid aides to care for the most feeble. Most young married couples elect to separate from their families and, in doing so, lose precious resources that might considerably lighten the burden of child care and the financial demands of setting up and maintaining a home.

We are not capitalizing on the special gifts of our oldest citizens—especially their accumulated wisdom and willingness to share the responsibilities of family life, particularly child rearing. Instead we hire outside workers to care for children and make the older family members feel unwanted and unneeded. A wise old physician said: "It takes one mother to raise six children, but not one of them can be found to care for her when she is old."

For the elderly, the urge to remain functional and a vital part of the work force or partake in some enriching activity is universal. Not long ago, I asked a colleague when he planned to retire. He answered: "Why would I retire? So I could be one of those guys who doesn't know what he's talking about anymore and is the worst golfer on the course?"

The accumulated wisdom of a lifetime can turn out to be a valuable asset: Corporations that once imposed mandatory retirements are trying to retain older workers with accommodations such as flex time and telecommuting. CNN's Shaheen Pasha commented recently: "With more than one worker out of four reaching retirement age by the end of the next decade, corporations are now in a mad dash to create a work environment that will convince older employees to forgo the leisurely pleasures of the golf course for the frenetic pace of the office."[3]

This is a good development for men, who often suffer most from the loss of professional identity. In a society where you are judged by how much you earn and how much power you wield, retirement can be a death sentence. Depression, feelings of worthlessness, and the physiological problems they create are serious issues. One of my patients who retired two years ago has become anxious, irritable, and so dependent on his wife that he follows her around the house and on the briefest errands. His wife, also my patient, bemoans the change in her hitherto reasonably happy marriage and now seriously wishes she could live alone. He has become reinterested in sex while remaining impotent, so that both find the attempts at intimacy frustrating, and she has begun to dread them.

> Depression in the elderly is underestimated and often misinterpreted as evidence of senility or dementia. Isolation, failing strength, and chronic illness, coupled with a feeling of being less useful to one's family and to society in general all impact the moods of older people.

Almost every older person worries and grieves over the gradual loss of function that accompanies aging: Vision loss, deafness, and even a decrease in the ability to smell and taste are all penalties exacted by longer life. Balance problems, loss of muscle mass and strength, and joints stiffened and painful with arthritis are all things many aging men have to deal with. It is a time when you want increased patience and gentleness from friends and children, not irritation with the more limited person you have become as you've grown older.

A friend who retired from teaching at an important academic medical center, where he was beloved by both peers and students who repeatedly nominated him "teacher of the year," has wilted in retirement. Within a year he was on beta-blockers for a failing heart, which left him so weakened that he planned only one excursion a day: Going for his groceries was enough of an outing, and he calculated how to get to the store without climbing a hill or having to walk very far. His appetite decreased; he ate much less than he had in the past. He seldom left the apartment. His calls to his children became less and less frequent. They had to be reminded that his medicines as well as his heart failure had blunted his vitality and tremendously increased the effort he had to put into even the simplest tasks of everyday living. To add to his isolation, he retained a lifelong reluctance to complain of any illness or discomfort or to ask for help when he was ill. Once, as a younger man, he had had severe gastroenteritis, and lay on the floor of his bathroom for almost three days until his family intervened.

I watch many of the children of my friends discuss the terms of their parents' wills—such as who will inherit what—often openly, in front of those parents. It is as though the younger generation regards the last years of their parents' lives as a burden and looks beyond them to a consideration of the benefit death will provide. While powers of attorney, health care proxies, and intelligent ordering of estates are all necessary, they have to be discussed in a loving, sensitive manner, and should include the older person's opinions and wishes every step along the way.

At least 14 percent of older people are significantly depressed and would benefit from either psychotherapy or an antidepressant.[4] A Dutch study of 4,051 older people over a six-year period found that depression was potentially lethal in men and was associated with a 1.67-fold increase in mortality—which was not true for depressed women.

Americans resist aging—and many of them handle it badly. Any book that promises ways to be younger, prettier, or stronger for a longer time is an automatic bestseller. A friend of mine calls this phenomenon "Doctor Bomba's magic elixir: drink this and live forever." I had lunch with a 46-year-old man recently who told me he plays tennis and swims every day. "It keeps my thinking sharp and the stiffness in my joints at bay," he told me. "But it takes me longer to recover after a match than it did before," he added ruefully. "I keep at it because I resist getting older." My office is filled with patients of both sexes who want to know what vitamins to take, what foods to eat, and what cosmetic procedures I would advise to keep them looking and feeling young. I was amused to see a joke in the *New Yorker* magazine that showed an impatient husband in black tie waiting for his wife's personal cosmetician to finish injecting Botox into her forehead as a prelude to their going out that evening. It is not uncommon for men and women to agree enthusiastically to investing thousands of dollars in cosmetic procedures but balk at a fraction of that fee for an office visit to their internist to treat their hypertension or an infection.

Women and men alike feel uncomfortable telling me their true ages, and the most welcome thing I can say to them is that they look younger than the number they give me. I was amused by a man's was amused to listen to a man's effort to estimate my age by asking the ages of my children. I watched him do the mental calculation as soon as I gave him the answer! Another man, who loves to flirt, announced that he had looked me up on the Internet to find out how old I was and pleasantly informed me that he was surprised at the answer: "You look great for your age," he assured me. I answered that he looked good for his, too.

> Growing older has many advantages. We are no longer discombobulated by the passionate intensity of youth that clouds our judgment. No longer does every incident seem worthy of an enormous amount of energy.

Sometimes I think youth is exhausting: I never cease to marvel at the effort my children put into decisions that should be simple and virtually automatic. With age comes a liberating detachment from social status and material things. I've watched countless older patients begin to give away things they would never have dreamed of parting with when they were younger. Real estate agents always say of estate apartments: "He didn't do anything to improve it for thirty years!" That should not surprise us. It is characteristic of the increasing detachment from possessions that is a hallmark of this time of life.

This calmer, steadier persona is a very useful resource for other family members, especially its youngest members. Many children find their grandparents' homes a serene port in a storm; my own children periodically ran away to my mother's apartment (located safely within the same apartment complex as my own) to take refuge from problems or an anticipated punishment they found overwhelming. In due course, my mother would telephone me and I would arrive at her home to find my son or daughter engrossed in a game of Parcheesi, sipping ginger ale, and eating half-melted

chocolate ice cream—much reassured that the world was not ending after all. Often my mother's advice had solved the problem that
had seemed so earthshaking only hours before.

One of the things we need less of in old age is sleep. Older members of the family can function as a kind of sentinel in the home.
When my daughter was young and awake at the crack of dawn, my
mother was there with her to feed the birds while they breakfasted
together. My children still recall the time spent with their grandmother as among their fondest childhood memories. Far from only
sitting at home baking cookies (which they did with her), my mother
took them on amazing adventures all over the world. She bought a
small boat and kept it in Bermuda. When they visited her there every
August the three of them would set out to explore beaches, swim in
newly discovered coves, observe schools of fish, and in general share
sunny hours of common tasks and constant discovery. On the few
occasions when I was permitted to tag along, I was impressed most
by the serenity of my mother and the calm, warm affection that
underlay everything the three of them did together. It was a welcome
relief for them from my much more pressured approach to life.

My older patients are also keen to preserve family history and
transfer it to their children: Stories of how their families were
formed and shaped, of adventures they had in youth, and of
the milestones of their lives begin to flow to all who will listen. As
she aged, my mother began to write out stories of her childhood on
yellow legal pads; these stories were some of the most interesting
I've ever read. One tale told of how a man came weekly to wind
and set the many clocks in her mother's town house. They still stick
in my mind. The images of that six-year-old little girl following the
clock master through the house, and of watching a craftsman apply
individual squares of gold leaf to her home's foyer, are more vivid
for me than even the many learned and scholarly lectures she
delivered in the prime of her career.

My grandmother, too, delighted me with stories of what she called
"the importance of dressing for business" at the turn of the century.

"Just the right hair comb was tremendously important to find," she laughed. My grandfather, who had been one of the original teamsters driving horse-drawn carts in New York City at the turn of the century, regaled us with stories of how he was shot by union organizers when he ran one of the first picket lines; he painted a vivid picture of the difficulties workers faced before unionization. His stories of the police, of politicians, and of how young people met and courted in the New York of the early 1900s rivaled, for me at least, Dickens's rich portraits of British society a half-century earlier. The past is important to know about and understand, and one of the most profoundly important functions of the older person is to tell us about it.

Age brings with it a sense of urgency, too. "If not now, then when?" is a question many older people begin to ask. Knowing that what seemed an endless span of time at 20 is, in fact, limited to only a decade or two more makes us much more efficient in deciding on what we'll spend our time and energies.

Whatever we think of old age, medical progress has made it ubiquitous. People alive at 85 make up the largest group in the population of most industrialized countries, and that population uses most of our health-care resources.[5] Most of the aged are women. Half of all men die before the age of 85 in the United States. By 90, two-thirds of them are gone.[6]

A comprehensive study of American men of Japanese ancestry, tracing their health for a 40-year period, identified coronary artery disease, stroke, cancer, chronic obstructive pulmonary disease, Parkinson's disease, and diabetes as the six most common afflictions.[7] Out of this group, 58 percent died by age 85 and 18 percent lived with some disability until that age. Only 11 percent survived to 85 with none of the chronic diseases I have listed and with cognitive and physical function intact. These men were called "exceptional survivors" and had several features in common: a strong grip (which was presumed to show higher levels of physical fitness compared to the other men in the cohort), a lean body, and good sensitivity to the action of insulin, as evidenced by low levels of serum triglycerides, glucose, and uric acid. Smoking and excessive alcohol consumption were important features in the lifestyle of those who died earlier. Educated individuals fared better than their brothers. An interesting formula was derived from the data: Men with no risk factors in midlife had a 60 percent chance of survival to age 85. With six or more risk factors, only 10 percent or less were expected to survive to that age.

(ANDROPAUSE)

The gradual loss of testosterone and other hormones that characterizes the process of male aging has been called *andropause*. An authority on male aging and fertility, Professor Harry Fisch, director of the Male Reproductive Center in the Department of Urology at Columbia University Medical Center of New York Presbyterian Hospital in New York City, points out that while men do not undergo the same dramatic change in physiology as women do in menopause, their change of life crisis is more complex and riddled with difficulties.

> Testosterone declines by about 1 percent in men after the age of 30. Lower levels of the hormone produce a significant group of symptoms, most of them very similar to the symptoms of estrogen-depleted women. Breast size enlarges in men, as the impact of the small amounts of estrogen that had been kept at bay by testosterone becomes evident. Bones begin to thin: Men account for 25 percent of all cases of osteoporosis, which culturally we have been trained to think of as a women's disease. And of course the many other symptoms we discussed earlier, such as a decrease in libido and a rise in depression, are also signs of a crisis.

It's not unusual for the oldest of the group to experience hot flashes: At a dinner party that included several octogenarian men, one 70-something male announced that he had never had a hot flash. The man facing him looked up and said wryly: "Just wait." Testosterone levels will fluctuate throughout your life, and its ups and downs are responsible for shifts in mood. After the sixth decade or so, as the hormone starts to decline rapidly, it is important to monitor its slide. Speaking with your doctor about what to expect is a good idea. He or she will probably want to do a test. Normal values range from 300 to 1100 nanograms in a decileter sample of blood, which is how researchers measure testosterone. If a man's testosterone drops below 250, it is a sign of impending trouble: In a study that lasted eight years, scientists showed that such men had a 35% higher chance of death than men whose testosterone values exceeded 250.[8]

There is interest in wider use of testosterone replacement. Recently, a group of experts who had studied the impact of this treatment decided to begin a new 12-month study, hoping to determine whether we know enough to prescribe it safely.[9] They put it this way:

> Testosterone is often equated in the popular culture with the macho male physique and virility. Viewed by some as an *anti-aging tonic*, the growth in testosterone's reputation and increased use by men of all ages in the United States has outpaced the scientific evidence about its potential benefits and risks.

The hormonal changes of aging are complex, and involve much more than a decline in testosterone. The adrenal gland itself changes. The levels of other hormones it produces change, including dehydroepiandrosterone (DHEA), a growth hormone (GH, secreted by the pituitary), and androgens (particularly testosterone). There are real gaps in our knowledge of how deficiencies of any of these contribute to the decline of strength, bone mass, cognition, and the other infirmities that characterize old age. Throw into the mix the general wear and tear caused by smoking, inactivity, poor nutrition, and excessive alcohol intake, and you begin to understand the complexity of the problem.

Testosterone can act directly on cells, or it can be changed into one of two other hormones: dihydrotestosterone (DHT), whose primary factories in the body are the prostate, skin, and reproductive organs; and estrogen, most abundant in fat, liver, and some parts of the central nervous system.

The impact of testosterone on cognition can be seen in female-to-male transsexuals: In one study in which assessments were done before and three months after testosterone administration, there was a significant increase in success with solving problems that had to do with spatial relationships and concepts, while there was a decrease in word and sentence production, a facility often better developed in women than in men.[10]

In spite of fears that administering testosterone to men might increase their risk for cardiovascular disease, short-term studies have shown the opposite. Testosterone infused directly into the coronary arteries dilates them, and the hormone increases the rate at which clots dissolve and lowers the levels of triglycerides in the blood.[11]

Because testosterone is rapidly broken down by the liver when taken orally, chemists are developing gels, patches, and injections. One popular way of delivering the hormone is through the skin. A patch containing testosterone is applied either to the scrotum or another part of the body; while the scrotal patch takes advantage of the high permeability of that skin to testosterone, it may cause higher-than-normal levels of DHT because of the scrotum's high concentration of an enzyme that converts testosterone to this more masculinizing hormone. These high levels of DHT may predispose users to prostatic and other cancers. Gels are popular delivery forms, but the problem is that the testosterone in them can be transferred to others by skin-to-skin contact.

A newer and perhaps safer class of compounds are called selective androgen receptor modulators (SARMS). They perform discrete androgenic actions on specific targets—muscle, sexual function and libido, and bone—without causing any harm to the prostate.

Unfortunately, the SARMS are still in the developmental stages, but hold out the promise of safer and more precisely targeted results.

Deciding whether a man will benefit from testosterone replacement requires a sophisticated and knowledgeable physician. Normal aging is associated with many of the same symptoms as testosterone deficiency, and many aging men may have hormonal levels that are as high as those of young men.

> **Testosterone or any of the precursor compounds that increase the levels of testosterone should never be used in men with normal levels of the hormone.** Low amounts of the hormone may be a *marker* rather than a cause of illness. For example, obesity, steroid use, diabetes, or excessive drinking can all lower testosterone levels.

Some experts use clomiphene citrate (Clomid), a hormone that stimulates the pituitary gland to produce two important fertility hormones: follicle-stimulating hormone (FSH), which in men stimulates the testes to produce sperm, and leutinizing hormone, which increases testosterone production. The result is often better quality and more abundant sperm. Clomid uses the patient's own internal mechanisms for improving testosterone production and thus eliminates many of the side effects associated with giving testosterone itself to the patient. A patient of mine had been using androgel for years when he complained of increasing abdominal fat, an inability to lose weight and an increase in the size of his breasts. His cells were importing the extra testosterone and converting it to estrogen via the action of a hormone present in fat cells, aromatase. In fact, what had been happening was that the externally administered testosterone was actually *feminizing* him rather than helping his erectile dysfunction and lowered libido.

Clomid has to be used judiciously, just as other forms of testosterone replacement. As Doctor Fisch points out in his superb book,

The Male Biological Clock,[12] it must be used only in men with lower-than-normal testosterone levels and those not at risk for cardiovascular disease, stroke, prostate cancer, or breast cancer. The treatment is relatively new, and the patients receiving it should have regular digital examinations and blood levels of prostate-specific antigen (PSA) measured to monitor them for any untoward effect on the prostate.

Prolactin, another hormone produced by the pituitary, is important because if levels rise (as in the case of a pituitary tumor, for example), lowered testosterone levels, impaired libido, problems achieving orgasm, and enlarged breasts can all result.

Many men have asked my opinion about using synthetic hormones to raise their vim and vigor. This is certainly reasonable, as we all want to maximize our body's potential, but many if not all are precursors to testosterone and can produce the same unwanted side effects as excess testosterone itself. Another favorite, human growth hormone, works on *all* the tissues of the body, and is dangerous because it will stimulate the growth of both benign and malignant tumors that might be present in the body.

THE AGING BRAIN

One of my colleagues, probably one of the best-known clinicians in the country, was growing old. I found him in the hospital one day tremendously upset. "I've made mistakes in recording a patient's history. Will you go up to the floor with me and help correct what I put in the chart?" I tried in vain to comfort him, and some weeks later met him on the street. "Will you have dinner with me?" I asked. "No," he said, "this isn't the time." We looked steadily into each other's eyes for a moment, and then quietly said goodbye. He committed suicide a week later, I am sure because he understood that his ability to care for patients, around whom he had built his whole brilliantly effective life, had ended.

Almost without exception, people have trouble with memory as they grow older. Most of it has to do with names. But some loss of memory is progressive, much more profound, and accompanied by other defects in brain function. A decline in the ability to reason, remember, and maintain emotional equilibrium can have many causes. The disorders that cause any of these symptoms are described by the blanket term dementia.

The fear of losing one's mind preoccupies everyone who is growing older. We forget the names of actors we grew up watching in our favorite movies or even of acquaintances. A friend of mine mentioned a woman we both knew who used to sell us fashion eyeglasses. Neither of us was able to remember her name. When we finally extracted it from the depths of our collective memory, we both laughed heartily about it, and exchanged rueful comments about that particular quirk of age. Patients confide in me daily about their fears that they, like their own parents or grandparents, will develop one of the dementias of old age. Usually they fear Alzheimer's, which is the most common cause of loss of cognition in the older person.

I received a call one afternoon about a colleague, a brilliant scholar, who had come to work as usual one day but had been unable to find her office. She was such an intelligent person that she had been able to hide her growing disability until it was far advanced—and, even with me, she had been too proud to share her growing fear that she was growing senile.

As my mother grew older she was unable to write checks and follow her investment accounts. On the day I took her checkbook out of her desk and began to pay her bills, I looked over at her sitting on the couch. She was wearing the same nightgown and robe she had refused to change for days. "What's the matter, Mother?" I asked. She looked back at me and answered: "I'm such a mess," with a look of profound distress I can remember to this day.

Here are some ways to decide whether you are experiencing the loss of cognition that accompanies normal aging or have a more serious problem.[13]

- Forgetting names is not unusual, but if you begin to forget appointments or have periods of confusion, it's worth noting.
- Forgetting to turn the heat off under a pot of milk is one issue, but forgetting that you put the milk on the stove at all is more serious. Absent-mindedness is common in people who are very busy and preoccupied with many details about which they think all day long. Those of us with intensely busy lives have to make a special effort to concentrate on what we're doing instead of reviewing some issue or crisis while we are making coffee or retrieving the newspapers.
- Forgetting where you put things is one of the most irritating features of aging. But putting objects in totally inappropriate places (like eyeglasses in the icebox) is a sign of a real problem.
- Changes in mood, particularly if they are rapid and without apparent cause, are another sign of trouble. Pronounced and dramatic changes in personality are another indication of brain dysfunction. Some of these changes, surprisingly, are rather welcome; I have had dominating, strong-willed patients become inexplicably sweeter and gentler with the advances of dementia.
- A profound loss of interest in the world around them is a hallmark of the demented individual. Even when they can still dress appropriately and answer questions rationally, a demented person becomes characteristically silent and withdrawn at family dinners or other celebrations, particularly if there are people present whom they don't know well. Often, demented patients become extremely anxious.

Describing the symptoms you experience or things you fear to your physician in detail is very important. In the first place, modern testing makes it possible to distinguish between what you suspect and what you're actually suffering. Many patients resist taking the test because they fear the answer, but the reality check will reassure you. You will know which issues need treatment and which are acceptable and expected for your age. The other reason to work closely with your physician on the nature and extent of your difficulties is that there are some diseases that can be significantly slowed with the proper treatment. One of these is Alzheimer's.

ALZHEIMER'S DISEASE

Alzheimer's disease accounts for 1.5 percent of all deaths in men.[14] It is caused by the accumulation of a substance in the brain called beta amyloid, the so-called plaques that characterize the disease. In a way that isn't completely understood, the excess of beta amyloid increases the amount of calcium inside brain cells, leading to their destruction. The plaques appear in the hippocampus, a brain structure that helps us form memories, and in areas of the brain used in reasoning and decision making. The supporting tissue that keeps nerve cells properly oriented is also attacked by this illness, and "tangles" of neurons are created that lose communication with other nerve cells. They die and further impair brain function.

Although there is no cure for this terrible disease, new drugs can slow the course and improve brain function in many individuals. Sophisticated imaging techniques of the brain in real time are primarily used as research tools at this time, but may eventually be used to document the course of the illness in individual patients.

Treatments include a range of medicines that exploit the fact that levels of acetylcholine, one of the chemicals in the brain that transmits messages between nerve cells, is very reduced. Acetylcholine is essential to memory formation; the FDA-approved drugs to increase its levels in the brain include tacrine (Cognex), donepezil (Arecept), rivastigmine (Exelon), and galantamine (Razadyne). Another medication, memantine (Namenda), works by regulating levels of glutamate, another chemical involved in memory formation.

Other ancillary drugs are being investigated to see if they will help reduce the risk for or progression of Alzheimer's; these include folate, vitamins B6 and B12, and the powerful new drugs called statins that retard or reverse atherosclerosis in the arteries of the heart and brain. Finally, some studies are working with nerve growth factor, which promotes the differentiation of nerve cells, increasing the number of dendrites and the length of axons on the neuron, both of which improve communication between cells.

Since Alzheimer's is incurable, it's worth considering joining the clinical trials being conducted on the disease to test the impact of new drugs, investigate gene therapy, and even to assess the idea of making a vaccine that will prevent the illness. A list of trials in progress is listed on the website of the Alzheimer's Association: www.nia.nih.gov/Alzheimers/ResearchInformation/ClinicalTrials.

PARKINSON'S DISEASE

This terrible affliction is essentially a loss of muscular control due to the destruction of a specific region of the brain called the substantia nigra, which produces the chemical called dopamine, a substance that ensures smooth, fluid, and coordinated muscular movement. The result is a characteristic coarse tremor, often called "pill rolling" because the index and thumb finger are apposed and perform a repetitive motion that seems as if the patient were rolling a tiny object between his fingers. It is fascinating to watch the tremor disappear when the patient performs a specific, intended movement. Theoretically, a Parkinson victim can perform even delicate operations like surgery because of this. Parkinsonians have problems starting to walk; often they have a repertoire of bizarre, flailing movements of their arms and upper bodies to enable them to begin the first step. When they do finally begin to move, they have a peculiar, shuffling gait. Their appearance is quite dramatically characteristic: Their faces are without expression and often they drool because of their inability to activate facial muscles. Even their handwriting is altered, becoming small and cramped because of the effort of modulating the muscular movement needed to create script.

Treatment for the illness depends on the principle that increasing the neurotransmitter dopamine in the brain will improve symptoms. Several medications are available to achieve this; among them are several modifications of levodopa, which is converted to dopamine in the brain. Other medications work in a similar way as dopamine; these include such medicines as bromocriptine (Parlodel), pergolide (Permax), and apomorphine (Apokyn). Various manipulations of the brain itself make up newer and promising therapies: Some destroy small regions of the brain that have abnormal activity in Parkinsonism. Another newer treatment entails implanting a set of wires in the brain to electrically stimulate it; none of the wires are in the substantia nigra, but all regions of the brain are "paced" back into normal activity by the implanted wires, and there is a relief of tremor, rigidity, and gait disorder. The process of implanting the wires is fascinating; it is done on a conscious patient and the effect of wire placement is carefully monitored while the brain's signals are played on an audible monitor. The treatment is successful enough in certain patients to be covered by Medicare.

OSTEOPOROSIS

One of my oldest and most admired colleagues had several falls during the last years of his life. Each time he fell, he broke several bones in his back. None of the physicians caring for him ordered a study of his bone density, however, and the diagnosis of osteoporosis was made much too late in his life to make effective treatment, much less prevention, possible. I found this remarkable because he had been a heavy smoker since his youth, and when he called to say he had fallen yet again and broken several vertebrae, I urged him to get his bone density tested.

Osteoporosis is a dangerous and often deadly affliction. Not only do we underestimate its reach, but many believe men are not affected by the thinning of bones that is so common in middle-aged and older women. Our bodies remodel our skeleton every day in an intricate process of buildup and breakdown, calibrated exactly to the force of the tug of muscle on bone that we produce throughout our day. If we do nothing but watch TV all day and sleep, bones thin and become dangerously fragile. This is true at all ages; one of my colleagues, Dr. Paul Killian, immobilized young soldiers in full body casts during the Vietnam War and documented a significant loss of bone density within days in these otherwise healthy young men.[15]

The skeleton is different in men and women, and so the vulnerability to an osteoporotic fracture is somewhat different, too. The bone of the vertebral bodies of males is thicker and stronger to begin with than that of females, which is the reason men do not usually suffer the compression fractures of the backbone that are so characteristic of elderly women with the disease and that create the "dowager's hump." There is no such protection from hip fractures, though, and one-third of them occur in men. They are also more deadly.[16] By the time they are 60, men have a 29 percent chance of having an osteoporotic fracture during their remaining years.[17]

In academic medicine, experts always discuss the value of testing for a specific disease, and opine about whether or not the test or tests needed to look for a possible illness are "cost effective." I've never had much patience with that kind of reasoning: We know that as men age they are more likely to have osteoporosis and that they are more likely to die of a fracture than are women.

Mysteriously, however, we are less likely to order bone density examination for men over 65, particularly those at special risk, such as those who have been given steroids for an illness or those who have smoked or who have drunk excessive amounts of alcohol for many years. As these experts put it:

> Thus, despite the importance of the problem of osteoporosis in men, clinical decision making is hampered by a lack of evidence-based cost-effectiveness analyses of common diagnostic and therapeutic interventions. The lack of consensus concerning this issue is reflected in very low rates of clinical intervention for osteoporosis in men.[18]

The International Society for Clinical Densitometry[19] and the Canadian Osteoporosis Society[20] have recommended bone densitometry for all men over the age of 70 and 65, respectively. If men in this age group have had a fracture or are at particular risk for osteoporosis, they should have a screening bone density examination. Men at increased risk for osteoporosis should have a bone density test *at any age*; jockeys, for example, are a class of men who suffer from eating disorders in an effort to keep their weight at a minimum. As a result, even at very young ages, they may have osteoporosis, as do anorexic young women.

Once osteoporosis, or a less-than-optimal bone density (called osteopenia), is diagnosed, it should be followed by an assessment of the patient's vitamin D levels, which are often low because we now advise less exposure to sun due to the increasing incidence of skin cancers in both sexes. Without adequate levels of this vitamin, we do not absorb enough calcium to replace lost bone. Calcium supplements and the newer category of medications called bis-phosphonates, which increase bone density and lower the fracture rate, are also helpful. Doctors should also screen for high levels of the hormone that regulates calcium metabolism and that comes from the hyperactivity of the parathyroid gland. This is done by a simple blood test. Patients with overactive thyroid glands or who take thyroid hormone may also suffer excessive bone loss and are a target for careful surveillance. Low testosterone levels predispose men to osteoporosis, as does overactivity of the adrenal gland. Finally, it's important for physicians to realize that even when they prescribe bisphosphonates to their osteoporotic patients, they must also be sure that calcium supplies are adequate, or the bisphonsphonate will not be effective.

Four ways to combat aging:

- **Keep up your exercise routine**: loss of strength and muscle mass happens more quickly as men age, but is not inevitable. Falls due to weakness are more and more common as you get older unless you are diligent about staying fit.
- As you age, your levels of testosterone may fall, with an impact on body shape. Your breasts enlarge and your midsection expands. Feelings of sadness, irritability, and more difficulty concentrating may begin to emerge. **See your doctor for a test of your testosterone levels**. If they are low, hormone therapy may be in order. There are other regimens available now that will increase your own production of testosterone rather than making simple replacement necessary.
- **Make sure that you have regular eye examinations and hearing tests**; if needed, wearing glasses and using the newer, almost undetectable hearing aides can prevent the isolation that leads to depression.
- **Confide in your spouse if you have feelings of sadness and anxiety.** Often wives bear the brunt of their spouse's anxiety about age and decreasing strength. Your doctor can help restore your confidence and will structure a routine to improve and maintain your functioning.

CODA

Writing this book has made me think about my experiences with my father, my husband, my son, my brothers, and the other men I've taken care of or interviewed. When I finished writing, I had a new view of men: of what makes them uniquely strong and competent and at the same time singularly vulnerable throughout their lives. The first time I consulted the CDC table that lists "Leading Causes of Death by Age Group, All Males—United States," I discovered that 6 percent of the boys who die before age 10 are murdered; that for men between the ages of 15 and 34, suicide and homicide are the leading causes of death after what the table calls "unintentional injuries"; and that heart disease begins to claim men when they are only 35 years old.[1] The data shocked and appalled me. As a physician, I find this state of affairs unacceptable.

I want this book to bring to everyone who reads it a new view of men, one that illuminates your unique value in our social structure and the price you pay for keeping us safe. We owe you our gratitude. You willingly perform the most dangerous jobs, and do so at a heavy cost—often giving your lives—and do it without complaint. I want men and the women who love them to read this book and understand why it is so important to concentrate research efforts on what makes men so vulnerable. I want them to understand that you often pay a terrible price for the tremendous services you provide.

We are in a new age of medicine, one that brings hope for longer and healthier lives. Understanding the structure and function of the DNA that makes us who we are has been among our most spectacular achievements. We are at the dawn of an era when health care can be individualized, based on a better understanding of what makes each person genetically unique. Scientists tell us that a minuscule sample of our DNA will reveal all of our distinctive, individual vulnerabilities and strengths so that doctors can focus on the prevention and treatment of disease. Gender-specific medicine is the first clue in the puzzle of how we are different from one another—the first essential pass at learning what makes men different from women. Inevitably, such understanding will change the way we take care of patients.

My father, practicing medicine in the 1930s, could only offer aspirin, morphine, and nitroglycerine to a man dying of a heart attack. Less than a century later, we physicians have learned how to open closed arteries and support failing hearts until we can transplant new ones. Most recently, we are learning how to generate new hearts from an individual's own cells so that he can be rescued with a new organ made from his own tissue! In my own lifetime, the things that we know and what we can do have expanded exponentially—well beyond our wildest speculations and imaginings. In the 1920s, Nobel laureates Frederick Banting and Charles Best discovered that insulin could save the lives of diabetics. I met Dr. Best just after I graduated from college. He had done this amazing work when he was a medical student; by the time I saw him, he was at the end of his life; a tall, grave man of few words but of enormous dignity and presence. Much more recently I met Marshall Nirenberg, another Nobel laureate, who was awarded the prize for cracking the genetic code. Every time I talk to him, the power of his intellect and the passion he brings to his science remind me once again of the tremendous creative potential of the human brain. We race forward, piling undreamed-of successes and breakthroughs atop one another so quickly that we haven't even time to think of how to use our new powers carefully and thoughtfully. We used to be taught in medical school that there was a natural end point to human life that was predictable and inevitable, no matter what our skills. Now we know that in fact, there is no fixed limit to how long we can live; we simply have to use our intellect to understand how to combat what kills us. Over the past century, we have nearly succeeded in doubling the lifespan of both sexes.

I wish my father were alive and could read this book. I am sure he would have some interesting insights, framed in his terse, trenchant, and profoundly intelligent prose, that would expand my own view of what we have still to accomplish and how to accomplish it. When I was an intern and the time came for me to perform my very first operation, an appendectomy, the chief resident assured me that he would "talk me through it." But I was not convinced I was ready for what seemed a huge challenge and responsibility. I went to a telephone booth in a driving rain just outside of the hospital and called my father to ask his advice. He took me step by step through all the maneuvers that would bring my patient safely (without his appendix) out of the operating room. He never repeated himself, never used an extra word, and above all, never voiced a doubt that I could do what needed to be done. He just told me what to expect and assumed that I would be equal to the task. It was just as he said it would be. I have thought in some detail about what he was like and how he lived as I put this book together and, just as on that rainy night of my first operation, I think he taught me a great deal.

We've done a spectacular job learning about the unique biology of women in the past 20 years; it's now time to turn a gender-specific lens on men. Let's use that same methodology to learn how best to improve and prolong their lives. I want us to think about and ultimately understand why men die first. It's more than time to acknowledge and to correct that grim statistic.

NOTES

ONE   THE STRONG, POWERFUL—AND MORE VULNERABLE—MALE

1. Leading Causes of Death by Age Group, All Males-United States, 2004, http://www.CDC.gov/men/lcod/o4all.pdf
2. Theresa M. Wizemann and Mary-Lou Pardue, eds., *Exploring the Biological Contributions to Human Health: Does Sex Matter?* Committee on Understanding the Biology of Sex and Gender Differences, Board on Health Sciences Policy (Washington, D.C.: Institute of Medicine National Academy Press, 2001), p. x.
3. Nadav Kashtan, Elad Noor, and Uri Alon, "Varying environments can speed up evolution," *Proceedings of the National Academy of Sciences* 104(34) (August 21, 2007): 13711–13716.
4. H. Skalestsky, T. Kuroda-Kawaguchi et al., "The male-specific region of the human Y chromosome is a mosaic of discrete sequence classes," *Nature* 423(19) (2003): 825–837.
5. R. J. Aitken and J. A. Marshall Graves, "Human spermatazoa: The future of sex," *Nature* 415(963) (February 28, 2002).
6. A. Lam, "Size matters: The impending death of the Y chromosome," *Science Creative Quarterly* (June 20, 2005), http://bioteach.ubc.ca/quarterly, p. 19
7. R. J. Aitken and C. Krausz, "Oxidative stress, DNA damage and the Y chromosome," *Reproduction* 122 (2001): 497–506.
8. Bryan Sykes, *Adam's Curse: A Future without Men* (New York: W. W. Norton, 2004), p. 311.
9. Maureen Dowd, *Are Men Necessary?: When Sexes Collide* (New York: Penguin Books, 2005).

10. B. T. Lahn and D. C. Page, "Functional coherence of the Y chromosome," *Science* 278 (1997): 675–680.
11. Robin Marantz Henig, "The real transformers," *New York Times Magazine*, July 29, 2007.
12. Arthur Miller, *Death of a Salesman.* Certain Private Conversations in Two Acts and a Requiem. (Penguin Books, 1976) (first published in 1949 by Viking Penguin) Act One, p. 59.

TWO BEGINNINGS: SURVIVING THE WOMB AND THE FIRST WEEKS OF LIFE

1. B. M. Friedrich and F. Julicher, "Chemotaxis of sperm cells," *Proceedings of the National Academy of Sciences* 104(33). (August 14, 2007): 13256–13261.
2. P. H. Jongbloet, "Over-ripeness ovopathy. A challenging hypothesis for sex ratio modulation," *Human Reproduction* 19(4) (2004): 769–774.
3. University of Pittsburgh Cancer Institute, Center for Environmental Oncology, http://www.environmentaloncology.org/faqdeclinefull, accessed 12/23/2007.
4. E. Arlsen, A. Giwercman et al., "Evidence for decreasing quality of semen during past 50 years," *BMJ* 305 (1992): 609–613.
5. L. G. Yueliang, H. Ping-Chi et al., *The Lancet* 356(9237) (2000): 1240–1241.
6. R. M. Sharpe and N. E. Skakkebaek, "Are oestrogens involved in falling sperm counts and disorders of the male reproductive tract?" *The Lancet* 341 (1993): 1392–1395.
7. S. A. Kidd, B. Esekanzi, and A. J. Wyrobek, "Effects of male age on semen quality and fertility: A review of the literature," *Fertil Steril* 75(2) (2001): 237–248.
8. A. Coale, "Excess female mortality and the balance of the sexes in the population: An estimate of the number of 'missing females,' " *Population and Development Review* 17(3) (1991): 517–523.
9. G. C. DiRenzo, A. Rosati et al., "Does fetal sex affect pregnancy outcome?" *Gender Medicine* 4(1) (2007): 19–30.
10. Vergani et al., "Risk factors for pulmonary hypoplasia in the second trimester and premature rupture of membranes," *American Journal of Obstetrics and Gynecology* 170 (1994): 1359–1364.
11. Y. Tremblay, "Andorgens and glucocorticoids in the developing lung: Gender-specific delay in synthesis between male and female," *Gender Medicine* 4(1) (2007): S36.
12. J. N. Quinones et al., "Is fetal gender associated with adverse perinatal outcome in intrauterine growth restriction?" *American Journal of Obstetrics and Gynecology* 193 (2005): 1233–1237.

13. A. Matteii and S. Gerli, "Pregnancy outcome: Is there any difference depending on the gender of the fetus?" *Gender Medicine* 4(1) (2007): S36.

14. J. A. Steier, P. B. Bergsjo et al., "Human chorionic gonadotropin in maternal serum in relation to fetal gender and utero-placental blood flow," *Acta Obstetricia et Gynecologica Scandinavica* 83(2) (2004): 170–174.

15. D. Owen and S. G. Matthews, "Glucocorticoids and sex-dependent development of brain glucocorticoid and mineralocorticoid receptors," *Endocrinology* 122(7) (2003): 2775–2784.

16. T. Hesketh and Z. W. Xing, "Abnormal sex ratios in human populations: Causes and consequences," *Proceedings of the National Academy of Sciences* 103(56) (2006): 13271–13275.

17. T. Walch, "Y. educator to report on China male surplus," *Deseret Morning News,* April 15, 2006. BNET business network, http://findarticles.com/p/articles/mi_qn4188/is_20060415/ai_n16166502, accessed 2/17/08.

18. J. Graffelman, "A statistical analysis of the effect of warfare on the secondary sex ratio," *Human Biology* 72(3) (2000): 433–435; and B. MacMahon and T. F. Pugh, "Human sex ratio," *American Human Genetics* 7 (1954): 284–292.

19. L. Ellis and S. Bonin, "War and the secondary sex ratio: Are they related?" *Social Science Information* 43(1) (2004): 115–122.

20. K. H. Cui, "Size differences between human X and Y spermatozoa and prefertilization diagnosis," *Molecular Human Reproduction* 3 (1997): 61–67.

21. H. S. Kochhar, K. P. Kochhar et al., "Influence of the duration of gamete interaction on cleavage, growth rate and sex distribution of in vitro produced bovine embryos," *Animal Reproduction Science* 771(1) (2003): 33–49.

22. R. L. Trivers and D. E. Willard. "Natural selection of parental ability to vary the sex ratio of offspring," *Science* 179(4068) (1973): 90–92.

23. K. Christensen, K. H. Orstavik, and J. W. Vaupel, "The X chromosome and the female survival advantage. An example of the intersection between genetics, epidemiology and demography," *Annals of the New York Academy of Sciences* 954 (2001): 175–183.

24. T. J. Mathews, F. Manacker et al., "Infant mortality statistics from the 2001 period linked birth/infant death data set," *National Vital Statistics Reports* 52(2) (September 15, 2003).

25. U.S. Bureau of the Census, *Statistical Abstract of the United States, 2000,* 120th ed. (Washington, D.C.: U.S. Bureau of the Census, 2000), pp. 84–86.

26. D. K. Stevenson, J. Verter et al., "Sex differences in outcomes of very low birthweight infants: The newborn male disadvantage," *Archives of Disease in Childhood, Fetal Neonatal Edition* 83 (2000): F182–F185.

27. J. S. Torday and H. C. Nielsen, "The sex difference in fetal lung surfactant production," *Experimental Lung Research* 12 (1987): 11–19.

28. B. Zaren, G. Lindmark, and L. Bakketeig, "Maternal smoking affects fetal growth more in the male fetus," *Paediatric Perinatal Epidemiology* 12 (2000): 118–126.

29. G. Koren, I. Nulman, J. Rovet et al., "Long-term neurodevelopmental risks in children exposed in utero to cocaine," The Toronto Adoption Study, *Annals of the New York Academy of Sciences* 846 (1998): 3006–3313.

30. E. Nagy, K. A. Loveland et al., "Different Emergence of fear Expressions in infant boys and girls," *Infant Behavior & Development* 24 (2001): 189–194.

31. R. J. Agate, W. Grisham et al., "Neural, not gonadal, origin of brain sex differences in a gynandromorphic fish," *Proceedings of the National Academy of Sciences* 100(8) (April 15, 2003): 4873–4878.

32. P. Dewing, W. K. Charleston et al., "Direct regulation of adult brain function by the male-specific factor SRY," *Current Biology* 16 (2006): 415–420.

33. G. Aranoff and J. Bell, "Endocrinology and growth in children and adolescents," in M. Legato, ed., *Principles of Gender-Specific Medicine* (London: Elsevier Science & Technology Books, 2004), p. 12.

34. P. Shaw, D. Greenstein et al., "Intellectual ability and cortical development in children and adolescents," *Nature* 440 (March 30, 2006): 676–679.

35. Dennis Garlick, "Understanding the nature of the general factor of intelligence: The role of individual differences in neural plasticity as an explanatory mechanism," *Psychological Reviews* 109(1) (2002): 116–136.

36. Edge: The Third Culture. The Science of Gender and Science. Pinker vs. Spelke. A Debate 5.16.2005, http://www.edge.org/3rd_culture/debate05/debate05_index.html, accessed 2/18/08.

37. L. Dong and J. Diorio, "Maternal care, hippocampal glucocorticoid receptors and hypothalamic-pituitary-adrenal responses to stress," *Science* 277(5332) (1997): 1659.

38. Francis, D. D., Young, L. J. et al. "Naturally occurring differences in maternal care are associated with the expression of oxytocin and vasopressin (L1a) receptors: Gender differences," *Journal of Neuroendocrinology* 14(5) (2002): 349–353.

39. D. Deviterne and D. Desor, "Selective pup retrieving by mother rats: Sex and early development characteristics as discrimination factors," *Developmental Psychobiology* 23(4) (2004): 361–368.

40. C. P. Wiedenmayer and G. A. Barr, "Ontogeny of defensive behavior and analgesia in rat pups exposed to an adult male rat," *Physiology & Behaviour* 63(2) (1998): 261–269.

41. J. D. Bremner, M. Steinberg et al., "Use of the structured clinical interview for DSM-IV dissociative disorders for systematic assessment of dissociative symptoms in posttraumatic stress disorder," *American Journal of Psychiatry* 150 (1993): 1011–1014.

42. J. D. Bremner, J. H. Krystal et al., "Neural mechanisms in dissociative amnesia for childhood abuse: Relevance to the current controversy surrounding the 'False Memory Syndrome,'" *American Journal of Psychiatry* 153(7) (1996): FS71–FS82.

43. Department of Health and Human Services, *Child Maltreatment 1997: Reports from the States to the National Child Abuse and Neglect Data System* (Washington, D.C.: Government Printing Office, 1999).

44. A. J. Sedlack and D. D. Broadhurst, *Third National Incidence Study of Child Abuse and Neglect* (Washington, D.C.: Government Printing Office, 1996).

45. W. C. Holmes and G. B. Slap, "Sexual abuse of boys. Definition, prevalence, correlates, sequellae and management," *JAMA* 280(21) (1998): 1855–1862.

46. A. J. Sedlack and D. D. Broadhurst, *Third National Incidence Study of Child Abuse and Neglect* (Washington, D.C.: Government Printing Office, 1996).

47. T. J. Shors and Miesegaes, "Testosterone in utero and at birth dictates how stressful experience will affect learning in adulthood," *Proceedings of the National Academy of Sciences* 99(21) (2002): 13955–13960.

48. H. L. MacMillan and the Members of the Canadian Task Force on Prevent Health Care, "Preventive health care 1000 update: Prevention of child maltreatment," *Canadian Medical Association Journal* 163(11) (November 28, 2000).

49. P. Florsheim, P. Tolan, and D. Gorman-Smith, "Family relationships, parenting practices, the availability of male family members and the behavior of inner-city boys in single mother and two parent families," *Child Development* 69(5) (1998): 1437–1447.

50. K. Meyer, "Male Martha Stewarts?" *The Wall Street Journal*, August 22, 2007.

51. C. A. Boyle and P. Decoufle, "Prevalence and health impact of developmental disabilities in US children," *Pediatrics* 93(3) (1994): 399–403.

52. S. Kraemer, "The fragile male," *BMJ* 321 (2000): 1609–1612.

53. N. Marlow, D. Wolke et al., "Neurologic and developmental disability at six years of age after extremely preterm birth," *New England Journal of Medicine* 352 (2005): 9–19.

54. L. M. Schrott, V. H. Denenberg et al. "Environmental enrichment, neocortical ectopias and behavior in the autoimmune NZB mouse," *Brain Research Developmental Brain Research* 67(1) (1992): 85–93.

55. S. L. Einfeld, A. M. Piccinin et al., "Pscyhopathology in young people with intellectual disability," *JAMA* 296(16) (2006): 1987–1989.

56. F. X. Castellanos, P. P. Lee et al., "Developmental trajectories of brain volume abnormalities in children and adolescents with attention-deficit/hyperactivity disorder," *JAMA* 288(14) (2002): 1740–1748.

57. T. Grandin and N. Scariano, *Emergence: Labeled Autistic* (Novato, CA: Warner Books, 1996).

58. M. Yeargin-Allsopp, C. Rice et al., "Prevalence of autism in a US Metropolitan area," *JAMA* 289(1) (2003): 49–55.

59. S. Baron-Cohen, *Male and Female Brains and the Truth about Autism* (New York: Basic Books, 2004).

60. M. Peterson, "What men and women value at work: Implications for workplace health," *Gender Medicine* 1(2) (2004): 106–124.

THREE　EDUCATING BOYS: HOW WELL ARE WE DOING?

1. P. Kristensen and T. Bjerkedal, "Explaining the relation between birth order and intelligence," *Science* 316 (June 22, 2007): 1717.
2. H. W. Hanlon, R. W. Thatcher, and M. J. Cline, "Gender differences in the development of EEG coherence in normal children," *Developmental Neuropsychology* 16(3) (1999): 479–506.
3. C. R. Clark, R. H. Paul et al., "Standardized assessment of cognitive functioning during development and aging using an automated touchscreen battery," *Archives of Clinical Neuropsychology* 21(5) (2006): 449–467.
4. Ariniello L. Society for Neuroscience. Brain Briefings May 2000, http://web.sfn.org/content/Publications/BrainBriefings/music_training_and_brain.htm, accessed 9/15/07.
5. Hyde, J. S. and Linn, M. C., "Gender similarities in mathematics and science," *Science* 314:599–600.
6. M. Gurian and P. Henley, *Boys and Girls Learn Differently. A Guide for Teachers and Parents* (New York: Jossey-Bass, 2001), p. 56.
7. H. Gardner, *Multiple Intelligences: New Horizons* (New York: Basic Books, 2006).
8. Ibid., 345.
9. Ibid., 120–121.
10. L. Chliwniak, "Higher education leadership: Analyzing the gender gap," *ERIC Digest,* http://www.eriddigests.org/1998–1/gap.htm, accessed 9/22/07.
11. The Nation's Report Card, *12th-Grade Reading and Mathematics 2005*, The National Center for Education Statistics, Institute of Education Resources, U.S. Department of Education, NCES 2007-468.
12. S. Mead, "Evidence suggests otherwise: The truth about boys and girls," http://www.educationsector.org/analysis/analysis_show.htm?doc_id=378705, accessed 9/22/07.
13. J. P. Gee, G. A. Hull, and C. Lankshear, *The New Work Order: Behind the Language of the New Capitalism* (Boulder, CO: Westview Press, 1996), pp. 125–126.
14. M. Weaver-Hightower, "The 'boy turn' in research on gender and education," *Review of Educational Research* 73(40) (Winter 2003): 471–498.
15. Ibid., 480.
16. D. J. Carter and R. Wilson, "Minorities in higher education. 1993 twelfth annual status report," http://eric.ed.gov/ERICWebPortal/custom/portlets/recordDetails/detailmini.jsp?_nfpb=true, accessed 9/22/07.

17. R. S. Byrd and M. L. Weitzman, "Predictors of early grade retention among children in the United States," *Pediatrics* 93(3) (1994): 481–487.

18. C. Goldin, L. F. Katz, and I. Kuzimeko, "The homecoming of American college women: The reversal of the college gender gap," Revision of May 2005 draft, March 2006. The National Bureau of Economic Research. www.nber.org/papers/212139.

FOUR   THE MALE ADOLESCENT: THE DANGEROUS GULF BETWEEN IMPULSE AND JUDGMENT

1. S. Ross, M. Bloomsmith et al., "Adolescent male chimpanzees: A scientific study with management implications," *Connect* (October 2006): 16–18.

2. R. E. Dahl, "Adolescent brain development: A period of vulnerabilities and opportunities," *Annals of the New York Academy of Sciences* 1021 (2004): 1–22.

3. A. Schlegel and H. Barry, *Adolescence: An Anthropological Inquiry* (New York: Free Press, 1991).

4. J. M. Fuster, *The Prefrontal Cortex: Anatomy, Physiology and Neuropsychology of the Frontal Lobe* (New York: Raven, 1989).

5. J. F. Leckman and L. Scahill, "Possible exacerbation of tics by androgenic steroids," *New England Journal of Medicine* 322 (1990): 1674.

6. B. S. Peterson, "Steroid hormones and Tourette's syndrome: Early experience with antiandrogen therapy," *Journal of Clinical Psychopharmacology* 14 (1994): 131–135.

7. G. M. Alexander and B. S. Peterson, "Testing the prenatal hormone hypothesis of tic-related disorders: Gender identity and gender role behavior," *Development and Psychopathology* 16 (2004): 407–421.

8. C. P. Bayer, F. Klasen, and H. Adam, "Association of trauma and PTSD symptoms with openness to reconciliation and feelings of revenge among former Ugandan and Congolese child soldiers," *JAMA* 298(5) (2007): 555–559.

9. United Nations Convention on the Rights of the Child, UN General Assembly Document A/RES/44/25, 1989.

10. J. B. Jemmott, L. S. Jemmott, and G. T. Fong, "Reductions in HIV risk-associated sexual behaviors among black male adolescents: Effects of an AIDS prevention intervention," *American Journal of Public Health* 83(3) (1992): 372–377.

11. W. S. Pollack, "Male adolescent rites of passage. Positive visions of multiple developmental pathways," *Annals of the New York Academy of Sciences*, 1035 (2004): 141–150.

12. M. Stevens, "Policing of special populations: Juveniles," http://ncwc.edu/mstevens/205/205lect10.htm, accessed 12/29/07.

13. D. A. Gentile, P. J. Lynch et al., "The effects of violent video game habits on adolescents' hostility, aggressive behaviors and school performances," *Journal of Adolescence* 27(1) (2004): 5–22.

14. J. L. Maggs, D. M. Almedia, and N. L. Galambos, "Risky business: The paradoxical meaning of problem behavior for young adolescents," *Journal of Early Adolescence* 15 (1995): 344–362.

15. S. A. Brown, "Recovery patterns in adolescent substance abuse," in J. S. Baer et al., eds., *Addictive Behaviors across the Life Span: Prevention, Treatment and Policy Issues* (Newbury Park, CA: Sage Publications, 1993), pp. 161–183.

16. B. F. Grant and D. A. Dawson, "Age at onset of alcohol use and its association with DSM-IV alcohol abuse and dependence: Results from the National Longitudinal Alcohol Epidemiologic Survery," *Journal of Substance Abuse* 9 (1997): 103–110.

17. A. D. McNeill, "The development of dependence on smoking in children," *British Journal of Addiction* 86 (1991): 589–592.

18. L. Lamberg, "Medical news and perspectives. New tactics help curb adolescent substance abuse and dependence," *JAMA* 298(7) (2007): 729–730.

19. National Center for Injury Prevention and Control (for suicide deaths) and Bureau of the Census (for population figures), "USA suicide rates—Averages for period 1980–1996 by sex and age group," http://fathersforlife.org/suicides/US_suicide_deaths.htm, accessed 10/1/2007.

20. S. J. Blumentahl and D. J. Kupfer, eds., *Suicide over the Life Cycle* (Washington, D.C.: American Psychiatric Press, 1990).

21. D. K. Curran, *Adolescent Suicidal Behavior* (New York: Hemisphere, 1987).

22. L. A. Willis, D. W. Coombs et al., "Ready to die: A postmodern interpretation of the increase of African-American adolescent male suicide," *Social Science and Medicine* 55 (2002): 907–920.

23. C. W. Runyan, M. Schulman et al., "Work-related hazards and workplace safety of US adolescents employed in the retail and service sectors," *Pediatrics* 119(3) (2007): 526–534.

24. J. Windau, E. Sygnatur, and G. Toscano, "Profile of work injuries incurred by young workers," *Monthly Labor Review* 126 (1999): 3–10.

25. T. R. Nasel, M. Overpeck et al., "Bullying behaviors among US young. Prevalence and association with psychosocial adjustment," *JAMA* 285(16) (2001): 2094–2100.

26. D. Olweus, "Bullying among schoolchildren: Intervention and prevention," in R. D. Peters et al., *Aggression and Violence throughout the Life Span* (London: Sage Publications, 1992), 100–125.

27. M. Beckman, "Crime, culpability and the adolescent brain," *Science* 305 (2004): 596–599.

28. Institute on Women and Criminal Justice, N. Frost, J. Greene, and K. Pranis "HardHit: The growth in the imprisonment of women," 1977–2004. http://www.wpaonline.org/institute/hardhit/index.htm, accessed 12/29/07.

FIVE   MALE DEPRESSION: ITS CAUSES, EXPRESSION, AND TREATMENT

1. H. G. Koenig, L. K. George et al., "Depressive symptoms and nine-year survival of 1,001 male veterans hospitalized with medical illness," *American Journal of Geriatric Psychiatry* 7(2) (1999): 124–131.

2. K. Hawton, "Sex and suicide: Gender differences in suicidal behavior," *British Journal of Psychiatry* 177 (2000): 484–485.

3. A. Gray, J. A. Berlin et al., "An examination of research design effects on the association of testosterone and male aging: Results of a metaanalysis," *Journal of Clinical Epidemiology* 7 (1991): 671–684.

4. D. Farrelly and D. Nettle, "Marriage affects competitive performance in male tennis players," *Journal of Evolutionary Psychology* 5(1) (2007): 141–148.

5. Personal communication with Colonel Jacobs, New York City, Spring 2007.

6. A. Mazur and A. Booth, "Testosterone and dominance in men," *Behavioral and Brain Sciences* 21(3) (1998): 353–397.

7. J. M. Dabbs, Jr., R. L. Frady et al., "Saliva testosterone and criminal violence in young adult prison inmates," *Psychosomatic Medicine* 49(2) (1987): 174–182.

8. L. Ellis, "Gender differences in smiling: An evolutionary neuroandrogenic theory," *Physiology and Behavior* 88(4–5) (2006): 303–308.

9. Braudy L. *From Chivalry to Terrorism. War and the Changing Nature of Masculinity* (London: Vintage Books [Random House], 2005), p. 62.

10. Personal communication with the author, New York City, Winter 2006.

11. "Leading Causes of Death by Age Group, All Males—United States," 1004, http://www.cdc.gov/nchs/datawh/statab/unpubd/mortabs.htm, accessed 10/28/2007.

12. K. Hawton, "Sex and suicide. Gender differences in suicidal behavior," *British Journal of Psychiatry* 177 (2000): 484–485.

13. W. S. Pollack, "Male adolescent rites of passage. Positive visions of multiple developmental pathways," *Annals of the New York Academy of Sciences* 1036 (2004): 141–150.

14. G. E. Murphy, "Psychiatric aspects of suicidal behaviour: Substance abuse," in K. Hawton and K. Van Heeringen, eds., *The International Handbook of Suicide and Attempted Suicide* (Chichester: John Wiley Sons, 2000), 135–146.

15. M. DeHert and J. Peuskens, "Psychiatric aspects of suicidal behaviour: Schizophrenia," in K Hawton and C. Van Heeringen, eds., *The International Handbook of Suicide and Attempted Suicide* (Chichester: John Wiley & Sons, 2000).

16. Institute of Medicine, *Reducing Suicide: A National Imperative* (Washington, D.C.: National Academies Press. 2000), 99.

17. A. Booth, D. R. Johnson, and D. A. Granger, "Testosterone and men's depression: The role of social behavior," *Journal of Health and Social Behavior* 40(2) (1999): 130–140.

18. S. Nishizawa, C. Benkelfat et al., "Differences between males and females in rates of serotonin synthesis in human brain," *Proceedings of the National Academy of Sciences* 94 (1997): 5308–5313.

19. D. Winkler, E. Pjrek, and S. Kasper, "Anger attacks in depression—Evidence for a male depressive syndrome," *Psychotherapy and Psychosomatics* 74(5) (2005): 303–307.

20. S. A. Madsen and T. Juhl, "Paternal depression in the postnatal period assessed with traditional and male depression scales," *Journal of Men's Health and Gender* 4(1) (2007): 26–31.

21. P. Ramchandani, A. Stein et al., "ALSPAC Study Team. Paternal depression in the postnatal period and child development: A prospective population study," *The Lancet* 365 (2005): 2201–2205.

22. U. Schweiger, M. Deuschle et al., "Testosterone, gonadotrophin and cortisol secretion in male patients with major depression," *Psychosomatic Medicine* 61 (1999): 292–296.

23. C. W. Hoge, J. L. Auchterlonie, and C. S. Milliken, "Mental health problems, use of mental health services and attrition from military service after returning from deployment to Iraq or Afghanistant," *JAMA* 295(9) (2006): 1023–1032.

24. W. Winkenwerder, "Post-deployment health reassessment (memorandum)," Washington, D.C.: Department of Defense, March 10, 2005, HA Policy 05–011.

25. J. M. Lyness, E. D. Caine et al., "Psychiatric disorders in older primary care patients," *Journal of General Internal Medicine* 14 (1999): 249–254.

26. S. N. Sediman and B. T. Walsh, "Testosterone and depression in aging men," *American Journal of Geriatric Psychiatry* 7(1) (1999): 18–33.

27. J. Unutzer, "Late-life depression," *New England Journal of Medicine* 357 (2007): 2269–2275.

28. W. Jiang, R. K. Krishnan, and C. M. O'Connor, "Depression and heart disease: Evidence of a link and its therapeutic implications," *CNS Drugs* 16 (2002): 111–127; B. S. McEwen, "The neurobiology of stress: From serendipity to clinical relevance," *Brain Research* 886 (2000): 172–189; G. Cizza, P. Ravn et al., "Depression: A major, unrecognized risk factor for osteoporosis?" *Trends in Endocrinology and Metabolism* 12 (2001): 198–203.

29. J. Hippisley-Cox, K. Fielding, and M. Pringle, "Depression as a risk factor for ischaemic heart disease in men: Population based case-control study," *BMJ* 316 (1998): 1714–1719.

30. Tausk M., "Hat die Nebenniere tatsachlich eine Verteidigungsfunktion?" *Das Hormon* (Organon Holland) 3 (1951): 1–24.

31. S. M. Michiel Korte, J. M. Kooklass et al., "The Darwinian concept of stress: Benefits of allostasis and costs of allostatic load and the trade-offs in health and disease," *Neuroscience & Biobehavioral Reviews* 29(1) (2005): 3–38.

32. T. R. Insel and D. S. Charney, "Research on major depression. Strategies and priorities," *JAMA* 289(23) (June 18, 2003): 3167–3168.

33. A. S. Young, R. Klap et al., "The quality of care for depressive and anxiety disorders in the United States," *Archives of General Psychiatry* 58 (2001): 55–61.

34. F. J. McMahon, S. Buervenich et al., "Variation in the gene encoding the serotonin 2A receptor is associated with outcome of antidepressant treatment," *The American Journal of Human Genetics* 78 (2006): 804–814.

35. H. G. Nurnberg, P. L. Hensley et al., "Treatment of antidepressant-associated sexual dysfunction with sildenafil. A randomized controlled trial," *JAMA* 289(1) (2003): 56–64; A. L. Montejo-Gonzalez, G. LLorca et al., "SSRI-induced sexual dysfunction: Fluoxetine, paroxetine, sertraline and fluvoxamine in a prospective, multicenter and descriptive clinical study of 344 patients," *Journal of Sex and Marital Therapy* 23(3) (1997): 176–194.

SIX   THE MALE LIBIDO: MEN AND SEX

1. J. T. Curtis, Y. Liu et al., "Dopamine and monogamy," *Brain Research* 1126(1) (2006): 76–90.

2. T. H. Clutton-Brock, "Mammalian mating systems," *Proceedings of the Royal Society B Biological Sciences* 236(1285) (1989): 339–372.

3. J. L. Shifren, G. D. Braunstein et al., "Transdermal testosterone treatment in women with impaired sexual function after oophorectomy," *New England Journal of Medicine* 343 (2000): 682–688.

4. L. J. Young, Z. Wang, and T. R. Insel, "Neuroendocrine bases of monogamy," *Trends in Neurosciences* 21 (1998): 71–75.

5. I. Savic, H. Berglund et al., "Smelling of odorous sex hormone-like compounds causes sex-differentiated hypothalamic activations in humans," *Neuron* 31(4) (2001): 661–668.

6. B. D. Neff and T. E. Pitcher, "Genetic quality and sexual selection: An integrated framework for good genes and compatible genes," *Molecular Ecology* 14(1) (2005): 19–36.

7. H. Fisher, "The drive to love. The biology and evolution of romantic love." 2006. Stony Brook Mind/Brain Lecture Series. 10th Annual Lecture, www.Thescwartzfoundation.org/mind-brain-2006-asp, accessed 2/19/08.

8. T. F. Lue, "Erectile dysfunction," *New England Journal of Medicine* 342(24) (2000): 1802–1813.

9. A. E. Benet and A. Melman, "The epidemiology of erectile dysfunction," *Urological Clinics of North America* 22 (1995): 699–709.

10. C. B. Johannes and A. B. Araujo, "Incidence of erectile dysfunction in men 40 to 69 years old: Longitudinal results from the Massachusetts Male Aging Study," *The Journal of Urology* 163(2) (2000): 460–463.

11. E. O. Laumann, A. Paik, and R. C. Rosen, "Sexual dysfunction in the United States: Prevalence and predictors," *JAMA* 281(537) (1999).

12. O. I. Linet and L. L. Neff, "Intracavernous prostaglandin E1 in erectile dysfunction," *The Journal of Clinical Investigation* 72 (1994): 139–149.

13. D. Haden, *Pox: Genius, Madness and the Mysteries of Syphilis* (New York: Basic Books, 2003).

14. R. S. Van Howe, "Circumcision and HIV infection: Review of the literature and meta-analysis," *International Journal of STD and AIDS* 10 (January 1999): 8–16.

15. P. M. Fleiss, F. M. Hodges, and R. S. VanHowe, "Immunological functions of the human prepuce," *Sexually Transmitted Infections* (London) 74(5) (1998): 364–367.

16. Fact sheet No. 243, "Effectiveness of male latex condoms in protecting against pregnancy and sexually transmitted infections," June 2000, http://www.who.int/mediacentre/factsheets/fs243/en/.

SEVEN HITTING 40: NEW CHALLENGES

1. D. J. Kruger and R. M. Nesse, "An evolutionary life-history framework for understanding sex differences in human mortality rates," *Human Nature,* 17(1) (spring 2006): 74–97.

2. Ibid.

3. D. J. Kruger and R. M. Nesse, "An evolutionary framework for understanding sex differences in Croatian Mortality Rates," *Psychological Topics* 15(2) (2006): 351–364.

4. M. G. Marmot, M. Kogevinas, and M. A. Elston, "Social/economic status and disease," *Annual Review of Public Health* 8 (1987): 111–135.

5. B. R. Migeon, "Why females are mosaics, X-chromosome inactivation and sex differences in disease," *Gender Medicine* 4(2) (2007): 97–105.

6. J. C. Wingfield, S. Lynn, and K. K. Soma, "Avoiding the costs of testosterone: Ecological bases of hormone-behavior interactions," *Brain, Behavior, and Evolution* 57(5) (2001): 239–251.

7. W. Hurst, *The Heart, Arteries and Veins*, 10th ed. (New York: McGraw-Hill, 2002).

8. D. A. Lawlor, S. Ebrahim, and G. Savey Smith, "Sex matters: Secular and geographical trends in sex differences in coronary heart disease mortality," *BMJ* 323 (2002): 541–580.

9. H. Hemingway and M. Marmot, "Evidence based cardiology: Psychosocial factors in the aetiology and prognosis of coronary heart disease. Systematic review of prospective cohort studies," *BMJ* 318 (1999): 1460–1467.

10. The Coronary Drug Project Research Group, "The coronary drug project. Findings leading to discontinuation of the 2.5 mgm day estrogen group," *JAMA* 226 (1973): 652–657.

11. S. Kraemer, "The fragile male," *BMJ* 321 (2000): 1609–1612.

12. W. Osler, "The Lumleian Lectures on Angina Pectoris. Delivered before the Royal College of Physicians of London by William Osler, M.D., F.R.S., Regius Professor of Medicine in the University of Oxford. Lecture 11* Delivered on March 15," in R. H. Major and C. Thomas, eds., *Classic Descriptions of Disease*, 3rd ed. (Springfield, IL: Charles C. Thomas, 1945).

13. American Heart Association, "Risk assessment tool for heart attack of coronary artery disease," http://www.americanheart.org/presenter.jhtml! identified=3003499.

14. P. S. Seth, G. P. Aurigemma et al. "A syndrome of transient left ventricular apical wall motion abnormality in the absence of coronary disease: A perspective from the United States," *Cardiology* 100(2) (2003): 61–66.

15. W. B. Cannon, "Voodoo Death," *American Anthropologist*, New Series 44 (2) (April–June 1942): 169–181.

16. S. J. Bunker, D. M.Colquhoun et al., "Stress and coronary heart disease: Psychosocial risk factors," National Heart Foundation of Australia position statement update, *MJA* 178 (2003): 272–276.

17. R. L. Wang, E. Bohn et al., "Noncompliance with antihypertensive medications: The impact of depressive symptoms and psychosocial factors," *Journal of General Internal Medicine* 17 (2002): 504–511.

18. R. I. Horowitz, C. M. Viscoli et al., "Treatment adherence and risk of death after a myocardial infarction," *The Lancet* 336 (1990): 542–545.

19. A. Styron, "Life and letters. Reading my father. A writer's triumphs and his torments," *The New Yorker*, December 10, 2007, 50–60.

20. D. E. Ford, L. A. Mead et al., "Depression is a risk factor for coronary artery disease in men," *Archives of Internal Medicine* 158(13) (1998): 1422–1426.

21. J. Hippisley-Cox, K. Fielding, and M. Pringle, "Depression as a risk factor for ischaemic heart disease in men: Population based case-control study," *BMJ* 316 (1998): 1715–1719.

22. R. J. Glynn, G. J. L'Italien et al., "Development of predictive models for long-term cardiovascular risk associated with systolic and diastolic blood pressure," *Hypertension* 39 (2002): 105–110.

23. SHEP Cooperative Research Group, "Prevention of stroke by antihypertensive drug treatment in older persons with isolated systolic hypertension: Final results of the Systolic Hypertension in the Elderly Program (SHEP)," *JAMA* 265 (1991): 3255–3264.

24. National Heart, Lung and Blood Institute, Lipid Metabolism Branch, Division of Heart and Vascular Diseases, "The prevalence study: Aggregate distribution of lipids, lipoproteins and selected variables in 11 North American populations," in *The Lipid Research Clinics Population Studies Data Book*, vol. 1 (Bethesda, MD: National Institutes of Health, 1980), 1–36.

25. P. Barter, A. M. Gotto et al., "HDL cholesterol, very low levels of LDL cholesterol and cardiovascular events," *New England Journal of Medicine* 357 (2007): 1301–1210.

26. P. L. Canner, L. C. Gatewood et al., "Fifteen-year mortality in coronary drug project patients: Long-term benefit with niacin," *Journal of the American College of Cardiology* 8(6) (1986): 1245–1255.

27. S. M. Grundy, "Cholesterol and coronary heart disease," *Archives of Internal Medicine* 157 (1998): 1174–1178.

28. K. M. Flegal, M. D. Carroll et al., "Prevalence and trends in obesity among US adults," *JAMA* 288(14) (2002): 1723–1727.

29. C. I. Ogden, K. M. Flegal et al., "Prevalence and trends in overweight among US children and adolescents," *JAMA* 288(14) (2002): 1728–1732.

30. R. L. Atkinson, "Viruses as an etiology of obesity," *Mayo Clinic Proceedings* 82(19) (2007): 1192–1198.

31. S. Lamon-Rava, P. W. F. Wilson, and E. T. Schaefer, "Impact of body mass index on CHD risk factors in men and women," *Arteriosclerosis, Thrombosis and Vascular Biology* 16 (1996): 1509–1515.

32. J. A. Berlin and G. A. Colditz, "A meta-analysis of physical activity in the prevention of coronary heart disease," *American Journal of Epidemiology* 132 (2004): 612–628.

33. C. A. Schoenborn and P. M. Barnes, "Leisure-time physical activity among adults: United States, 1997–1998," advance data from vital and health statistics, no. 325 (Hyattsville, MD: National Center for Health Statistics, 2002).

34. P. H. Stone, J. E. Muller et al., "The effect of diabetes mellitus on prognosis and serial left ventricular function after acute myocardial infarction: Contribution of both coronary disease and diastolic left ventricular dysfunction to the adverse prognosis: The MILIS study group," *Journal of the American College of Carodiology* 13 (1989): 49–57.

35. M. J. Legato, A. Gelzer et al., "Gender-specific care of the patient with diabetes: Review and recommendations," *Gender Medicine* 3(2) (2006): 131–158.

36. S. S. Bassuk and J. E. Manson, "Gender and its impact on risk factors for cardiovascular disease," in Marianne J. Legato, M.D., ed., *Principles of Gender-Specific Medicine* (New York: Elsevier Academic Press, 2004), p. 193.

37. L. Rosenberg, D. W. Kaufman et al., "The risk of myocardial infarction after quitting smoking in men under 55 years of age," *New England Journal of Medicine* 313 (1985): 1511–1514; A. J. Dobson, H. M. Alexander et al., "How soon after quitting smoking does risk of heart attack decline?" *Journal of Clinical Epidemiology* 44 (1991): 1247–1253.

38. J. S. Gill, Shipley et al., "Cigarette smoking: A risk factor for hemorrhagic and nonhemorrhagic stroke," *Archives of Internal Medicine* 149 (1989): 2053–3057.

39. C. H. Hennekens, "Risk factors for coronary heart disease in women," *Cardiology Clinics* 16 (1998): 1–8.

40. A. Evans, H. Tolonen et al., "Trends in coronary risk factors in the WHO MONICA project," *International Journal of Epidemiology* 1 (suppl. 20) (2001): 535–540.

41. R. C. Ellison and M. Martinic, eds., "The harms and benefits of moderate drinking: Summary of findings of an international symposium," *Annual Epidemiology* 17 (suppl.) (2007): S1–115.

EIGHT   MEN AND CANCER

1. Center for Disease Control, "Health disparities in cancer," http://www.cdc.gov/cancer/health disparities/statistics/men.htm, accessed 10/3/2007.

2. A. Jamal, R. Siegel et al., "Cancer statistics," *CA: A Cancer Journal for Clinicians* 57 (2007): 43–66.

3. W. E. Sakr, D. J. Grignon et al., "High grad prostatic intraepithelial neoplasia (HGPIN) and prostatic adencarcinoma between the ages of 20–69. An autopsy study of 249 cases," *In Vivo* 1003(8) (1994): 439–443.

4. A. Jemal, T. A. Murray et al., "Cancer statistics 2002," *CA: A Cancer Journal for Clinicians* 52 (2002): 23–47.

5. G. D. Steinberg, B. S. Carter et al., "Family history and the risk of prostate cancer," *Prostate* 17 (1990): 337–347.

6. A. W. Hsing, L. Tsao et al., "International trends and patterns of prostate cancer incidence and mortality," *International Journal of Cancer* 85 (2000): 60–67.

7. J. M. Chan, E. L. Giovannucci, "Vegetables, fruits, associated micronutrients and risk of prostate cancer," *Epidemiologic Reviews* 23 (2001): 82–86.

8. W. E. Gardner, Jr., and B. D. Bennett, "The prostrate-overview, recent insights and speculations," in R. S. Weinstin and W. A. Bardner, Jr., eds., *Pathology and Pathobiology of the Urinary Bladder and Prostate* (Baltimore, MD: Williams & Wilkins, 1992), pp. 129–148.

9. L. L. Banez, R. J. Hamilton et al., "Obesity-related plasma hemodilution and PSA concentration among en with prostate cancer," *JAMA* 298(19) (2007): 2275–2280.

10. A. Bill-Axelson, L. Holmberg et al., "Radical prostatectomy versus watchful waiting in early prostate cancer," *New England Journal of Medicine* 352 (2005): 1977–1984.

11. C. Warlick, B. J. Trock et al., "Delayed versus immediate surgical intervention and prostate cancer outcome," *Journal of the National Cancer Institute* 98 (2006): 355–357.

12. "Recent trends in mortality rates for four major cancers by sex and race/ethnicity—United States, 1990–1998," *Morbidity and Mortality Weekly Report* 51 (2002): 49–53; reprinted in *JAMA* 287(11) (2002): 1391–1392.

13. http://medicineworld.org/cancer/colon/epidemiology-of-colon-cancer.html, accessed 2/17/08.

NINE SPORTS: THE PRICE MEN PAY

1. B. Campbell, M. O'Rourge, and M. Rabow, "Pulsatile response of salivary testosterone and cortisol to aggressive competition in young males," paper presented at the Annual Meeting of the American Association of Physical Anthropologists, Kansas City, 1988.

2. L. Klaiber, D. Broverman et al., "Effects of infused testosterone on mental performances and serum LH," *Journal of Clinical Endocrinology* 32 (1971): 341–349.

3. A. Mazur, "A biosocial model of status in face-to-face primate groups," *Social Forces* 64 (1985): 377–402.

4. P. C. Bernhardt, J. M. Dabbs, Jr., et al., "Testosterone changes during vicarious experiences of winning and losing among fans at sporting events," *Physiology and Behavior* 65(1) (1998): 59–62.

5. M. Roderick and I. Waddington, "Playing hurt. Managing injuries in English professional football." *International Review for the Sociology of Sport* 35(2) (2000): 165–180.

6. B. J. Maron, K. P. Carney et al., "Relationship of race to sudden cardiac death in competitive athletes with hypertrophic cardiomyopathy," *Journal of the American College of Cardiology* 41 (2003): 974.

7. R. Eckart, S. L. Scoville et al.; "Sudden death in young adults: A 35 year review of autopsies in military recruits," *Annals of Internal Medicine* 141 (2004): 829.

8. V. E. Friedwald, B. J. Maron, and W. Roberst, "The editor's roundtable: Sudden cardiac death in athletes," *American Journal of Cardiology* 100 (2007): 1451–1459.

9. Pu Gardner, "Recent deaths put health risks in spotlight soccer," *The New York Sun*, September 4, 2007, www.nysun.com/article/61838.

10. B. J. Maron, P. D. Thompson et al., "Cardiovascular preparticipation screening of competitive athletes: A statement for health professionals from the Sudden Death Committee and Congenital Cardiac Defects Committee (cardiovascular disease in the young)," *American Heart Association*, circulation 94 (1996): 850–856.

11. "Brain Injury in Sports," www.headinjury.com/sports.htm, accessed 2/18/08.

12. R. C. Cantu, "Head injuries in sports," *British Journal of Sports Medicine* 30 (1996): 289–296.

13. K. Leblanc, "Concussions in sports: Guidelines for return to competition," *American Family Physician* 50 (1994): 801–808.

14. A. H. Ropper and C. Gorson, "Concussion," *New England Journal of Medicine* 356 (2007): 166–172.

15. J. Ibanez, F. Arikan et al., "Reliability of clinical guidelines in the detection of patients at risk following mild head injury: Results of a prospective study," *Journal of Neurosurgery* 1000 (2004): 825–834.

16. For a detailed summary of these guidelines, see Roderick, *Playing Hurt.*

17. P. R. McCrory and S. F. Berkovic, "Second impact syndrome," *Neurology* 50 (1998): 677–683; and the American Orthopaedic Society for Sports Medicine. Summary of management of concussion in sports. 1998. "Brain injury in sports," www.headinjury.com/sports.htm, accessed 2/18/08.

18. K. M. Guskiewica, S. L. Bruce et al., "National athletic trainers' association position statement: Management of sport-related concussion," *Journal of Athletic Training* 19(3) (2004): 280–297.

19. J. Macur, "Doping officials question drug policy in baseball," *New York Times*, November 17, 2007, D3.

20. G. J. Mitchell, "Report to the commissioner of baseball of an independent investigation into the illegal use of steroids and other performance enhancing substances by players in major league baseball," DLA Pipers US LLP, December 13, 2007, http://www. mlb.mlb.com/mlb/news/mitchell/report. jsp, accessed 1/12/08.

21. L. D. Johnston, P. M. O'Malley et al., "Monitoring the future: National survey results on drug use, 1975–2005," "Volume 1: Secondary school students," (Bethesda, MD: National Institute on Drug Abuse, 2006), NIH publication 06–5883.

22. J. A. Lombardo, "Anabolic-androgenic steroids," *National Institute on Drug Abuse Research Monograph* 102 (1990): 60–73.

23. New York State Department of Health. Bureau of Narcotic Enforcement. "Anabolic steroids and sports: Winning at any cost," http://www.nyhealth.gov/publications/1210, accessed 2/18/08.

24. R. F. Heller, N. Miller et al., "Coronary heart disease in 'low risk' men," *Atherosclerosis* 49(2) (1983): 187–193.

25. World Anti-Doping Agency, "The world anti-doping code," http://www.WADA-AMA.org/RETContent/document/WADA_Code_2007_3.0.pdf, accessed 11/20/07.

TEN MEN'S WORK: WHAT ARE THE HAZARDS?

1. T. DeLeire and H. Levy, "Gender, occupation choice and the risk of death at work," NBER Working Paper No.8574, issued in November 2001, NBER Program (HC), http://www.nber.org/papers/W8574.pdf, accessed 11/18/07.

2. H. Luntz, *Seamen's Compensation Review* (Canberra: Australian Government Publication Services, 1988).

3. A. Otterland, *A Sociomedical Study of the Mortality in Merchant Seafarers* (Goteborg: Scandinavian University Books, 1960).

4. H. L. Hansen, "Surveillance of deaths on board Danish merchant ships, 1986–93: Implications for prevention," *Occupational and Environmental Medicine* 53 (1996): 269–275.

5. Costantinos Poulakis, personal communication.

6. F. Reimer, "Suizide bei jugendlichen seeleute," *International Journal of Prophylatic Medicine and Soziahygiene* 6 (1962): 7–11; G. Wickstrom and A. Leivonniemi, "Suicides among male Finnish seafarers," *Acta Psychiatrica Scandinavica* (1985): 575–580.

7. J. M. Lincoln and G. A. Conway, "Preventing commercial fishing deaths in Alaska," Centers for Disease Control and Prevention, National Institute for Occupational Safety and Health, Anchorage, AL, jxw7@cdc.gov.

8. L. Rosenstock and J. Olsen, "Firefighting and death from cardiovascular causes," *New England Journal of Medicine* 356(12) (2007): 1261–1263.

9. "Firefighter fatality retrospective study," prepared for the Federal Emergency Management Agency, United States Fire Service, National Fire Data Center, Arlington, VA, TriData Corp., April 2002.

10. S. N. Kales, E. S. Soteriades et al., "Emergency duties and deaths from heart disease among firefighters in the United States," *New England Journal of Medicine* 356 (2007): 1207–1215.

11. A. Duenas-Laita, J. L. Perez Castrillon, and M. Ruiz Mambrilla, "Heart disease deaths among firefighters," *New England Journal of Medicine* 356 (2007): 2535–2537.

12. L. W. Raymond, T. A. Barringer, and J. C. Konen, "Letter to the editor," *New England Journal of Medicine* 356 (2007): 2535–2537.

13. S. N. Kales, E. S. Soteriades et al., "Firefighters and on-duty deaths from coronary heart disease: A case control study," *Environmental Health* 2 (2003): 14–35.

14. T. Tate, "Suicide prevention training," http://www.cophealth.com/sp.html, accessed 11/20/07.

15. J. M. Violanti, J. F. Vena, and S. Patralia, "Mortality of a police cohort: 1950–1990," *American Journal of Industrial Medicine* 33 (1998): 366–373.

16. R. Davis and F. K. Mostifi, "Cluster of testicular cancer in police officers exposed to hand-held radar," *American Journal of Industrial Medicine* 24 (1993): 231–223.

17. W. D. Franke, S. L. Ramey, and M. C. Shelley, "Relationship between cardiovascular disease morbidity, risk factors and stress in a law enforcement cohort," *Occupational and Environmental Medicine* 44 (2002): 1182–1189.

18. J. M. Violanti, "Stress patterns in police work: A longitudinal analysis," *Journal of Police Science and Administration* 11 (1983): 211–216.

19. J. M. Violanti, J. E. Vena, and J. R. Marshall, "Suicide, homicides and accidental deaths: A comparative risk assessment of police officers and municipal workers," *American Journal of Industrial Medicine* 30 (1996): 99–104.

20. W. H. Kroes, *Society's Victim: The Police* (Springfield, IL: Charles C. Thomas, 1986).

21. J. M. Violanti, "Dying from the job: The mortality risk for police officers," http://www.cophealth.com/articles/articles_cying_a.html, accessed 11/20/2007.

22. National Institute for Occupational Safety and Health of the CDC, "Worker Health Chartbook 2004," Publication No.2004–145, http://www2.cdc.gov/niosh-Chartbook/ch4/ch4–2.asp, accessed 11/25/07.

23. R. Noe, A. L. Cohen et al. "Skin disorders in construction workers following hurricanes Katrina and Rita. An outbreak investigation in New Orleans, Louisiana," *Archives of Dermatology* 143(11) (2007): 1392–1398.

ELEVEN ANDROPAUSE AND THE AGING MALE

1. US Census Bureau, Facts for Features, "Oldest baby boomers turn 60," CBO6-FFSE.01–2, January 3, 2006.
2. US Census Bureau, American FactFinder, http://factfinder.census.gov/home/saff/main.html, accessed 12/8/07.
3. S. Pasha, "Corporations woo baby boomers," CNNMoney.com, September 29, 2005, http://money.cnn.com/2005/09/29/news/fortune500/babyboomers_companies/index.htm, accessed 12/3/07.
4. R. A. Schoevers, A. T. F. Beekman et al., "Association of depression and gender with mortality in old age. Results from the Amsterdam Study of the Elderly (AMSTE)," *The British Journal of Psychiatry* 177 (2000): 136–342.
5. J. W. Vaupel, "The remarkable improvements in survival at older ages," *Philosophical Transactions of the Royal Society B Biological Sciences* 352 (1997): 1799–1804.
6. U.S. Census Bureau, American FactFinder, http://factfinder.census.gov/home/saff/main.html, accessed 12/2/07.
7. B. J. Wilcox, Q. He et al., "Midlife risk factors and healthy survival in men," *JAMA* 296(19) (2006): 2342–2350.
8. M. M. Shores, A. M. Matsumoto et al., "Low serum testosterone and mortality in male veterans," *Archives of Internal Medicine* 166 (2006): 1660–1665.
9. Committee on Assessing the Need for Clinical Trials of Testosterone Replacement Therapy, *Testosterone and Aging: Clinical Research Directions*, Institute of Medicine of the National Academies, ed. C. T. Liverman and D. G. Blazer (Washington, D.C.: National Academies Press, 2004).
10. S. H. M. VanGooze, P. T. Cohen-Kettenis et al., "Activating effects of androgens on cognitive performance: Causal evidence in a group of female-to-male transsexuals," *Neuropsychologia* 32 (1994): 1153–1157.
11. F. F. Pasqualotto, A. M. Lucon et al., "Risks and benefits of hormone replacement therapy in older men," *Revista do Hospital das Clínicas* 59(1) (2004): 32–38.

12. H. Fisch, *The Male Biological Clock* (New York: Free Press, 2005), 58.

13. Modified from "About Dementia," http://www.dementia.com/bgdisplay. jhtml?itemname=dementia_about, accessed 12/8/07.

14. Centers for Disease Control and Prevention, "Leading Causes of Death for Males," June 2007, sourced in U.S. Department of Health and Human Services, "Top 10 Heath Concerns of Men," http://www.4woman. gov/mens/physical/index.cfm, accessed 12/8/2007.

15. Paul Killian, personal communication.

16. J. A. Kanis, A. Oden et al., "The components of excess mortality after hip fracture," *Bone* 32(5) (2003): 468–473.

17. G. Jones, T. Nguyen et al., "Symptomatic fracture incidence in elderly men and women. The Dubbo Osteoporosis Epidemiology Study (DOES)," *Osteoporosis International* 4(5) (1994): 277–282.

18. J. T. Schousboe, B. C. Taylor et al., "Cost-effectiveness of bone densitometry followed by treatment of osteoporosis in older men," *JAMA* 298(6) (2007): 629–637.

19. N. Binkley, J. P. Bilezikian et al., "Official positions of the International Society for Clinical Densitometry and executive summary of the 2005 Position Development Conference," *Journal of Clinical Densitometry* 9(1) (2006): 4–14.

20. J. P. Brown and R. G. Josse, "2002 clinical practice guidelines for the diagnosis and management of osteoporosis in Canada," *CMAJ* 167(suppl.) 10 (2004): 51–534.

CODA

1. Leading Causes of Death by Age Group, All Males-United States, 2004, http://CAC.gov/men/LCOD/o4all. pdf.

INDEX